Praise for Griffith REVIEW

'Essential reading for each and every one of us.' *Readings*

'A varied, impressive and international cast of authors.' *The Australian*

'*Griffith REVIEW* is a must-read for anyone with even a passing interest in current affairs, politics, literature and journalism. The timely, engaging writing lavishly justifies the Brisbane-based publication's reputation as Australia's best example of its genre.' *The West Australian*

'There is a consistently high standard of writing: all of it well crafted or well argued or well informed, as befits the various genres.' *Sydney Review of Books*

'This quarterly magazine is a reminder of the breadth and talent of Australian writers. Verdict: literary treat.' *Herald Sun*

'*Griffith REVIEW* editor Julianne Schultz is the ultra-marathoner of Australian cultural life.' *Canberra Times*

'At a time when long form journalism is under threat and the voices in our public debate are often off-puttingly condescending, hectoring and discordant, *Griffith REVIEW* is the elegant alternative.' *Booktopia Buzz*

'*Griffith REVIEW* is a consistently good journal. There is some terrific writing on display as well as variety and depth to the issues being grappled with.' *The Age*

'Australia's most important literary essay magazine.' *Courier-Mail*

'At once comfortable and thought-provoking, edgy and familiar, [it] will draw the reader through its pages.' *Australian Book Review*

'*Griffith REVIEW* is a wonderful journal. It's pretty much setting the agenda in Australia and fighting way above its weight... You're mad if you don't subscribe.' Phillip Adams

'Once again, *Griffith REVIEW* has produced a stunning volume of excellent work. The pieces are diverse, the stories unique and real. But one thing remains constant – superb writing.' *Weekend Herald* (NZ)

SIR SAMUEL GRIFFITH was one of Australia's great early achievers. Twice the premier of Queensland, that state's chief justice and the author of its criminal code, he was best known for his pivotal role in drafting agreements that led to Federation, and as the new nation's first chief justice. He was also an important reformer and legislator, a practical and cautious man of words.

Griffith died in 1920 and is now best remembered in his namesakes: an electorate, a society, a suburb and a university. Ninety-six years after he first proposed establishing a university in Brisbane, Griffith University, the city's second, was created. His commitment to public debate and ideas, his delight in words and art, and his attachment to active citizenship are recognised by the publication that bears his name.

Like Sir Samuel Griffith, Griffith REVIEW is iconoclastic and non-partisan, with a sceptical eye and a pragmatically reforming heart and a commitment to public discussion. Personal, political and unpredictable, it is Australia's best conversation.

GriffithREVIEW43

Pacific Highways

Co-edited by Julianne Schultz and Lloyd Jones

GriffithREVIEW43

INTRODUCTION

7 **Looking east**
JULIANNE SCHULTZ: Changing the focal length

At the crossroads
LLOYD JONES: Winds of change

ESSAY

12 **To a neighbour I am getting to know**
ROBERTO ONELL: Letter from Chile (Translated by Ross Woods)

27 **On masks and migration**
HARRY RICKETTS: Learning to stand upright

33 **Patterns of migration**
GREGORY O'BRIEN: Notes on eels, on the way to the Kermadecs

38 **Cable stations**
LYNNE McDONALD: The encircled earth

48 **Primate city**
FINLAY MACDONALD: Gorilla in the midst

67 **Hitching a ride**
REBECCA PRIESTLEY: Nature knows no borders

88 **A Kiwi feast**
DAVID BURTON: Paua with wild silverbeet, samphire & sea grapes

105 **Thinking about waves**
LYNN JENNER: Knowing when to leave

123 **Born to run**
JOHN SAKER: The remarkable tale of Steve Adams

136 **Walking meditations**
HINEMOANA BAKER: Fingernails, feet and fossils

148 **Sea of trees**
ASHLEIGH YOUNG: The road not taken

154 **O Salutaris**
IAN WEDDE: Between here and there

164 **Pure brightness**
ALISON WONG: Conversations with ghosts

182 **School report**
BERNARD BECKETT: Cracking the literacy code

194 **Tectonic Z**
ROD ORAM: Creating a zone of hope

210 **We are all Stan Walker**
DAMIEN WILKINS: Why you should have watched the most hated show on television

261 **First, build your hut**
LYDIA WEVERS: New Zealand's missing great nineteenth century novel

270 **Simply by sailing in a new direction**
KATE DE GOLDI: The search for Storyland

281 **The lie of the land**
HAMISH CLAYTON: Jim's wife by another name

290 **An A-frame in Antarctica**
MATT VANCE: Getting away from it all

296 **Reading Geoff Cochrane**
CARRIE TIFFANY: A constant companion

MEMOIR

116 **The beach**
LEILANI TAMU: States of transition

129 **Fitting into the Pacific**
PETER SWAIN: Some things you ought to know

179 **Postcard from Beijing**
KATE WOODS: Artistic villages and empty mansions

218 **Open road**
BRIAN TURNER: No pain, no gain

224 **Whale Road**
KATE CAMP: Things to do in Iceland

254 **Place in time**
PAMELA 'JUDY' ROSS: Abridged interview from the Avonside Project

REPORTAGE

16 **On my way to the border**
STEVE BRAUNIAS: Learning by osmosis

237 **Amending the map**
SALLY BLUNDELL: A city of becoming

249 **Portrait of an artist**
GLENN BUSCH: Photographer, documentary-maker, storyteller

FICTION

61 **Anxiety** CK STEAD

144 **Waiheke Island** EMILY PERKINS

206 **Getting to yes** WILLIAM BRANDT

POETRY

15 **Clearing at Dawn** YA-WEN HO

46 **Demarcations** JAMES BROWN

75 **L'Anima Verde** CLIFF FELL

94 **Whale Survey, Raoul Island, with Rosemary Dobson** GREGORY O'BRIEN

113 **The uprising** DINAH HAWKEN

232 **Green light** JAMES BROWN

259 **There, being Monday morning** VINCENT O'SULLIVAN

268 **Encounter above the Hurunui** CLIFF FELL

295 **Erebus voices** BILL MANHIRE

299 **Equinoctial** GEOFF COCHRANE

PICTURE GALLERIES

95 **When the swimmer reaches shore** BRUCE FOSTER

233 **Christchurch Christmas, 2012** ANNE NOBLE

griffithreview.com

More great stories and poetry are available in *PACIFIC HIGHWAYS Vol. 2*
as a **free download** at www.griffithreview.com

GriffithREVIEW43 AUTUMN 2014
GriffithREVIEW is published four times a year by Griffith University
in conjunction with Text Publishing. ISSN 1448-2924

Publisher	Marilyn McMeniman AM
Editor	Julianne Schultz AM
Co-editor	Lloyd Jones
Deputy Editors	Erica Sontheimer, Nicholas Bray
Production Manager	Paul Thwaites
Publicist	Susan Hornbeck
Publication & Cover Design	WH Chong, Text Publishing
Text Publishing	Michael Heyward, Kirsty Wilson, Shalini Kunahlan
Proofreading	Alan Vaarwerk
Editorial Interns	Coco McGrath, Madeleine Watts, Alana Brekelmans, Nicholas Ivanovic, Jessica O'Neill, Sam Hooshmand, Kirra Smith
Administration	Jane Hunterland
Typesetting	Midland Typesetters
Printing	Ligare Book Printers
Distribution	Penguin Australia
Cover Image	Bill Hammond, *Watching for Buller*, 1993, (Detail), Oil on canvas, 1000 x 1200mm. Courtesy of Collection of the James Wallace Arts Trust

Contributions by academics can, on request, be refereed by our Editorial Board.
Details: www.griffithreview.com

GRIFFITH REVIEW
South Bank Campus, Griffith University
PO Box 3370, South Brisbane QLD 4101 Australia
Ph +617 3735 3071 Fax +617 3735 3272
griffithreview@griffith.edu.au www.griffithreview.com

TEXT PUBLISHING
Swann House, 22 William St, Melbourne VIC 3000 Australia
Ph +613 8610 4500 Fax +613 9629 8621
books@textpublishing.com.au www.textpublishing.com.au

SUBSCRIPTIONS
Within Australia: 1 year (4 editions) $111.80 RRP, inc. P&H and GST
Outside Australia: 1 year (4 editions) A$161.80 RRP, inc. P&H
Institutional and bulk rates available on application.

FEEDBACK AND COMMENT www.griffithreview.com

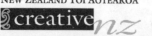

Looking east

Changing the focal length

Julianne Schultz

FOR a number of years I travelled on a New Zealand passport. It wasn't so much that I identified with the land of my birth, but for pragmatic reasons: when I first needed a passport to travel – fittingly to the Pacific – I was a student, and a New Zealand passport cost less than half an Australian one, and lasted twice as long. Even if I hadn't been back since I left at age four, for a penurious twenty-year-old, this was as good a reason as any to identify internationally as a Kiwi.

In the 1970s the boundaries between being a Kiwi and being an Aussie were blurred, and had been for half a century. Citizenship seemed interchangeable, with accompanying rights and responsibilities. My Australian parents happened to be living in Hamilton when I was born, so I was entitled to both, before opting to be officially stamped Australian.

Long before the formal free trade agreements, which focused on goods, services, capital and quarantine, there was effectively a free movement of people that bound the countries together. It was an uneven trade that benefitted Australia, as more left New Zealand than arrived – Australians flocked to even more distant shores.

The movement of people has continued, although the rules have changed – official Australian Government web pages bristle with daunting category classifications – but seem to have done little to stem the flow. More than 650,000 New Zealanders call Australia home, while 60,000 Australians have made a permanent journey east across the Tasman.

The dream of a united Australasia may have withered in the nineteenth century, but the sense of interchangeability lingers – like cousins who keep in touch, but keep a distance – bumptious and pushy city types on the western shores of the Tasman, versus the kids from the bush on the east.

NEW ZEALAND REMAINS Australians' preferred holiday destination, and as they pour off the planes, will readily agree it is arguably, inch for inch, the most beautiful country in the world. Green, watery, hilly, lush – the opposite to the ancient, flat, dry plains of Australia.

When they notice the country at all, Australians still tend to talk down to New Zealand, imagining we are in the big league; a continent, rather than a sparsely populated country on the edge of Asia. So while Australians were busy looking north and west, to the east something changed. New Zealand not only made a virtue of its environment, but became home to some of the best wines, movie directors, writers, footballers, sailors, scientists, educators and female leaders in the world.

It not only maintained, but developed its history of social innovation. It found new depth in the richness of its human and environmental capital. It continued its evolutionary path – since seafaring Polynesians followed the stars and currents to arrive in Northland about a thousand years ago, followed hundreds of years later by settlers from Europe, Asia and the Americas – to become an even more innovative, humane society at the crossroads of the Pacific, Tasman and Great Southern Oceans.

In an evolutionary sense, modern Australia and New Zealand grew out of similar stock. Notwithstanding a very different Indigenous history and the legacy of convict settlement in Australia, a hundred years ago they were recognisably similar, inheritors of the Enlightenment, and southern outposts of the British Empire. Despite close economic ties, they have now diverged in ways that to Australian eyes are unexpected and rewarding and truly original. New Zealand is not a depleting white society, as Australians may once have thought, but an emerging polyglot nation of four and half million people where all children learn Māori in school, where cultural diversity has taken deep root, where the natural environment is a resource to be treasured and there is water everywhere.

This edition of *Griffith REVIEW* has been shaped by Lloyd Jones' passionate connection to his country, and showcases some of the best writers a highly literate society has produced. It does not shirk from the challenges, but celebrates the evolution of New Zealand into a truly connected hub more than able to provide imaginative sustenance and hold its place in the global village.

From an Australian perspective this edition has provided a wonderful opportunity to change the focal length in the way we see New Zealand. It jettisons the old clichés, and even more recent ones – there is not a sheep, hobbit, bottle of sauvignon blanc, ski field or rugby player to be found – displaced by something that is surprisingly rich, sophisticated and passionate.

From a New Zealand perspective, I hope that this edition provides a mirror on the evolution of a remarkable and resilient society through the eyes and words of your own; we are just holding the mirror so you can see from a slight distance. And from my point of view, I am pleased to synthesise these two elements of my own life.

Sydney, 2 December 2013

At the crossroads

Winds of change

Lloyd Jones

THE oldest highway across the Pacific is perhaps as old as the planet. A jet stream circles the Pacific Rim. The amazing godwit hurtles along at an airborne speed of five hundred kilometres an hour on its journey from Siberia along the western littoral of the Pacific to a landing strip on Christchurch's Brighton Beach – one of the longest non-stop flights of any migratory bird. Each spring, until its near destruction in the 2011 earthquakes, bells from the cathedral would ring to announce the arrival of the godwits.

The highways favour one species or another. Eels slither out of farm creeks, cross fields, wriggle and worm their way through shingle to reach the sea where they ditch their land-crawling apparatus and take on seafaring equipment to swim thousands of kilometres to their breeding ground south of Tonga. Secondary lanes of importance conduct crayfish on their long distance crawl.

Sea lanes had to be invented with the assistance of the stars; the Southern Cross caught the eye of the earliest navigators and led them to imagine pit stops across the length and breadth of the Pacific. Around these pit stops are smaller local lanes and off ramps, minor traffic, inter-island causeways. Crays on their marathon crawl often encounter cables. These highways of chatter connect every point around the Pacific Rim and beyond. Tidal movements push flotsam around the Pacific. Hitchhiking species jump from one pit stop to another. Sailing ships were blown on and off course; some crashed ashore.

On the beach new communities grew; a mix of journeying and settler genes. Colours were mixed and new breeds took to sea lanes to continue the journey. Gradually, over a period of thousands of years, a facial *moko* with its origins in modern-day Taiwan appear on faces dwelling on the two largest southern-dwelling islands in the Pacific.

Names are conveyed along the same route. Words are dropped on this island, and are carried on to the next. Along the Pacific highways landmass and sea and air are not considered to be separate entities, but one big soup of dynamic exchange of people, language, custom and memory.

WATER IS A reflective substance, and New Zealand abounds in lakes, rivers and coast. Many of our legends and histories speak of watery origins. No town or farm in New Zealand is more than a couple of hours' drive from the sea. But our sense of place is informed by more than what greets us out the window.

However secure and deep-rooted we may feel about this place we are a nation of immigrants. Elsewhere is reflected in our faces. One decade into the twenty-first century New Zealand is more diverse than ever before.

Thinking about who we are and where we live requires that we consider *who* lives here, and *who* gets to say. And, which places does memory hark back to? The answers were different in my parents' day, as they are in my children's lifetime. The story of departures and arrivals is ongoing. New arrivals set about modifying and fitting into it; the country makes its own adjustments.

In the imagination of the northern hemisphere geography has always placed New Zealand at a disadvantage, on the edge of the planet and its consciousness. Present, but slightly out of view. A destination, but not necessarily one for tomorrow or the next day; a popular choice on some bucket lists along with riding an elephant and seeing the Taj Mahal.

IN THE TWENTY-FIRST century New Zealanders have less reason to think of themselves as marginal – they are present and noted everywhere.

Auckland took three decades to become the city with the largest Polynesian population of any in the Pacific. In little over a decade it has become one of the most cosmopolitan cities in Australasia, boasting 160 ethnicities – 40 per cent of the city's residents were born overseas. Change to the composition of the population inevitably delivers new cultural reference points, new interpretations of history. We see ourselves in relation to new places; the gaze travels in new directions: north and east as well as the time-honoured gaze west across the Tasman.

This issue of *Griffith REVIEW* attempts to track some of these changes and to position New Zealand in the more exciting place it now occupies. One where it is possible to think of New Zealand as a hub in a mesh of highways spanning the littoral of South America, Asia, and Australia. There lies the future, as economists used to say.

Perhaps it is time to acknowledge what is even more obvious. The future is here.

Wellington, 2 December 2013

Lloyd Jones commissioned the authors published in *Griffith REVIEW 43: Pacific Highways* and the e-book *Pacific Highways: Volume Two*. His most recent book is *A History of Silence: A Memoir* (Text, 2013).

ESSAY

To a neighbour I am getting to know

Letter from Chile

Roberto Onell

A UN VECINO QUE EMPIEZO A CONOCER

Voy a contarte una historia de agua, una historia de olas, unas olas de piel que se desplaza y regresa, una historia que aun desconociéndola sé que sabes, sé que escuchas; sé que la palpas desde un día a la noche que vuelve, salpicada de sal y de espuma, en ese universo de ojos que se nos abren como un día que no deja de venir a nuestra orilla.

Original Spanish continued in full at www.griffithreview.com

I AM going to tell you a story of water, a story of waves, human waves, a story I know you are already familiar with. I know that you feel it night and day, splashed with salt and foam.

The moment I first saw the sea is lost from memory – that's memory sometimes – a bottomless chest where we mislay all that we want to preserve. The sea was the Pacific: of that I am certain. I was born in Santiago, the Chilean capital, a city placed in the centre of the country, in a valley enclosed by the great Andes Mountain Range to the east, and by the smaller Chilean Coastal Range to the west. As *santiaguinos*, we live surrounded by peaks, some higher, some smaller. To get to the beach from Santiago means going to the Litoral Central, the coastal line that runs from Santo Domingo in the south, and to Mirasol in the north.

I saw the sea for the first time probably from a car on a trip with my parents. I can't remember the moment, but of the journey I remember the anticipation: leaving behind the Central Valley, negotiating the Coastal Range and its pleasant, small valleys, the sea imminent, and there it is – blue, throbbing, always foreign, always impressive. With the hills behind me now, from the back seat I look out between my parents' heads, the ocean fills the windscreen – distant, calm, inexorable. The sea quenched the thirst in our eyes – the Pacific Ocean, *that other*.

San Antonio was the usual entrance to the coast, but I was disappointed by the never-ending stench and the dregs of the port. The route through the Valle de Casablanca was the one I liked more: it was green, more panoramic. We arrived at Algarrobo, a pretty hamlet where a few months earlier they had installed the first traffic light.

Our stay varied between a few hours and a couple of weeks. To be on the beach itself, to bathe in the sea provided me with reverence and fear; firstly, because at that time I hadn't learned to swim, and, secondly, because of the history it contained. It scared me and continues to – its perpetual movement, in its constant instability, in its coming and going – *that other* flooding my body and consciousness.

ROBERT LOUIS STEVENSON and Daniel Defoe were the first authors of the sea that I read, at twelve years of age. Authors *with* sea that I remember. And that I now remember because they take me away from the beach; they take me sailing and exploring, to live with sailors and passengers. *Treasure Island* and *Robinson Crusoe* were etched in my spirit, surely, for no other reason than for the fact that they put me aboard and let me experience the shipwreck… I remember, suddenly, 'The Marine Chilote', a song from Chilean folklore that I've heard since kindergarten, in which the sea is a setting for the protagonist, a fisherman and seal hunter; it's a nice little waltz, except that, he doesn't *enter* the sea. After Stevenson and Defoe came Jules Verne and Francisco Coloane, eminent figures; later, a certain vitality found in Herman Melville and Ernest Hemingway; the lyricism of Coleridge, of Rafael Alberti, of Vicente Huidobro's 'Monument to the Sea', Nicanor Parra's 'They Sing to the Sea', of some melancholy lines by Raul Zurita; and more recently, the vicissitudes captured by Jorge Amado and Joseph Conrad. But 'The Ocean Road', from Pablo Neruda's *Canto General* (1950), continues to be, for me, the best entry to the Pacific, because it doesn't speak of the sea: it translates it, turns it in to language. Well, compared with the landlocked literature of the countryside and the city, these are the poetic and maritime voices of *that other*.

AT THIS POINT, *Rotation* (2010) comes to mind, my book of poems. Poems full of water or, better still, containers that can hold no more. Each time a poem says 'sea', 'wave', 'tide,' it never says 'Pacific' nor the name of any city, but for someone who lives in Chile, it is impossible to say all that without seeing the Pacific Ocean. In fact, I remember clearly that the poem 'Dream of the Return' was born on the shores of the Pacific. Of course I saw myself as such a part of the ocean – that was the idea – that its name didn't matter. In a poem, the name doesn't matter, because it is never a real name. The real name is *that other* always in search of a voice.

And now I write this letter to a reader from another horizon. Someone who speaks to me in another language, in that other English of New Zealand, to me, an inhabitant of Spanish, but of another Spanish, the Chilean. It is a word that puts us face to face – the Pacific. I greet you, friend, from my shore.

Santiago, Chile
October 2013

Translated by Ross Woods

Roberto Onell teaches Chilean and Hispano-American Poetry at the Pontificia Universidad Católica de Chile and holds a joint doctorate from this institution and the University of Leipzig for research on Pablo Neruda's *The Heights of Macchu Picchu* (1967). He has published a number of academic and newspaper articles on literature. In 2010, he published *Rotation* (*Rotación*, Ediciones Tácitas) and is currently working on his second collection of poems.

Ross Woods is a lecturer in Spanish at Victoria University of Wellington and is the author of a number of studies on twentieth-century Spanish literature. Also a translator of contemporary Hispanic poetry, his first collection of translations, of Pablo Valdivia's *Breathing Underwater*, will appear in 2014.

Ya-Wen Ho

Clearing at Dawn

曉晴
李白
野涼疏雨歇，春色偏萋萋。
魚躍清池滿，鶯吟綠樹低。
野花妝面濕，山草紐斜齊。
零落殘雲片，風吹掛竹溪。

A Clear Dawn

Li Po

The bush is cool, the light showers have stopped – a panorama of
Spring.

The clear waters boil with leaping trout; birds chirp, the fern fronds droop.

The bush flowers dapple their dewy petals; the hill tussocks give a
crisp salute.

Above the cabbage tree and creek, wisps of cloud gently scatter in the wind.

(translation Ya-Wen Ho)

Clearing at Dawn

Li Po

The fields are chill, the sparse rain has stopped;

The colours of Spring teem on every side.

With leaping fish the blue pond is full;

With singing thrushes the green boughs droop.

The flowers of the field have dabbled their powdered cheeks;

The mountain grasses are bent level at the waist.

By the bamboo stream the last fragment of cloud

Blown by the wind slowly scatters away.

(translation Arthur Waley)

Ya-Wen Ho's essay, 'Poetry as social experiment', can be read in the e-book *Pacific Highways: Volume 2*, available free at www.griffithreview.com

Ya-Wen Ho is a twenty-six-year-old poet. She is a graduate of the University of Auckland. She came to New Zealand from Taiwan at the age of seven. Li Po (Li Bai), 701- 762 AD, is a revered classical Chinese poet of the mid Tang Dynasty, known as the golden age of cosmopolitan civilisation. Arthur Waley first translated 'Clearing at Dawn' into English in 1922.

On my way to the border

Learning by osmosis

Steve Braunias

I GOT up, dressed, and walked to the airport. Everyone else was driving as fast as they could to beat it out of the city, out of New Zealand, to catch the first flight leaving for the colonies – Sydney, Brisbane, Melbourne, even Darwin. There were incredible statistics. Every week, thirty thousand people – equal to the population of Gisborne, that lovely, beachy city on the East Coast, where Captain Cook first made landfall – were fleeing New Zealand, wanting away, deserting the ship that wasn't so much sinking as going round in circles.

Poor old New Zealand. The money wasn't as good as the Australian dollar. The weather wasn't as warm, the natives were a lot less restless. The various assorted claustrophobias of living in a narrow archipelago north of the South Pole could get you down. Everyone knew each other's business; nosiness and complaint were the New Zealand condition. It was also a form of entertainment. The most popular and longest-running TV show was *Fair Go*. Reality TV before it became a named genre, it dealt with consumer affairs, and made a cult out of shonky service and broken promises. But the numbers streaming every week to Auckland International Airport suggested *Fair Go* had spawned an even more popular sequel: Go Away.

I wasn't in any hurry to get there. I had no intention of leaving. I just wanted to make my way to the border, on foot, and take in the view on the way. It was the last the émigrés would see of New Zealand, the last few kilometres of road and creek, countryside and strip mall. It was also the first that new arrivals would see of New Zealand; not the tourists wanting to gawk at mudpools, snow, and hobbits further south, then leave, but the new New Zealanders, humble and not necessarily downtrodden, here to set up shop, coming from Asia and Africa, the Pacific and the Middle East, the ESOL generation with prayer mats and dim knowledge of an island nation on Chile's latitude.

New Zealand, the obscure country. It makes a fetish of its station in life; class-conscious, race-conscious, self-conscious above all of being in the bottom right-hand corner of the atlas, the two islands like a couple of crumbs scattered on the wide Pacific. Does it have small-man syndrome? Is that why it constantly feels the need to assert itself, make belligerent noises about 'punching above its weight'? But that belligerence is, for the main part, provincial. The cities are too busy. They just go about their business, none more so than Auckland, the city with the most people, about a third of the country's population hammering away on an isthmus. We're doing our best to send the kids to school and put food on the table. We're Aucklanders, and we're stuck in traffic.

But I was free to walk. I closed the front door. The light was soft; moisture collected on the broad, fat leaves of the massive rubber tree in front of our house, its roots muscling in on the foundations. *Must chop tree.* It was a pale morning in late summer, 19 degrees and rising, the fructifying heat of subtropical Auckland yet to come in on the tide that filled the mangrove swamps with green water.

ONE OF THE neighbours was out at the letterbox. He was barefoot and one toe was bandaged. He gave a long speech about having six stitches after the removal of his ingrown toenail. He is Māori, works on the rubbish trucks, and has three sons – West, Wonder, and Wrath. Come out fishing, he said, and yanked his thumb at his aluminum dinghy on the front lawn. I wondered idly about the possibility of sailing to the airport. Could it be done, in this city of waterways, creeks and rivers?

I live on a peninsula. It's shaped by the sucking tide. Thick, oozing mud gathers on the banks of the creeks, and out of it grows the native mangrove,

Avicennia marina, with its ingenious system of roots known as pneumato-phores. The pneumatophores drink saltwater on the incoming tide; when the tide retreats, the salt is despatched through the plant, and spat out on the surface of the leaves. A mangrove is a saltworks. They are all over Auckland, gathering at bays and on the sides of creeks and rivers, hunched and woody, a steaming forest of pale green – wait a while, and before long, you'll see a flash of white. It's a face. The white-faced heron roosts on top of mangroves, an expert spear-fisher, feeding on crabs that scuttle out of the mud.

I was about to consult the neighbour's opinion on navigating a course to the airport when I saw the old sailor approaching. The old sailor had a red nose as big as a doorknob. He was a familiar sight. He walked around the neighbourhood all day; he lived alone in a house concealed behind a bottle-brush tree, and you'd see him bailing up strangers on the street, his doorknob glowing, an ancient mariner talking about his days in the navy, and about the wife who left him to fend for himself and their handicapped daughter. The daughter left him, too. The bottle-brush tree surrounded the house. He was desperate for company. I left him and the neighbour to it.

It struck me that the first two people I met on my airport voyage, both of them New Zealanders born and bred, were hobbled and wretched. Were they like Lawrence's crippled Lord Chatterley – fairly crude and not especially subtle metaphors of impotence and failure, signs that the New Zealand way of life was on the fritz? Did it follow that I would meet Mellors in blackface, an immigrant, some raw, calloused son of the soil from the other side of the world?

MONARCH BUTTERFLIES AND bright Australian parrots poured colour inside a cool, dark pine forest. Further along, I came to a river. Green water trembled in the shadows of the mangroves. Layers of history flowed in on the tide. I was standing at a river mouth where Māori once took flaming torches to frighten bar-tailed godwits off the shellbanks; the birds would fly into nooses made from the leaves of cabbage trees.

Houseboats were moored alongside the banks. A seventy-year-old resident had recently been in the news; on his way back from KFC, he lost his grip on the handrail of his boat, fell into the mangroves, and couldn't move. He was stuck there for twenty-four hours. He drank rainwater. A mate found him. He said, 'He's only a little fella, and he's fairly plumpish. He's not fat but he had plenty of meat on him to keep him going.'

I crossed the bridge, and into an industrial estate lined with an estimated eight hundred factories. It was watery, leafy, fertile. The harbour sparkled to my left, a creek mooched slow and dreamy to my right, the two waterways shaping the estate into one of Auckland's most graceful peninsulas. 'The flats are not to be beaten for carrots and cabbages,' declared a visitor in 1891, when the dark, damp earth was tilled as a vast market garden. Tomatoes were staked to ti-trees, citrus went berserk. Grapefruit and lemon trees are still all over the peninsula, and so were oak, wattle, magnolia, Moreton Bay fig, gum… I had arrived at an industrial heartland, but was on a nature walk.

Behind the trees, factories were filled with hoses, surfboard bags, cages, fasteners, resin, windscreens, mannequins, trampolines, forklifts, rifles, drinking chocolate; the lovely, woozy scent of dried herbs emanated from the doorway of a low warehouse. I called in.

Mr Wang, forty-four, wearing a collarless jacket with tartan lining, led me to the upstairs kitchen for a cup of green tea. There was a faux grandfather clock. It had stopped. In the timeless room, Mr Wang said he had only recently arrived in New Zealand, from Shanghai. His sister owned the warehouse. He was its new manager. Downstairs were sacks and trays of medicinal herbs with exquisite names – phoenix-tail, wintersweet flower, charred hawthorn, hollybark. What did they do, exactly? 'I don't know,' he said.

He was shocked when I asked him whether he was married. 'Is a personal question!' I said I was sorry. He said, 'No. No wife.' He had bought a house. How much? That was an okay question to ask. '$790,000. I think is good price.' He was, I told him, an eligible bachelor. He sighed, 'The right woman…where is she?'

The loneliness of the long-distance immigrant was played out again, ten minutes later, when I came across Mr Odiah. He was at his letterbox. He wasn't looking for mail or the morning paper. It was just something to do. He looked up and down the long boring street. 'No one is here,' he observed, correctly. He was from Nigeria. He had been in Auckland for four years. He knew some other Nigerians.

He lived in a row of battered wooden villas and peeling stucco flats. The grass in front yards was thick. I saw a dead rat. Curtains were ripped and torn, fences were smashed, there were packets of cigarette papers on the pavement. I bent down to pick up a toy gorilla. Ants marched around it. A silverfish approached. It intercepted a crumb passed between two ants, and rode off.

The front door to a flat was open. Manjoola, seventeen, small and shrewd, lay on the couch in pyjamas and sheepskin boots; her sister Sophie, twenty, shy and rather large, stood in the kitchen, wearing a yellow terry-towelling dressing gown. They were beautiful girls, Indians from Fiji, and there seemed such decadence in their sleepwear. But they were shiftworkers, at Burger King and KFC – perhaps Manjoola sold the old man in the house-boat what was nearly his last supper – and they lived with their parents in a dark two-bedroom flat that cost $280 a week.

I asked about their neighbours. There was an old New Zealand man who hung his gigantic white underpants on a line they could see from their kitchen. There was a Cook Islander couple with a big dog. 'Tinnie house,' said Sophie, meaning they sold dope. How did they know? 'Pair of sandshoes tied up on the power lines outside,' said Manjoola. There were also three Chinese girls, very young, very pretty. I told Manjoola and Sophie about Mr Wang, and said, 'He is looking for love.' Manjoola said, 'They sell it for an hour.'

The sisters laughed. It felt like such a happy house. There was a prayer room and candle set up inside the broom cupboard. What did they pray for? 'Mum and Dad and Manjoola,' said Sophie. Manjoola said, 'Mum and Dad and Sophie and Mr Wang.'

THREE OF AUCKLAND'S dormant volcanoes rose round and grassy as I stood on top of a rise and admired the view. You could see flat, stunned suburbs, the rectangles of sports fields, and the oval of an abandoned racetrack. I was loving the walk, the fresh air, the smell of crushed figs fallen from Moreton Bay fig trees – they smelled of coconut. The sun was high. Warm air waggled above the pavements.

An old woman on a mobility scooter waited at the traffic lights. The crone held onto the leash of her pitbull. I was entering a zone of high security and low expectations. A retirement village, cruelly, was on Ash Road. A few doors down, I called in on Noel, an old man who I saw sitting inside a hut. It had a phone in it and a calendar. Noel wore a Texan tie and – how do you do, Lord Chatterley? – a neck brace.

He sold fences and gates. He was very cynical. 'The crime scene in New Zealand is wonderful,' he said. 'We can't keep up with it. Ten years ago if you said you wanted razor wire, you'd be run out of town. Now everyone wants it. People are desperate for security.'

The hut was his office. His home was on the other side of town, on the same Auckland street as New Zealand's millionaire Prime Minister, John Key. Even there, he said, there was a crime wave. Two days ago he counted six cars which had been broken into. 'Key, he wouldn't know a bloody thing about it. Walking disaster. Idiot. But they love him. Wake up, New Zealand!'

I NEEDED A rest. I'd walked about eight kilometres, a third of the way, and stopped in at a Korean dumpling restaurant in a row of five shops. There was a superette, a bakery, a hair salon, and that constant in any low-income precinct: a coin-operated laundromat. No one was in it. The salon was closed. An elderly Chinese woman with an angry face, framed beneath a hairnet, glared above a tray of large sugar doughnuts at the bakery. The superette was a miracle of tidiness, every object perfectly positioned, the floor spotless; an Indian woman with exquisite make-up waited for customers.

I read the paper at the restaurant. 'Very bad man,' said the woman who brought out a bowl of dumplings. She stabbed her finger at a photograph of a man in a business suit. It was the investment analyst who had become an overnight villain. Famously, he had driven his Saab over a Korean man who had marched over and angrily banged on his bonnet. The businessman had panicked, and fled, not realising that the 'small bump' he felt beneath the wheels was the legs of the Korean. His victim, who sold cigarette lighters and batteries to convenience stores, suffered terrible injuries.

The finger stabbed again at the photo. I pointed at another picture, of the Korean, and said, 'Very angry man.' I hated the simple little morality tale of the press coverage. The businessman lived in a $2 million house with a pool, earned a $100,000 bonus every six months; the Korean slept in a warehouse, and couldn't afford his medical bills. A jury found the businessman guilty of reckless driving. He was given a community sentence. The law, howled the mob, was an ass. Throughout, the businessman had failed to give the mob what it wanted: an apology. He had transgressed some deep New Zealand code by not admitting fault. 'Very bad man.' We are all Koreans now.

MAD DOGS BARKED in the midday sun behind razor wire, possibly sold by old Noel, and the heat climbed. But Mr Sione was wrapped up like Scott of the Antarctic as he ambled along the pavement.

He said, 'Oh, is so cold in New Zealand! I go home Saturday to Tonga. I been visiting family for three months.' Where was he headed today? 'To Pak'NSave,' he said. 'I arks my brother, is it far? He say, "A walk do you good".' He smiled, and wrapped his coat around his shoulders. 'It don't do me good.' *I arks my brother.* He spoke in a kind of fluent Tonglish.

I turned a corner, and walked among the servants of Allah. The next suburb I had come to was a little mecca, with its mosque and its halal gizzards, its Egyptians, Iraqis, Pakistanis, Palestinians; and an Ethiopian, Gabra, who arrived in New Zealand in 2001. She had very big round eyes. She wore a gold cross around her neck. I asked her about her faith, and she said, 'When I come here, life is dark. Everything was mess. Immigration say, "We don't accept you. No work permit for you." I waiting, waiting, waiting. I ask God, "Where are you?" That night I dream. God say, "You will win. I bless you." I am born again.'

Did this bring happiness? Gabra said, 'Not really. I'm not happy. I wanted to visit my mum when she was sick, but I didn't have the papers to leave and come back. My mum waited, waited, waited for me, until she died.'

I headed for the shining waters of an inlet, crossed a pedestrian bridge, swung east, and made for New Zealand's longest and most important road, an epic stretch of street laid in concrete one foot thick, first cut out of swamp and bush in 1843 – the Great South Road, made great in the 1860s, when Governor George Grey expanded it to move troops from Auckland to invade the Waikato, and smash the Māori resistance.

What layers of history moved on the tides of its past? Buried violence, foundations of lawless impulse. Scott Hamilton, in his brilliantly provocative and unashamedly intellectual blog *Reading the Maps*, has often written about the history and meaning of the Great South Road. He notes, 'Soldiers were regularly flogged for desertion, theft and drunkenness, and sometimes appeared in civilian courts accused of more serious offences. In January 1864, for instance, a member of the First Waikato Regiment named Michael McGuire was charged with raping a fourteen-year-old Pākehā girl in one of the settlements along the Great South Road.'

One of his blogs is a kind of open-letter proposal for funding. With director Paul Jarman, Hamilton wanted to a film a documentary about the Great South Road. He knew his subject. He writes, 'In the 1940s and '50s Māori from the Waikato and Northland began to settle in significant numbers in the new suburbs beside the Great South Road. In later decades of the twentieth century, South Auckland became the main destination for new immigrants to New Zealand. In the 1960s and '70s tens of thousands of Pacific Islanders were drawn by the promise of jobs in the area's burgeoning economy.' Despite the neoliberal restructuring of the economy in the late 1980s and the '90s, and the closure of railway workshops and factories in South Auckland, the flow of new citizens from the Pacific has continued, and has been complemented by immigration from Asia and the Middle East. 'With their linguistic and cultural diversity, the new communities along the Great South Road offer a glimpse of New Zealand's future.'

I kept my eyes peeled for glimpses. There was Khaled from Cairo, a confirmed Marxist and indifferent Muslim, smoking a waterpipe in front of a barbershop. 'These fanatics,' he said, squinting in the direction of the mosque, 'with their rules and hierarchies... Hypocrites!' I asked if he knew enough Marxists to form a cell. 'Please. Take me seriously,' he said, I apologised, and felt ashamed. He passed the waterpipe. It was orange flavoured. We talked about his barbershop. He said he sub-let a room above it to an Iraqi tailor. How much? 'Market value,' said Khaled.

Mr Singh sat on the front steps of his flat in a kind of row of barracks. He was only fifty-four, but looked decrepit; there were black hollows carved beneath his eyes, his mouth was thin and bitter. He came from Bangalore.

He arrived in Auckland with his wife in 2008. Their son, an engineer, flew them over, but he left last year for a better job in Australia. 'We have no relatives, no friends,' said Mr Singh. 'All the time staying at home. TV. But New Zealand is good country.' He wore a faded pink T-shirt. It mocked him; it read, COOL GUY.

The barracks were next to a river. Two Chinese men were fishing, and had filled half a bucket with twitching mullet. The brown water stirred, and up popped a shag, large and sleek and glistening. Afternoon rush-hour sent up wads of exhaust smoke; the sky darkened, and I walked past a massive brewery. There were grand houses with chipped fountains, an empty caryard, a Mongolian barbecue restaurant.

George from Rarotonga sat in his wheelchair – Lord Chatterley in blackface, but he wore a singlet, and his upper body was strong, athletic. He was twenty-three. Two years ago, in the Cook Islands, he was climbing up a waterfall but lost his footing, and fell. He was flown to New Zealand for emergency surgery, and stayed: he was paralysed from the hips down.

He said, 'Oh man, New Zealand's the best! Good food, and you get the benefit, not like fucken Raro.' Good food? 'KFC.' There was a scar on his forehead. 'Oh, that. I fell off a bridge once.'

TWENTY KILOMETRES DOWN, and just the last ten kilometre stretch to the airport to go. I looped back towards the west. There were planes overhead. Leaving, not landing: Gisborne had grabbed its hat, made its goodbyes, was out the door. On the ground, a finance lender brazenly advertised its services to BENEFICIARIES WITH BAD CREDIT, and a short, dazed Māori with tattoos around his neck came out of a dairy, stared at the traffic with his mouth wide open, and then walked upstairs to his room in a boarding lodge.

But there were palm trees in rude good health, and a cheerful shopping centre, selling pink taro and green coconuts. There were a lot of Dollar Shops. There were a lot of Pacific Islanders and Asians. I got to talking with Michele, half-Māori, half-Chinese, as she walked along the pavement with her shopping bags. They were stocked with porkbone, watercress, pumpkin, kumara, cabbage, carrots, beetroot and turnips. 'We grew up loving food,' she said. She was the youngest of twelve growing up in a market garden south of Auckland. 'Parsnips is where Dad made his name and his money. It's a hard vegetable to grow; it has a poisonous sap that can burn your skin – look,' she said, and rolled up her sleeve. 'I still have scars.'

Another inlet, another bridge, another round, grassy volcano. Golden light glowed on a stand of gum trees. A faint breeze stirred the Tongan and Samoan flags in a lawn cemetery.

I got to the last block of shops before the pastures and scrublands surrounding the airport. A homeless man walked into a park. A tough Māori woman wore a T-shirt which instructed readers, IF YOU TALK SHIT, YOU GET HIT. An Indian restaurant advertised goat curry. An Asian hair salon advertised LADIE'S HAIRCUTS. Outside a Catholic church, a statue of Mary was protected by a security fence – no razor wire, yet. The foundation stone of a Presbyterian church was inscribed in the unlovely mangled English of Corinthians: OTHER FOUNDATION CAN NO MAN LAY THAN THAT IS LAID WHICH IS JESUS CHRIST.

An office building advertised a Chinese medical university, Mrs Wong's Ballet Academy, and Mr Xu's tax accountancy firm. I walked in, and found Mr Xu behind a stack of papers on his desk. 'I'm so busy!' he wailed, and returned to his figures.

A few doors down, a young Indian loitered in the doorway. His hair was sleek and shiny. He looked fit, agile, happy. He said, 'Do you want to have fun?'

I asked what he had in mind. 'Come upstairs,' he said, and took a step backwards. He was nervous, breathy, strange.

No, I said, tell me here. He said: 'Man on man fun.' Here, at last, was the potent and orgasmic Mellors – but I was being cast as Lady Chatterley. I said, I don't think so. He said, 'I've never tried it! I was just curious…'

IT WAS A dismal way to end my tour of civilisation. The shops finished, and the fields began. There were three large glasshouses full of tomato plants. There were cows, spur-winged plovers, trucks. I stopped for a beer at a deserted airport hotel. There was a giant kiwi sculpture on the roof. The setting sun shone on its fat arse.

I tromped along a four-lane speedway to the airport. The traffic was hard and fast, making it too dangerous to walk on the side of the road, so I stuck close to the fence-line, and staggered the last four kilometres in a muddy ditch. My shoes got wet. I was happy. I'd gone for a thirty kilometre stroll. I got to Auckland International Airport and sat down and didn't move for nearly an hour. Six flights had left for Sydney that day, and another three were scheduled; the numbers were only slightly less for Brisbane and Melbourne. There were flights to Perth, the Gold Coast, Cairns, Adelaide. A flight arrived from Guangzhou, another from Kuala Lumpur. It wasn't a bad exchange. The new world was arriving, and New Zealand was getting out of the way.

The new New Zealanders moved slowly, cautiously. The departing New Zealanders, any minute about to become ex-New Zealanders, brayed and stuck out their stomachs and stocked up at duty free. They were taking the New Zealand way of life with them, including the belligerence and complaint, the aggression and claustrophobia, and their large stupid children with wizened, bitter faces.

It had got dark. It was a beautiful summer's evening. I looked at the anxious Kiwi fatties heading for the door, and thought: *You must be mad leaving all this behind.*

For a walk of a different kind, read 'Nocturnal' by Owen Marshall, in the e-book *Pacific Highways: Volume 2*, available free at www.griffithreview.com

Steve Braunias is the author of *Civilisation: 20 Places on the Edge of the World* (Awa Press), judged best non-fiction book of the year at the 2013 *New Zealand Post* national book awards. He works as a staff writer at *Metro* magazine and lives in Te Atatu, Auckland.

On masks and migration

Learning to stand upright

Harry Ricketts

WINTER, *a small grocery shop in suburban New Zealand*: the opening stage direction of Jacob Rajan's enduringly popular solo piece *Krishnan's Dairy*, first performed at Bats in Wellington in 1997. A short song describes how Gobi and Zina Krishnan came to New Zealand from India and set up their quintessential Kiwi dairy. Rajan as Gobi appears behind the counter. His face is in half-mask, he puts on a scarf, starts to sing 'I Say a Little Prayer for You', forgets the words, hums, mimes opening and closing the dairy door, puts out buckets of cut flowers, stares at the moon. Soon – deftly switching between masks – Rajan will also be Zina, the emperor Shah Jahan and his wife Mumtaz Mahal (in whose memory he built the Taj Mahal), and, at the end of the play years after Gobi is shot by a burglar, Apu, Gobi's and Zina's grown-up son.

Theatrically, the use of masks links *Krishnan's Dairy* to classical Greek tragedy, Commedia dell'arte, Japanese Noh drama, also religious ritual and observance in many parts of the world. Equally, the masks point up the front, the persona, that immigrants often, perhaps always, feel required to adopt on coming to a new country, to New Zealand, for instance. Gobi's mask also suggests the stereotypical image that locals sometimes project onto new arrivals: Indians are highly strung, English are snooty, Germans are efficiency-mad, Asians drive badly…

The immigrant mask can take many forms. In her 1980 short story 'The

Spy', the Danish-descended Yvonne du Fresne, lightly fictionalising her child-self as Astrid, describes how in the 1930s she tried to model herself on an English neighbour, girl of the Empire, making her 'spine a ramrod of steel' and rehearsing 'a new light, cool voice': 'I prayed that I might choke on one of the afternoon tea cakes, and be brought back from the Dead by a smart thump on my back by Hilary, and recover, and say "Don't worry – it was nothing." For that was what Hilary and her friends said when they were thrown by their Shetland ponies.'

THAT CERTAINLY WASN'T the approved model or mask fifty years later when I moved to New Zealand from the UK in 1981 – in fact, rather the reverse. This was made clear to me sometimes playfully, sometimes pointedly. One early friend liked to tease me about not grasping that 'He's a good joker' didn't mean someone was funny, just that he was a good bloke. At a poetry reading I took part in a couple of years later in Christchurch, I was ticked off by a local poet for how English my poems sounded and, by implication, my speaking voice. The experience transmogrified itself into a poem called 'The Reading', suggesting in the penultimate line a comic version of the image or mask that the immigrant may find reflected back at them:

> The audience has been most polite;
> and why not? – jacket, short hair, English, I'm safe enough;
> my poems won't bite…
> In the second half (a bit drunk) I start to bluff;
> tell a risqué story – which falls flat.
> The audience is getting bored,
> and so am I. I wonder if I were to strip
> – decide it hasn't come to that.
> There are what appear to be two huge tusks growing down over my
> > upper lip.
> I stop. The audience, relieved, applaud.

My kids learned the trick much quicker and more successfully, soon switching accent and idiom between school and home as neatly as Jacob Rajan switched masks.

Accent is always a powerful marker of difference: Gobi's and Zina's Indian English; my modified public school English; the German, Polish, Czech, Austrian and Hungarian accents of the Hitler-fleeing refugees Ann Beaglehole chronicles so movingly in *A Small Price to Pay* (Allen & Unwin, 1988). One of these, Gerry Gilbert, apparently 'rejoiced when days passed without being asked *Where are you from?* every time she spoke.' For some of the wartime German refugees Beaglehole interviewed the situation was further complicated by their vehement desire to forget their native language, refusing to speak it themselves and refusing to teach it to their children. 'Don't say it in Russian, don't say it in German / Say it in broken English', as Marianne Faithfull later famously sang in a different context.

Beaglehole makes the obvious but crucial distinction between voluntary and involuntary immigration: 'It is the absence of free choice that distinguishes a refugee from a migrant.' In my case, with a growing family, I was (partly at least) running away from what seemed like a paralysed, already Thatcheritic England which seemed a dispiriting place to bring up children. And I was lucky enough to be running towards a job, a university lectureship.

I was also, like other immigrants before and since, just running. I was born into a post-WWII, fag-end-of-Empire world, and, until he retired, my mother and I followed my British army officer father from posting to posting: London, Ipoh, London, Worcester, Hong Kong, finally Worcester again. From an early age, my inner circuitry was programmed for a move every few years, and as an adult I initially replicated the pattern: university in England, teaching in Hong Kong, teaching in England, teaching in New Zealand.

By contrast, remittance men, like Nicholas Mahs, form a rather special category of immigrant: neither quite voluntary nor involuntary, but forced, often bribed, to live in a colony like New Zealand because of some social misdemeanour or scandal. For Mahs, it was marrying beneath him, and his irate father packed him off from England at the age of thirty, together with his wife, to live out the next four decades in Dunedin. The mask that Mahs seems to have adopted, or simply maintained, was that of a gentleman of leisure. One consolation late in his exile came when Lord Kitchener, parading through the streets of Dunedin in 1910, spotted Mahs in the crowd and halted the procession to exchange a few words with his old acquaintance.

SUCCESSFUL REINVENTION IS one possible consequence of being an immigrant, previously unguessed-at energies and potentialities being released by a change of country, together with a lack of former constraints or inhibitions. The Yorkshire-born Russell Haley might be one example; he initially continued as a poet after coming to New Zealand in 1966 but really found his true vein when he turned to fiction. In one short story collection, *The Transfer Station* (1989), he even deliberately adopts a laconic, blokey persona and narrative voice reminiscent of the local short story writer and novelist Frank Sargeson. Such shifts are hinted at in *Krishnan's Dairy* since Gobi seems to be making a reasonable stab at his new shopkeeper role, as the initially reluctant Zina plainly does in the years following Gobi's death. Sometimes, for writers, the lost homeland can spring into sharper imaginative relief: Katherine Mansfield wrote her evocative Wellington stories after years in England. Sometimes the loss of a local idiom and audience has less rewarding effects, and reluctance to adapt in the new land, demonstrates a desire simply to replicate a previous role. That is one way to read Frank Sargeson's story 'The Making of a New Zealander', written in 1940 as an equivocal nod to that year's centennial celebrations. The heart of the story is an unresolved conversation between Dalmatian orchardist Nick and the narrator, an itinerant, local farm-worker, about whether either of them is really a New Zealander:

> 'You think that you and me are born too soon? What do you think?'
> He said it over and over, and I couldn't look him in the face. It had too much of that sadness … I mightn't have put it in the way Nick had, I mightn't have said I was born too soon, but Nick knew what he was talking about. Nick and I were sitting on the hillside and Nick was saying he was a New Zealander, but he knew he wasn't a New Zealander. And he knew he wasn't a Dalmatian any more.

This is one of those Sargeson stories in which, as Patrick Evans so adhesively put it in *The Penguin History of New Zealand Literature* (1990), 'Someone not very bright is going to tell us something about somewhere not very nice'.

That decade in New Zealand, the 1940s, was one especially preoccupied with questions of national identity. Allen Curnow's celebrated sonnet 'The Skeleton of the Great Moa in Christchurch Museum' (1943) riddlingly explored (at least for Pākehā New Zealanders) the identity problem, claiming that the representative speaker, like the extinct moa, though 'peculiarly New Zealand's', had 'failed to adapt', a point quietly underscored by the poem's persistent half-rhyme. The pay-off comes in the epigrammatic final couplet – 'Not I, some child born in a marvellous year, / Will learn the trick of standing upright here' – which both postpones the moment of balance (successful adaptation/assimilation) but also enacts it, since, to a New Zealand ear of the 1940s (though not, tellingly, to an English one), 'year' and 'here' make a perfect rhyme.

THIS QUESTION OF what does or does not constitute New Zealand identity persists. When my son Will, the percussionist in the local band Phoenix Foundation, tried to convert his long-term New Zealand residency into citizenship, he was officially told that touring with the band in the United States, UK and Europe (and promoting local music) meant he was spending too much outside New Zealand to qualify. Only after an eighteen-month campaign in the media and social media under the slogan 'Is Will a Kiwi?' and support from his local MP did common sense eventually prevail.

Citizenship, by birth or adoption, seems an obvious indicator of identity. But what that identity might amount to is still not always clear. A friend, who like me is a bounced Pom, suggested in a recent conversation that many Pākehā New Zealanders do not think they have a distinctive identity but in fact they do. The complication, he argued, arises from a clash between personal drive and the public need to assert a collective identity, to be 'just part of the team', 'one of the boys or girls', the recipient of a 'lucky pass'. Kiwis, he thought, want to be, even have to be, different but not tell anyone. The gold standard for such an attitude remains Edmund Hillary's throwaway comment after climbing Everest ('We knocked the bastard off'). Which partly explains why the great batsman Martin Crowe was often disparaged, not least by former team mates, as self-regarding, demanding, neurotic, insufficiently rugged. Crowe too disconcertingly asserted his difference, not least in his aesthetic of trying each time he batted to play the perfect innings. In other words, he did not adopt or promote the correct, the acceptable, stance.

Refugees and immigrants are not the only ones to wear masks. To a greater or lesser extent we all do every day, many times a day. I first became dimly aware of this in a German class at boarding school in England in the mid-1960s. We were studying Alfred Andersch's 1957 novel *Sansibar oder der letzte Grund* (Sanzibar or the Final Reason). The novel is set in 1937 in Rerik on the Baltic Sea. The Nazi presence presses in the background. Like the masks in *Krishnan's Dairy*, the narrative constantly switches between a small cast of belief-challenged characters. Most of these wish, literally or metaphorically, to escape: the local priest, two disillusioned Party members, a boy who wants to be free like Huckleberry Finn, a young Jewish girl on the run. A friend and I became very taken with a remark that Gregor, one of the faltering communists, makes: '*Wenn wir nichts mehr tun, gibt es uns auch nicht mehr*' ('If we don't do anything more, we won't exist anymore either'). How profound that seemed at fifteen, more profound perhaps for not being in English. We were rather earnestly trying to make sense of the world, to construct a presentable self, and, like Mrs Munt in Forster's *Howards End* (1910), which we were also studying, we 'collected new ideas as a squirrel collects nuts, and [were] especially *attracted* by those that are portable'. It never occurred to us at the time that our German master, whom we admired for his quicksilver banter and ability to improvise private codes out of lines from our set books (as my friend and I were busily doing), might be also putting on a mask, like Gregor, like Gobi, having to make himself perform.

Many years later, that same friend encountered our German master, now an old man, in a London superette. He told my friend that, months away from retirement, he had been sacked for propositioning one of the boys. Presumably, one day the mask just finally slipped.

References available at www.griffithreview.com

Harry Ricketts teaches English literature and creative non-fiction at Victoria University of Wellington and co-edits the review quarterly *New Zealand Books*. He has published twenty-five books, including a biography of Kipling, a group biography of a dozen British World War I poets, personal essays and nine collections of poems.

Patterns of migration

Notes on eels, on the way to the Kermadecs

Gregory O'Brien

AN eel, like an artist or writer, carries its immediate past around with it: if an eel wants to know where it has been, it just spins its head 180 degrees and stares down the length of its tell-tale body. At the same time, its slender, arrow-like form implies a course onwards. My painter-friend in Sydney, Noel McKenna, would probably align the unfurling cadence of the eel-body with Paul Klee's concept of the act of drawing as 'taking a line for a walk' or maybe, in this case, a swim.

With such an association in mind, Noel McKenna's map-like painting hung in the 2013 Wynne Prize, *Centennial Park*, offers a detailed account of the life-cycle of the long-finned eels of inner city Sydney. An inscription, lower right, notes how, before European settlement, Centennial Park had been part of a chain of wetlands which linked the reserve's pond-life directly with Botany Bay: 'The eels (female) still today, usually during a rainy autumn, set off across the park, cross into Randwick Racecourse, through the suburb of Kensington, across the Australian Golf Course, into swampy Eastlakes area and across the Lakes Golf Course. After this, through swamps alongside South Coast Drive then into Botany Bay…'

Presumably a ghost-like impression of Sydney-as-prehistoric-wetland remains embedded in their fish-brains. Not only do these eels have phenomenal memory, they also have stamina and timing enough to get around the airport-bound traffic on South Dowling Road and environs. From the mouth of Botany Bay they swim northwards, as far as the spawning grounds of New Caledonia. In due course, the next generation somehow finds its way back to Centennial Park, taking a left by the kiosk, skirting the horse-track, dodging the peloton…

A comparable migration occurs amongst the eels (or tuna) of Lake Wairarapa, not far from the New Zealand town of Masterton, where artist Robin White lives. In this case, the tuna gravitate towards Tongatapu, in the Tongan Islands. In good time, the next generation comes racing back – to the same bend in the stream, the same drainpipe… (These dextrous Wairarapa eels gained a cult following in 2012 for a different, but not unrelated, reason: after unseasonal February rain, they emerged, en masse, from the town's stormwater system, transforming suburban Masterton into a scenario that could have been lifted from a low-budget horror film – see 'Mo farking eels' on YouTube.)

There is much we can learn from these eel-citizens of the South Pacific. In the post-colonial world, their tenacious, migratory nature might be considered exemplary, as might their mobility, navigational skills, phenomenal homing instinct and a usefully amphibious constitution (when out of water, they breathe through their skins).

Stylised depictions of these Wairarapa tuna traverse Robin White's mural-sized work on tapa (hand-moulded paperbark), *Siu i Moana* (2011), a creation much preoccupied with such a pattern of migration – 'for the simple reason,' she says, 'it's not just about fish; it's about life on the planet and the connectedness of all things'. Made in collaboration with Ruha Fifita and a group of Tongan women, White's ongoing series of tapa works also encapsulates the human migrations of recent decades, and celebrates the links between the peoples of Aotearoa and those of the Polynesian islands. Her iconography encompasses oceanic life forms – fish (tuna in particular), birds, crabs – while also sampling cultural and material traffic; the labels on tinned foodstuffs, flip-flops and tea bags alongside religious symbols and nationalistic emblems.

In May 2011, Robin White and I were among a group of nine artists who hitched a ride on the Royal New Zealand Navy vessel *Otago*, destined for Tonga, via the Kermadec region – one of the last near-pristine marine environments on the planet. Through these munificent waters, we traced the migratory route of Robin's tuna-neighbours – from the maritime realm up through the sub-tropics and beyond. It set us thinking and talking about the ocean and New Zealand's particular place therein. If you take into account our territorial waters (which are the fifth largest of any country in the world), only one seventeenth of 'New Zealand' is made up of dry land. If not exactly water-dwellers, we are a nation of watersiders – hence a responsibility towards the ocean and a need to – in a sense – *claim it*, imaginatively as well as in a pragmatic sense.

Robin had lived seventeen years in Kiribati so she was used to lengthy voyages and pondering such oceanic realities. Over a thousand times larger than the total landmass that drains into it, the Pacific Ocean is beyond rational comprehension. It covers nearly a third of the planet. Just north of the Kermadec Islands the seabed is ten kilometres straight down. It's a hard place to get your head around. The challenge, for all the artists involved in the Kermadec project, was to find some way of gaining artistic purchase on this aquatic reality; to find a language that could impart something of the overwhelming oceanic experience.

Alongside the aforementioned long-range eel voyages, a different migratory narrative is worth relating here – this time stemming from the Great Crayfish Boom in the waters around New Zealand's Chatham Islands during the late 1960s. A year or two into this unregulated frenzy of cray-harvesting, suddenly the nets and pots started coming to the surface empty. It wasn't that the crays had all been caught (although a huge number had been), it was that the over-fishing had prompted the remaining crayfish population to ship out – to embark on a mass migration northwards across the ocean floor. A half-century later, many of these long-lived crays are probably still in transit, trudging slowly on. (Eventually the Chathams crayfish industry was able to resume, at a sustainable level – but it has never come anywhere near its earlier, ruinous glory.)

With this form of undersea foot traffic in mind, I was talking to another Sydney-based painter-friend, Euan Macleod, whose stock-in-trade for decades has been an archetypal perambulating figure, often striding across the ocean-floor (like Ulysses or any number of equivalents in Polynesian and other mythologies). I imagined Macleod's submarine figure in transit to Raoul Island (largest of the Kermadec group), wending his way among the smoking undersea volcanoes of the Kermadec Ridge, with a formation of Robin White's eels directly overhead and the migrating Chatham crays traipsing across the seabed around him. And I also imagined, in the ocean around this figure (who will resurface in my poem *Memory of a Fish*) an even slower migration of human detritus – of busted satellites, radioactive drums, shipping containers and Coca-Cola bottles as well as debris from the MV *Rena*, lately wrecked on Astrolabe reef.

Eel-like, an artist in the Pacific needs to be both marathon swimmer and deep-sea diver. There is an immense distance to cover and there are layers and depths to every square metre of it. The artist necessarily also becomes a map-maker, plotting a course through the unstable oceanic reality, with its infinite horizons, crosscurrents and contrariness. It was in the navigational stick-charts of the Marshall Islands and the traditional tapa-cloths of Tonga, Fiji and Niue that Robin White and Niuean-born John Pule – another artist on the Kermadec voyage – discovered a modus operandi (not surprisingly an indigenous one) suited to the Pacific, and responsive to its constantly vying realities: past and present, human and non-human, indigenous and exotic, and its omnipresent cycles of life and death.

Sometime after the voyage, it was tapa-cloth that also provided the imaginative blueprint for my documentary poem *Memory of a Fish*, with its weaving of different strands – elements from history, oceanography, current events, statistics, autobiography. The poem was written in the form of a letter to my son, Felix, who sailed to Raoul Island a year after I went ashore there. (We're a lucky family: far more people make it to the summit of Mount Everest than have set foot on any of the Kermadec islands.) Although I wanted something of an eel-like movement in the cadence and, visually, in the poem's form, it was the simultaneity of the tapa-cloth that offered the abiding creative model. Inspired by the all-encompassing tapa grid, the poem was built around proximity, juxtaposition and coincidence. It was the inconsequential fact that my son and I had sat on the same lawn on Raoul Island eating ginger slice that kicked the poem to life, that set the albatross to fly in the first line – taking skywards with it some lines of Charles Baudelaire, and onward from there.

In Polynesian traditions, the tapa is often used to wrap things that are precious: not only is it used to clothe the bodies of the living but also to enshroud and honour the dead. Tapa can be used as mats off which food is eaten; or it can be hung to provide shelter. Within the formality of its grid, it contains wisdom, family and village structures, religious beliefs, histories, recipes and genealogical information. In the spirit of the tapa, *Memory of a*

Fish seeks to cover great distances while, at the same time, rendering them intimate (therein lies a paradox at the heart of Oceania), to navigate simply the complexities of the Pacific while touching upon issues currently facing the region.

Since the Kermadec voyage and subsequent visits to Tonga, Rapanui (Easter Island) and Chile, my notion of the Pacific has changed. Instead of being a vast, silent *nowhere,* it has become a sentence stocked with a multitude of verbs and nouns, all of them contained within two geographical parentheses: on one side the curvilinear form of New Zealand and, on the other, the ribbon-like nation of Chile. Looking horizon-wards from either extremity, we might contemplate what artist Phil Dadson refers to as 'the pulsing current of the intelligence we're part of'. About 60 to 70 per cent of the human body is made of water, he reminds us, hence 'the tidal rhythms that connect us to the oceans'. Accordingly, we might consider the ocean as an animating principle as well as sustaining presence – 'the ocean within us', to borrow a phrase from Epeli Hau'ofa.

At this point we might bring together all the strands of human culture, history and voyaging that we can gather along with strands of non-human life: flight paths of sea birds, currents of ocean and air, migratory routes of tuna… On the intersecting tapa-matrix of these plotted lines, we could then locate ourselves as beings deeply rooted in a place (or space) but also migratory, transient, in flux. Integral to this permanent state of unfinishing, the ocean, *our ocean*, has no end – as Robin White told me, on the aft deck of HMNZS *Otago* – only loose ends.

'Memory of a fish' can be read in the e-book *Pacific Highways: Volume 2*, available free at www.griffithreview.com

Notes and suggested further reading are also available on the website.

Gregory O'Brien is a Wellington-based poet, essayist, painter and curator, whose recent publications include a collection of poems, *Beauties of the Octagonal Pool*, (Auckland University Press, 2012), and a monograph on painter Euan Macleod (Piper Press, Sydney, 2010). An earlier meditation on oceanic matters, *News of the swimmer reaches shore*, appeared from Carcanet (UK) and Victoria University Press in 2007.

Cable stations

The encircled earth

Lynne McDonald

Here in the womb of the world — here on the tie-ribs of earth
Words, and the words of men, flicker and flutter and beat
Warning, sorrow and gain, salutation and mirth

Rudyard Kipling, 1902

'**WANTED,** boys fifteen years of age to learn submarine telegraphy and serve overseas.' This type of advertisement attracted young men to serve in the Pacific Cable Board's (PCB) network of stations across the Pacific. Among them my great-grandfather, David Cuthbert, and my grandfather, Robert Cuthbert, who worked as cable operators, with David becoming a manager. The peregrinations of this cable family took them from Tobermory, Scotland, to Ballenskelligs in Ireland. From the snow in Halifax, Nova Scotia, to Bamfield, Canada, then later to the warmer climes of Southport in Queensland, Norfolk Island, Fiji and strangest of all, Fanning Island, nearly 2,000 kilometres from Honolulu.

Robert Cuthbert was born in Ballenskelligs in 1885. His son, Martin, my father, was born in Suva in 1918, and lived on cable stations in Fiji, Fanning Island, Halifax, Norfolk Island, and finally settled in Auckland when his father retired. As a child I was probably the only person at school who could point to Fanning Island on a map. I grew up in a 'Cable Family', and relished the stories my father told of his childhood including descriptions of huge coconut crabs that prowled around the houses on Fanning Island. My father built crystal sets for us, using skills passed to him by his father and his grandfather. I have been told that after he died, David Cuthbert's house in Auckland was festooned with aerial wires for crystal sets and other 'wireless' devices as his descendants carried on his fine tradition. A cable man's skills live on. Memories of life on Fanning Island stayed with my father and his sister. Both my great-grandfather and grandfather lived and worked there and my uncle David was born there, I can only look on my grandmother with awe at her courage to take her childen to live on isolated Fanning Island, let alone to deliver a baby there.

NEW ZEALAND WAS, like Australia, connected to Britain by the Eastern Extension Australasia and China Telegraph Company cable, which ran through the Middle East and across the Indian Ocean to Australia, and across the Atlantic to Nova Scotia. Its frequent breakdowns, however, meant that the New Zealand government was keen to support any endeavour that promised a more reliable connection.

The Pacific Cable Board was formed by the British and Canadian governments in 1896 with additional members from Australia and New Zealand.

With Britain's territorial possessions coloured red on the map in the nineteenth and much of the twentieth century, the dream was for a cable that touched only British soil – an 'All Red' route. The plan to establish a submarine telecommunications cable across the Pacific would realise this ideal and circumnavigate the globe. One of the first highways across the Pacific was the almost 'All Red' route of PCB cable. 'All Red' shipping lines were popular with tourists in the dying days of the Empire – from Australia to Fiji, Honolulu and Vancouver. The dream was, however, never fully realised. Ships had to refuel at non-British ports and airlines had to share facilities. These enterprises were 'All Red' in spirit only.

When the cable was connected in 1902 the *Brisbane Courier* described the cable as 'the world's great ocean highway'. In *The Tentacles of Progress* (1988), Daniel R Headrick described the British Empire as, 'stronger than death dealing war-ships (sic)…stronger even than the unswerving justice of Queen Victoria's rule are the…two or three slender wires that connect the scattered parts of her realm.' Headrick argued, 'The web of iron that tied the colonial empires together was [now] made of electricity as well as steam and iron.'

In pursuit of the 'All Red' cable line, the PCB needed relay station sites. Stations needed deep water so the cable did not snag on the seabed or get caught by the anchors, a sloping beach to bring the cable to shore; land to locate an office and connect the cable ends, and sites suitable for building staff residences. The most propitious seabed was soft and muddy, known as globigerina or radiolarian ooze, which allowed the cable to sink into the mud, protected from most damage, except volcanic eruption and earthquakes.

While it was relatively easy to select Bamfield in Vancouver for the first Pacific relay station in 1901, the next link was more perplexing. With cable-laying technology still embryonic, distance was critical. The nearest British territory on the route between Vancouver and Fiji was Fanning Island, but that would require the cable to be laid over nearly 6,500 kilometres. This was considered impossible at the time – the trans-Atlantic cable, laid by the ship the *Great Eastern* was only 3,680 kilometres long.

The alternative was to use an unclaimed island in the Hawaii group, Necker Island, which would have reduced the length of cable to 5,120 kilometres. Canadian Sir Sandford Fleming, a leading proponent of the cable, asked a colleague to travel to Necker Island and claim it for Canada, but discovered that Britain had already ceded sovereignty over the island to Hawaii and had only requested landing rights for the cable. When Hawaii learnt of Fleming's intentions, it sent the steamer ship *Iwalani* to take possession of the rocky island and ensure its sovereignty was protected.

Fleming's proposed route had been from Vancouver to Necker Island, then to Apamana Island in the Gilbert group, and on to San Cristobal in the Solomon Islands, then to Australia at Port Denison, Queensland. This would have bypassed New Zealand.

This route did not eventuate. Despite the higher cost of Fanning Island and a possibly a slower message rate, it was the chosen route.

In Vancouver, a site was selected at the junction of Bamfield and Grappler Creeks in Barclay Sound. The cable from Halifax, Nova Scotia, to Vancouver was operated by the Canadian Pacific Railway Company until 1910 when it was handed over to PCB. The Canadian Pacific Railway Company constructed the Vancouver cable station between 1901 and 1902 on the top of a cliff, including a fifty-room bachelors' quarters, with library, billiard and music rooms, for twenty men and twelve Chinese servants. There was also a manager's house. The married staff lived in twelve houses. One cable operator said that had PCB used isolation as one of the criteria for selecting Bamfield, it was a good choice, and it reduced the distance to Fanning Island by a few miles. Although money may have been saved on the cable, the station was very expensive to maintain. The staff included a plant engineer, fulltime carpenter, servants, a cook, two waiters, night duty cook, cook's helper, two laundrymen, and an office boy. There was also 'outside staff', a Chinese foreman and several workers. Everything was shipped by sea, using a 'three boat a month' service run by the Canadian Pacific Railway.

THE SELECTION OF the landing site in Australia was comparatively easy. Land at Southport was acquired and the Australian postmaster-general oversaw the project. This became the training school for the young operators from the British Empire. There was a gymnasium, tennis court, and library on site, which was close enough to town for the trainees to venture out on social occasions – dressed in navy blazers trimmed with red embroidery, a red crown on the breast pocket to indicate they were on imperial service.

The next relay station, Norfolk Island, was where three separate parts of the cable landed; the Queensland line, the New Zealand line and the Fiji line. Anson Bay was chosen, the only location on the island with a gently sloping sandy beach, but far from the island's main settlement and its 'easygoing indolent people'. Hopes that the station should become self-sufficient were expensive to realise. Staff needed a lot of extra assistance to be self-sufficient. Even more, apparently, than the isolated atoll, Fanning Island.

A survey of the Northland area by cable steamer *Britannia* led to Doubtless Bay being chosen as the New Zealand station in 1901. The isolation of Harris Green was likened to an island. The land was desolate, unable to support any form of agriculture, but there was space for station buildings.

Harris Green finalised the link between New Zealand and England by an (almost) 'All Red' line.

A new cable was eventually laid to speed messages between Southport and Sydney, and Doubtless Bay to Auckland. Harris Green cable station became redundant by 1912. In time, the cost of routing all messages from New Zealand to Australia through Norfolk Island became unsustainable. Instead a cable was laid directly from Bondi Beach in Sydney to Muriwai Beach in Auckland in 1912. Now New Zealanders flock to Muriwai Beach to surf, as they do to Bondi Beach. The favoured gathering points for young Australiasians were first linked by cable.

FIJI WAS MORE of a problem. A landing place for the cable at Suva was difficult to find because the cables had to be stored in tanks onshore to avoid them drying out, then floated out to the cable ship, which had to moor as close as possible because there was a limit to the time that the cable could drift in the sun. The best solution was to reclaim land which would also accommodate any future extensions, but this increased construction costs.

Britannia arrived at Fanning Island – an atoll almost 3,500 kilometres from Suva – on 23 August 1901, with a letter of introduction from the acting Western Pacific high commissioner which advised long-time resident, and one of the so-called 'Kings' of Fanning Island, William Greig, that the British government had the right to take any part of the land on Washington or Fanning Island for the cable. Known to the people of nearby Manihiki as Tabuaeran ('the place of the heavenly footprint') because of its shape, the area of land on Fanning Island is approximately 34 square kilometres with a lagoon covering about 110 square kilometres. The rim of useable land is about a kilometre wide. A site had been selected on an earlier visit by Captain Field on HMS *Penguin* who described the land as 'a howling wilderness of barren stone-covered ground' where Greig had established a sort of oasis, with enough soil to allow grass (of a sort) to grow. Shade from coconut trees created a pleasant site for the buildings, in comparison to the rest of the barren atoll. Greig imported potatoes and onions twice a year from San Francisco, and kept pigs, cattle and poultry, which fed on the meagre grass, leaves and other greenery.

There is no trace of an earlier occupation of the atoll. Several people had previously claimed the island for England, even purchased it from those already living there. Caroline Ralston described how Joseph Navarro, a member of the 'beach community' in Honolulu, was banished to Fanning Island in 1825 for assaulting his wife's lover. In 1848 George Collie and Edward Lucett from Tahiti stayed briefly, taking possession of the island for Britain. Lucett found a 'man of Crusoe habits' on the island, with his 'Kanak' wife from the Sandwich [Hawaiian] Islands and a large number of children and grandchildren. Henry English probably paid Lucett and Collie for possession in 1852, and set up a plantation using Manihikan labour. Later, the Scot William Greig and American G Bicknell and their families took over the island, and worked with JT Arundel to set up what became an unproductive guano business between 1879 and 1883.

The ownership of the little island continued to be subject to underhanded dealings and intrigue. In 1906 the *Los Angeles Times* published an article headed 'Fanning Island, A Queer Little South Sea Spot Which Is To Be Auctioned Off By England'. After several changes of ownership by 1935, Burns Philp purchased both Fanning and neighbouring Washington Islands, and formed Fanning Islands Plantations Limited. The cable station there operated until 1963.

The proposed site of the cable station, where the old guano works once stood, was one of the highest points on the island, and received the full benefit of any winds. Fresh water was scarce, so large cement underground tanks were needed. The construction of a wharf for unloading supplies from ships was also suggested, as it was dangerous for ships to approach too close to the shore. *Britannia* landed a building to house the shore ends of the cable.

The cable station buildings on Fanning Island included a manager's house, bachelor quarters, and houses for married staff. There were amenities to keep the men occupied, including a swimming pool, night and day tennis (on a court which was painted green to absorb the glare from the sun), billiards and movies. There was good fishing and the lagoon provided many pastimes – sailing and outrigger canoe racing. Some had their own dinghies with outboard motors for fishing trips and excursions.

The hall had a stage, piano and a pianola with several hundred rolls and a gramophone with twenty records. The married quarters and the doctor's house were on the same side as the lagoons – airy open concrete villas about ten feet above the ground surrounded by verandas. On the ocean side there were workshops, engine rooms and freezing chambers, boat houses, the cable hut and the little settlement where the Indian and Gilbertese servants lived. Alcoholic beverages were permitted, and because the island was considered to be a ship at sea for customs purposes, it was duty free and so each man could keep a good supply of 'liquid refreshments'. While my family stories were not recorded, the archives hold some tales from Fanning Island. The single men's quarters were spacious and built in three parts which soon acquired names, such as 'Snobs Alley', Posh Lane', and 'The Bastard's Retreat'. More recently, a retired telegraph operator recalled the 'Bomb' parties when Britain tested nuclear weapons on nearby Kiritimati Island in the 1950s and cable staff would celebrate by watching the explosions after listening to the countdown through the wireless equipment.

IN 1902 THE Pacific cable was ready for operation. On 3 March, the *Anglia* anchored offshore at Southport, ready to splice its end of the cable to the prepared one onshore. Landing the cable was more difficult than expected. There was big surf and the crew of the surf boat that rowed out to the ship with the cable aboard was unable to continue. The ingenious solution was to float a rope in from the ship, with the cable attached to a row of barrels. (A similar method was used in 1999 to land the new Southern Cross cable at New Zealand's Takapuna Beach.) The winch was not strong enough for the extra weight of the heavy rope, so twenty men helped heave the heavy rope on to the beach. As they pulled the row of barrels ashore, the waiting crowd cheered as the end of the cable appeared. The cable was tested and messages were successfully sent and received.

Despite its somewhat ignominious arrival, the cable was in place and *Anglia* departed for Norfolk Island, landing the shore end of the cable there two weeks later. Then *Anglia* steamed to Doubtless Bay and by the end of the month New Zealand was linked to Norfolk Island and Australia. The welcoming party included New Zealand postmaster-general Sir Joseph Ward who sent a message to his Australian counterpart deputy postmaster-general, HH Buzacott; 'I have attended at Doubtless Bay today and have had the pleasure of witnessing the landing of the Pacific cable between New Zealand, Norfolk Island and Austra-lia…' Messages captured the excitement and possibilities: 'The cable…will unite Canada with New Zealand and Australia', and this from Brisbane, 'this event will tend to bind closer these bonds of kinship between the contracting colonies.'

The *Anglia* sailed on to lay the cable to Suva, splicing the ends on 10 April. The first message sent over the cable was from the governor of Fiji to the governor of New South Wales, congratulating him on the success of the enterprise. There was then a delay of five months until the northern Pacific section was laid.

An understated but nevertheless triumphant message was sent from Suva on 31 October, 'The Pacific Cable was completed at 5.15 today'. The next day the shore end of the cable linking Fiji with Fanning Island was joined at Suva to 'unite the two hemispheres', as the *Fiji Times* reported. With the final splicing, the 'crimson thread which will bind Queensland in friendly handgrip with kinsmen beyond the seas…' was complete. One of the first messages was handed to King Edward VII on Newmarket Racecourse.

The *Brisbane Courier* waxed lyrical in its tribute. Headlined 'The Encircled Earth', the article spoke of breaking down boundaries, reconciliation of racial animosities. 'Puck's metaphor of putting a girdle around the earth in forty minutes became yesterday an embodied reality…'

On 3 November 1902, the cable was officially commissioned by the Australian postmaster-general, JG Drake. The celebrations were marked by speeches by politicians and the superintendent of Pacific Cable, in the presence of celebrities including soprano Nellie Melba and the famous body builder, Eugen Sandow.

A 'Great Ocean Highway' now crossed the Pacific; silence was replaced with chatter as messages sped back and forth under the sea between the islands. They brought the news of the sinking of the *Titanic*, the outbreak of World War I, and the panicked message sent by an operator as Germans entered the cable building at Fanning Island in 1914, about to cut the cable and destroy equipment. This message was received at the Bamfield cable station by its manager, my great-grandfather among others. The cable also brought up-to-date news and information about prices for export products from Australia.

This highway invigorated the Pacific, it connected previously isolated islands, and provided work for many New Zealanders, Australians and Canadians – 'Gentlemen On Imperial Service'.

Lynne McDonald studied Pacific history to Masters level at the University of Auckland, where one of her lecturers encouraged to use her family ties to the 'Cable' in her Masters thesis. She is currently undertaking a PhD at Massey University.

James Brown

Demarcations

1. The Violinist in Spring

It is not the blue notes, but the blue touch paper.
It is not the short fuse, but the long memory.
It is not the small bunch of forget-me-nots, but the bed of red hot pokers.
It is not the brand recognition, but the subconscious associations.
It is not the warm feelings, but the doubtful sounds.
It is not the diminished seventh, but the opening chord to 'Hard Day's Night'.
It is not what it has been, but what it will become.
It is not the leap of faith, but the wired landing.
It is not the abandoned airstrip, but the opencast mine.
It is not the tailings, but the percentages.
It is not the dance in the figures, but the figures in the dance.
It is not the twist, but the sacrificial rites.
It is not the heart in the mouth, but the fork in the tongue.
It is not between the lines, but between you and me.

2. Summer Near the Arctic Circle

It is not the distance between us, but the lack of distance between us.
It is not the bonds, but the restraints.
It is not the cucumber sandwiches, but the people passing round the
    cucumber sandwiches.
It is not the cut of the jib, but the angle of entry.
It is not the long division, but the brief comings together.
It is not the bare buttocks, but the bared buttocks.
It is not the offensive line, but the defensive line.
It is not the trench system, but the high water table.
It is not the insufficient fall, but the blocking high.
It is not the big picture, but the tiny ruins.
It is not the clues, but the puzzle.
It is not the correct answer, but the pencilled working.
It is not the sound reasoning, but the quiet mystery.
It is not the man in the moon, but the woman in the well.

3. Autumn Testament

It is not the farther to go, but the father to be.
It is not the longing, but the belonging.
It is not the clasp on the purse, but the purse on the lips.
It is not above suspicion, but under the pump.
It is not the unsettled stomach, but the unsettled mind.
It is not the need for god, but the desire for god.
It is not evidence of a divine creator, but evidence against a divine creator.
It is not the Gaza Strip, but Gazza whipping his shirt off.
It is not talking with your feet, but footing it with your mouth.
It is not the parting shot, but the passing shot.
It is not the power, but the spin.
It is not the slant, but the enchantment.
It is not the whale in the room, but the pea in the pod.
It is not under the mattress, but staring you in the face.

4. Mrs Winter's Jump

It is not the words that chill us, but the silence.
It is not the silence gathering on the rooftop, but the snow.
It is not the snow falling outside, but the snow falling inside.
It is not the deepening drifts, but the lengthening drifts.
It is not eternity, but the tight deadline.
It is not the lack of time, but the lack of humour.
It is not the obvious punchline, but the unforeseen impact.
It is not the sock in the eye, but the sock in the mouth.
It is not the cheap gag, but the cost of free speech.
It is not the failure of the imagination, but the imaginative posturing.
It is not the stroking of the chin, but the stroking of the ego.
It is not the slapped back, but the turned back.
It is not the personal preference, but the casual indifference.
It is not not caring, it is caring too much.

James Brown's latest poetry collection is *Warm Auditorium* (Victoria University Press, 2012). He has been a finalist in the Montana New Zealand Book Awards three times. He teaches the Poetry Writing workshop at the International Institute of Modern Letters at Victoria University and works as a writer at Te Papa, New Zealand's national museum.

Primate city

Gorilla in the midst

Finlay Macdonald

NOT long ago a TV current affairs program mounted a live studio debate about whether 'Auckland is sucking the life out of New Zealand'. Viewers were invited to vote and overwhelmingly agreed there was, indeed, an urban vampire in their midst. The studio audience – drawn from Auckland, naturally, since most of the national media are now based there – completely disagreed; if anything, Auckland was the real victim. As polls go it was hardly scientific. But it did point up the strange perceptual divide between much of New Zealand and its largest city.

More surprising than the result was that such a question was even being asked. Regional prejudice is one thing – denouncing the imagined Sodom and Gomorrah of the alpha city is a national pastime in many places – but what other country feels its very existence might be threatened? Even allowing for the hyperbole of primetime, the image of Auckland as a giant parasite was somewhat extreme. Conversely, what kind of city might inspire such paranoia and distrust?

That brilliantly misanthropic travel writer Paul Theroux offered this advice to the seeker of urban truths: '[The] only way to understand a city is to see its periphery, because that's where the workers generally live, the people who are employed to maintain it…' He was writing about the shanty camps of West Africa, where the edge of town tends to reveal unpalatable things about unsustainable migration, human desperation and the pitiless hierarchies of a slum planet. Were Theroux to apply his universal rule to contemporary Auckland, by contrast, the truth would be one of stultifying banality.

Built on a narrow isthmus between two harbours, the city's growth is dictated first and foremost by geography. The central east and west are the oldest residential areas, flanked by the Waitematā and Manukau harbours respectively. So the thousands of people who move to Auckland each year tend to gravitate towards its northern and southern boundaries, where the process of urbanisation is devouring once supremely fertile farmland like some peculiar form of architectural blight.

The new housing developments rising from old pastures — with names like Dannemora and Botany Downs — are now intruding into rural pockets that were once the preserve of the Range Rover and polo set; vast streetscapes of ostentatious tract housing, 'McMansions', built to the permissible limits of their sections, with colonnaded porticos and arched entranceways, like the boastful family mausoleums you find in certain cemeteries.

Albany to the north is much the same. Once the city's orchard belt, where as a child I would go with my parents to buy cheap fruit from the roadside stalls, it is now a conglomeration of steroidal subdivisions and sterile business parks, interspersed with the odd leftover green field, invariably staked out with developers' billboards and 'for sale' signs. I've worked in offices there, and was struck by the fact that the one thing everyone had in common was money — not so much the possession of it as the need to make it. There could be no other reason to be there.

At the inner extremities of Auckland's sprawl lie more traditional working class suburbs, older ones to the west and newer ones clinging to State Highway 1 as it snakes southward through Manukau and Manurewa. These are the parts of town where the middle classes prefer not to venture, where backyards accommodate the giant feet of the power pylons feeding the city, and where the news media tend to look for hard luck stories that suit the stereotypes.

But the trouble with trying to understand Auckland by studying its periphery is that the periphery keeps seeping across notional city limits like spilt paint. Villages and hamlets are subsumed in the process, built over and around, soon lost in the tangle of motorway exits and shopping mall car parks. The true frontiers of this still young city are always open to interpretation.

When I was growing up in the early 1970s, having moved to Auckland from Dunedin (and before that from London), we once had a summer holiday in Browns Bay. It felt far enough away from our home in the inner east to be a genuine change of scene. There was a camping ground with family cabins, and all the things one still associates with New Zealand's beach life – a dairy selling ice creams, people fishing from boats, a happy barefoot existence.

Browns Bay today is just another suburb on the city's northeastern coast. It drains of commuters in the morning and fills back up again when the motorway finally unclogs in the evening. It retains a pleasant, laidback seaside air, albeit modified by having become a haven for white South African immigrants who've opted to take their chances anywhere but the rainbow nation. But the idea of driving there for a holiday from somewhere in the same city would be risible now.

Just fifteen minutes further up the highway (assuming Auckland's notorious congestion doesn't delay you) is the turnoff to the Whangaparaoa Peninsula. If my parents had perhaps been quaintly English by choosing Browns Bay for a holiday, there was absolutely no doubt that the pretty coves and coastline of Whangaparaoa were sufficiently far from the CBD to qualify as *another place*.

My best friend's father had done well in business and owned a holiday house at Arkles Bay on the peninsula. Taking off for 'Arkles' was a proper mission – the loaded car, the back seat packed with kids, the windows down – and most of the journey was along normal open roads, not arterial routes. Again, much of Whangaparaoa is now dormitory suburbia, mainlined into the Auckland commuter grid, and a relatively easy run to the low-rise business zones of the upper north shore.

Much of this expansion has been facilitated by the steady building of motorways, which is what generally passes for urban planning in Auckland. The city now reaches beyond Orewa in the north, and is closing in on Warkworth, a town that not so long ago marked an imaginary dateline as you drove north. In the south the urban maw is beginning to snack on the old market garden region around Pukekohe. The main highway has become a ribbon development of towns and inhabited hinterland all the way to Hamilton, 120 kilometres away.

WHERE AUCKLAND ENDS and the world begins, then, depends on your point of view. The rest of the country enjoys disparaging Aucklanders for not caring about – or even being aware of – what happens beyond the Bombay Hills (the low southern range that once demarcated the city boundary). Like most national clichés, it's a half-truth that ignores its own petty chauvinism. But the more obvious absurdity of pretending its largest city is somehow separate from 'real ' New Zealand is the sheer demographic logic that Auckland is, in any number of ways, *becoming* New Zealand.

Such an utterance would almost certainly invite rebuke or maybe, in some particularly parochial parts of the country, an invitation to take it outside. Even avowedly metropolitan New Zealanders tend to cling to sentimental notions of national identity associated with a rural settler past and an enduring affection for the outdoors and the seaside.

To suggest to someone on the West Coast of the South Island, for instance, or in the Canterbury heartland, that the crowded, vain, acquisitive, gridlocked, polyglot, metrosexual metropolis to the north was at least as representative of New Zealandness as the woolshed or the small-town rugby club, would be the cue for a derisory snort at the very least.

If anything, in the minds of many non-Aucklanders, the city has come to emblemise everything that *isn't* authentic. Its denizens are labelled Jafas – just another fucking Aucklander – and the city is demonised as slick, superficial, corrupt, a rat race and a basket case. The feeling is (on the whole) not mutual. Aucklanders' attitudes to the rest of the country are as diverse as Aucklanders themselves, usually affectionate and often nostalgic. After all, the rest of the country is where so many of them come from.

Perhaps this is why Auckland's sense of identity remains so opaque. Every so often the city council or some tourism lobby tries to build a campaign around 'branding' Auckland. It is inevitably greeted with a mixture of cynicism and apathy. One that has half stuck is 'city of sails', a reference to the high per capita boat ownership and nautical pleasures of the Hauraki Gulf. The fact that most Aucklanders don't own boats, rarely sail on one, and, in the case of some of its less privileged youngsters, have not actually seen the sea, matters little. The motto simply isn't held dear enough to bother quibbling about.

The parodic alternative, 'city of snails', a wink at the ubiquitous traffic jams, hits a better self-deprecating note. Aucklanders are rapidly realising their city's ability to cope is being outstripped by growth and unmatched by any coherent political vision. While the city routinely tops international lifestyle surveys of desirable places to live, there is a dawning sense that smugness is no panacea for smog and wasted potential.

So where once the issues of urban planning, roads and public transport might have been the domain of council drears and local busybodies, now you will hear terms such as 'infrastructure' and 'rail corridor' and 'cycle way' bandied about with real passion at bars and dinner parties. One of the most popular local websites is the Auckland Transport Blog, which is filled with wonkish debate and proselytising zeal. As usual, the people are well ahead of their politicians.

Auckland's experience is not so unusual, of course. The exponential growth of cities, with all the challenges this presents, is a global phenomenon. Already half the world's population is coastal and urban, with the proportion rising inexorably in the coming decades. The loss of the best growing land, the pressure on resources and infrastructure, the economic implications of too many people vying for too few places to live – these are as true of supercities from São Paulo to Lagos as they are of a relatively small and benign conurbation in the South Pacific.

What does distinguish Auckland, however, is the city's size and pace of growth relative to New Zealand as a whole. With about 1.5 million inhabitants, the city represents a third of the country's total population. Already three quarters of New Zealanders live in the North Island, with the bulk of them north of Lake Taupō, and most within the powerful gravitational field of Auckland.

Estimates of how fast Auckland is growing vary between fifteen and twenty thousand people each year (1 to 2 per cent of its current population). It has been said the city grows annually by the equivalent population of Oamaru (the South Island town perhaps best known as the childhood home of Janet Frame). Logic dictates this calculus can't last, because Oamaru, like so much of provincial New Zealand, is experiencing population decline.

Damn lies and statistics being what they are, vested interests are prone to interpreting the projections to suit their own needs. Various Cassandras have suggested Auckland will have a million more inhabitants by 2030. The Auckland Council's latest urban plan is also predicated on that assumption.

If correct it would mean the entire country's predicted population increase (to five million by 2030) will occur in Auckland, which would then account for precisely half the total national population. Good grief! Where will the children play?

Calmer minds have said this is an extreme interpretation of demographic trends. Still, there's no disputing Auckland will be significantly bigger, in both sheer numbers and as a proportion of New Zealand in general, within twenty-five years. While this inevitability focuses attention on the bursting seams of the big city, you hear a lot less about its corollary – the likely impact on anywhere that isn't Auckland.

There are many exceptions – thriving, well niched little towns with sound economic DNA – but much of provincial New Zealand is threadbare. The marketing fairytale of purity, wide open country, boutique wineries and adventure tourism is only part of the story. The other is boarded-up shops, derelict factories, rural ghettos and aimless youth. You drive through these places on the way to somewhere else.

Right now Auckland is more than three times the size of New Zealand's next largest city (Wellington, followed closely by Christchurch). It is almost twice the size of the other main centres combined. It's by no means inconceivable that Auckland will be five times larger than its southern siblings within two decades. Such relative critical mass attracts more than people. It draws capital, talent, youth, knowledge, ambition and innovation towards itself and away from other places.

THERE IS A term for this phenomenon: the primate city. Coined in 1939 by an American geographer, Mark Jefferson, it describes the kind of city that dominates a nation demographically, politically, economically and culturally. The most extreme modern example is Bangkok, which is many orders of magnitude bigger than any other city in Thailand. But it is a First World phenomenon, too, with Paris and London both belonging to the urban primate species.

The main criteria by which primate cities are measured is that they be at least twice the size of the next largest centre and, according to Jefferson's original definition, 'at least twice as significant'. There's no doubt Auckland meets the first standard. While Christchurch and Wellington provide a modest counterweight to the country's top-heavy population distribution, beyond that New Zealand is really a collection of little towns about the size of an average Auckland suburb.

If the second sounds like the sort of claim that lights up radio talkback lines, a very good case can be made for it. Auckland's tax contribution alone means the country would implode without it. The country's major airport and port are in Auckland. Since the 1980s nearly all the head offices of major local or multinational companies have moved to Auckland, if they weren't already there. It is inarguably New Zealand's only international city.

A large proportion of Auckland's population growth comes from foreign migration. Almost unremarked on (other than by the odd xenophobic politician looking for a quick jump in the polls) the city has become one of the most diverse in the world (190 ethnic groups and counting). The sheer cultural energy this has generated, not to mention the business enterprise, is visible everywhere. Modern Auckland is immeasurably more interesting, as well as better fed, than the city I grew up in.

Auckland now accounts for nearly 40 per cent of New Zealand's GDP. All of the main media companies, from print to radio and television, are headquartered in Auckland (Radio New Zealand is the exception, still based in Wellington, but with a large Auckland bureau). By any measure – employment, retail activity, consumption, discretionary income – it is hugely significant.

The one aspect of Auckland's dominance that might be disputed is its political role. It's a given that no government can be elected without winning Auckland, so in that sense it wields enormous influence. John Key, the current prime minister, is from Auckland, as was Helen Clark before him. The new leader of the Labour Party opposition, possibly the next prime minister, David Cunliffe, is an Aucklander. For all that, Auckland is not the capital (though it was once, briefly, from 1840 to 1865) and has long been at the mercy of decisions made in Wellington.

Right now we are in the middle of another typical power struggle as the current mayor, the mild-mannered but strong-willed Len Brown, pushes through a major program to complete and expand the city's commuter rail service, and a 'unitary plan' to curb the city's ever-expanding girth by imposing new density codes designed to drive development up rather than out.

This grand scheme is the next phase of a massive restructuring of Auckland that began with the abolition of seven sub-city and district councils and their amalgamation into a so-called 'Super City'. The battle to control this new entity was fierce because the stakes were high – control of a massive budget and the influence and spending power that goes with it.

Even so, the projected cost of the rail upgrade is well beyond the means of Auckland's ratepayers, already stretched by very high housing and living costs, meaning the central government will have to contribute. Wellington has taken an extraordinary amount of convincing that decent public transport is a priority for Auckland, and remains similarly sceptical about allowing more intensive housing development within existing city limits.

There's little doubt the centre-left mayor is a thorn in the National-led government's side. But Brown has such a strong and loyal support base in South Auckland, where he began his political career, that it will be very difficult to unseat him. The notion that political control now resides in the largely brown and working class south of the city has undoubtedly been unsettling for the entitled classes. But until they find a candidate capable of winning hearts and minds outside their own comfort zone in the leafier suburbs, they will have to bide their time.

This is not to say the new council has complete autonomy. The super city model was deliberately hobbled by a central government nervous about losing control of such a large social and economic bloc. It is hard to avoid the conclusion that the very concept of a big city has been, and to some extent remains, alien and unnerving in an otherwise sparsely populated rural country on the edge of the world. Auckland's growth hasn't so much caught the rest of New Zealand by surprise as been willfully ignored.

THE ROOTS OF this haphazard development and strange neglect by successive governments go deep. Virtually from the moment New Zealand's first governor, William Hobson, decided to move to Auckland from the Bay of Islands in the 1840s there was self-interested grumbling and jealous in-fighting, the likes of which have more or less defined national politics ever since.

Partly because the South Island was flirting with secessionist ideas in the mid-nineteenth century, and partly because of the travel difficulties in a raw colony, the proposal to move the capital further south gained currency almost from the start. Resentment and suspicion of Auckland are nothing new.

While the colonial government imposed a certain order on Auckland's early development, it had limited expectations of the role of government. The settlers were too busy trying to make their fortunes to be much bothered with administrative responsibility, and when the capital moved south it was down to a local wealthy elite to fill the void. Auckland has always been a merchant town, with civic values and priorities to match.

The young city was also the major exception to a development model applied elsewhere by Edward Gibbon Wakefield's New Zealand Company. Land tenure was the means by which most towns and communities were founded, with the proceeds of sales used to fund infrastructure. Auckland's development, however, was largely driven by speculation, a legacy visible now in its role as the country's financial capital, its susceptibility to the boom and bust business cycle, and its inhabitants' obsession with real estate values and capital gains.

Given this history is it any wonder Auckland became the natural home of a rebellious coterie of free market liberals implacably opposed to the statist instincts of Wellington's nation builders? From their northern redoubt they watched and plotted and waited while the Labour government of 1935 to 1949 fought the Depression, established a welfare state and managed a Keynesian economy that delivered considerable prosperity. As one Labour politician observed after their eventual defeat in 1949, 'They walked to the polls to vote us in and drove to the polls to vote us out.'

The National government of Sid Holland is remembered mostly for having crushed the militant trade unions during a waterfront lockout in 1951. But there was another decisive (if less dramatic) ideological act that would have a profound effect on the future of Auckland, and that was to throw out a fully conceived housing and transport plan created in 1946 by Labour. Had this not happened the city today might be vastly different.

The Auckland historian and urban planner Chris Harris has made a study of this crucial historical juncture, and noted the rich irony of Wellington, so much smaller than Auckland, having an immeasurably better public transport system. 'It is hard to imagine Wellington without its trains, trolley buses and car-free downtown environs,' Harris has written, 'as it would be to imagine

Auckland without its motorway flyovers, inhuman streetscapes and rain-induced gridlock.'

The key to Wellington's efficient alternative was a version of the state-led mechanism of using land value gains to pay for public transport and amenities – the very plan rejected in favour of a speculative model in Auckland. While it was a relatively orthodox form of state capitalism, it patently smacked too much of socialism for some. The very notion of development planning became suspect, and various fundamental policies inherited from the previous government, from state housing to a form of capital gains tax, were rolled back.

A plan to develop Auckland along transport corridors, with rail loops and bus routes linking the spokes, was ditched. Rail fell out of favour. Motorways and the private car were promoted as the way of the future. Land speculation, held in check by wartime price controls, gathered pace as developers snapped up cheap rural acreages that could be sold for handsome profits once the motorways arrived. Those motorways were funded from road and petrol taxes, creating a self-sustaining cycle of road-based development – in effect, a public subsidy for private gain.

Visitors and locals alike often wonder why Auckland's state housing developments are dotted in and between many of its tonier suburbs, including a waterfront ridge with panoramic views of the Waitematā Harbour. Partly this was a deliberate plan to integrate the citizenry, but it is also the result of the way private developers leap-frogged the state housing zones to build middle class suburbs beyond them. As Harris observed so perfectly, this unintended pattern of growth meant the state housing rings 'acquired a transit-camp quality for migrant labour'.

In the 1960s a fatally destructive decision was taken to push the main north-south highway through the centre of the city to the harbour bridge, creating a tangle of feeder roads and slipways that quickly became known as 'spaghetti junction'. A visionary plan in the early 1970s by long-time mayor Dove Myer Robinson to build a 'rapid rail' network in anticipation of the city's predictable future needs was also torpedoed by the usual suspects – local political rivalry and government bias.

Within a very few years the city went from above average per capita public transport usage to levels lower than in Los Angeles. Harris quotes the report of an international planning consultancy as early as 1966 describing Auckland's CBD pedestrian environment as 'unpleasant to the point of being uncivilised'.

Nearly half a century on it would be hard to argue things have improved a lot. There have been sporadic attempts to beautify the 'golden mile' of Queen Street and its side streets, but all attempts to limit traffic volumes and create pedestrian malls have been defeated by a reactionary retail lobby and a civic bureaucracy hooked on parking revenues.

What is particularly tragic is that Auckland might now be one of the world's better preserved Victorian/Edwardian cities. Older photographs of the central city show a nicely proportioned streetscape, lined with the kind of solid stone and brick buildings that elsewhere have adapted well to modern office or apartment conversion.

Alas, a rip-shit-and-bust development boom in the 1980s, unleashed by the wholesale economic deregulation of David Lange's Labour government, saw great holes ripped in the city fabric, filled with tasteless mirror glass towers and cheap retail barns. Lovely heritage buildings were torn down in the dead of night to be replaced with car parks, flagrant breaches of town planning regulations went unpunished, and the last vestige of Felton Matthew's original (though never fully realised) street plan was buried under a nondescript shopping complex.

What survived was largely due to the share market crash in 1987, which stopped the construction cranes – in some cases literally – mid-swing. But a mini-boom in the 1990s saw another phase of council-sanctioned architectural vandalism, most notable for the erection of some of the worst inner city apartment blocks this side of Pyongyang.

These days one feels sorry for the perplexed tourists searching for the heart of a city amidst the chain stores, office blocks and fast food outlets that clog the main artery of town. God save them if they stray there after midnight, when the bars and pubs disgorge throngs of drunken 'revellers', as newspapers love to call them, despite the main forms of revelry being fighting, vomiting and passing out in doorways.

This combination of unchecked and unplanned suburban sprawl, careless road building and aesthetic negligence has inevitably encouraged a kind of low level anomie that ensures Auckland remains less than the sum of its parts. The writer and political commentator Chris Trotter characterised the city's 'chaotic' suburban satellites as 'breeding grounds for an antithetical sort of citizen' along the lines of Herbert Marcuse's 'one-dimensional man', first identified in the consumer belts of 1950s Southern California.

This is a vision of the primate city as a thousand-pound rogue gorilla – ugly, angry and alienated. On a bad day it is all too easy to see Auckland that way, too. It's vaunted status as the largest Polynesian city in the world, and its claim to being the capital of the South Pacific, can begin to sound like the boast of a bigger but similarly squalid Apia or Nadi.

And yet, on a good day, Auckland sparkles with all the promise it must have held for the earliest Māori settlers, drawn to its abundant waters and fertile volcanic soils; or for Hobson, spoilt for choice when it came to choosing the site for his new capital; or for the thousands of new migrants and refugees who have made a place for themselves and their children here, and are now in the process of remaking the city into a genuinely cosmopolitan corner of the new world.

You might not know it from reading Auckland's only daily newspaper, but much of the city's creative dynamism comes from the south, from Māori and Pacific Island musicians and artists, and the remarkable cross-cultural references they play with. The recent announcement that a northern branch of the national museum will open in Manukau rather than the city centre may well prove a tipping point of sorts.

If Auckland epitomises the yawning wealth gap now afflicting New Zealand, with mean streets and genuine poverty within spitting distance of palatial harbourside homes with four-car garages, it does at least have the makings of a functional post-colonial community, in which Māori and European have reached some kind of accommodation.

AS A SCHOOLBOY I witnessed the 'occupation' of a place called Bastion Point by members of the local Ngāti Whātua tribe. It lasted more than five hundred days and ended with a large-scale police eviction. The land overlooks the Hauraki Gulf, and had been requisitioned by the government in the 1880s as a defence outpost during the so-called 'Russian scare'. By rights it should eventually have been returned to its Māori owners. Instead, it was gifted to the city council, which later earmarked it for sale and subdivision.

This was a particularly odious move, as Ngāti Whātua had originally donated the three thousand acres Hobson used to establish his capital. The tribe later gave more land to the growing city. By the time of the Bastion Point protest it is fair to say their good faith had been sorely tested.

After much negotiation and a legal claim lodged under the Treaty of Waitangi, Ngāti Whātua won their land back. They had generously sought only the return of land that had not already been used for roads or housing, and the reserve where the protesters had been so roughly treated is now administered in partnership with a more enlightened city council. Auckland may struggle to find its true heart, but this might be the place to locate its soul.

Bastion Point is also the resting place of Michael Joseph Savage, the still revered prime minister whose government's vision of a better urban environment was thwarted in Auckland. The view from his memorial fulfils every tourism cliché; breathtaking, lovely, inspiring, uplifting. In the near distance is Waiheke, the unique island suburb that still retains a little of its old hippie ways despite large injections of arriviste cash. Ahead lies Rangitoto, the island volcano that fills the harbour entrance and the mind's eye of most Aucklanders when they think of their city.

Within a stone's throw is Auckland's (and New Zealand's) 'most expensive street', Paritai Drive, where the $50 million mansion of a distressed financier has just been advertised. Just as near is a state housing block as poor and rundown as you will find anywhere. Status anxiety of both kinds. Have and have not. White and brown. A tale of two cities. A tale of two countries. Find a spot somewhere between those places, squint hard against the glare from the water, and you might just catch a glimpse of the future.

Finlay Macdonald has worked as a journalist, author, broadcaster and publisher during his twenty-five-year career. He is a former editor of the New Zealand *Listener* magazine, was the commissioning editor at Penguin NZ, and is currently the local publisher for HarperCollins.

ANXIETY

CK STEAD

I'D HAD a successful trip to several South American countries and was boarding a LAN Air flight back to Auckland from Santiago, flying Economy as I always do, but reflecting that if my company, Preston Products, went on like this, bringing in new overseas orders, I would soon be able to think about an upgrade to Business. The time hadn't arrived when we would be instructed to switch our electronic gadgets to flight mode, or off, and I was catching up with a few messages. There were several old ones from Mahinārangi Marsden, signed Lucy Matariki, the name she'd recently taken. I regretted the change. Māori words very often have several meanings, sometimes quite distinct, and Mahinarangi could mean (or in my free translation I might read it as) 'gift of the sky'. But equally I could see it as 'maker of songs' – and among her many talents that's what she was. I liked both versions, and the sense that I did not have to choose: she could be both.

But I had to admire the cleverness of her reasons. Matariki, she had explained, was that little star cluster, the Pleiades, and its appearance in the night sky of mid June marked the beginning of the Māori new year – the shortest day, the exact equivalent of St Lucy's day in the northern hemisphere. It was the dark point after which (though the days might sometimes get colder) everything would slowly improve – days would get longer, nights shorter. 'If winter come can spring be far behind' was what it meant. So the new name, Lucy Matariki, was combining her Māori and her Pākehā heritages. But she cast a slightly grim light – or darkness – over this change when she told me there was always, in her mind and in her life, a doubt about whether the light would really return. So I would rather have been able to think of her as the gift of the sky and maker of songs than as our Māori St Lucy, the blind girl (as she was in the northern hemisphere mythology) representing mid-winter's day.

Mahina (as everyone still called her) had been our most useful IT person – very eccentric, often unsettling in the office, with great swings between what I, in my layman's shorthand, called her manic and depressive phases. She once told me she had been officially designated as 'somewhat bi-polar' – and we had both laughed at that word 'somewhat'. There were times when I had to warn her to ease off, quieten down, even take a day or two off work, because she was unsettling the staff. I sometime grumbled and even thought of being rid of her. But she was a constant source of entertainment. And finally, and I suppose most importantly from an employer's point of view, her work was always good. She could do things with computers which none of the rest of us in our little company were capable of. She was our mad, indispensible Mahina.

She was a frightful sentimentalist, so full of the milk of human kindness, and the honey as well, I had to protest and tease her about it. But I was careful too, aware that she was precarious. I treated her gently and with respect. In fact I'm afraid I rather prided myself on being 'good with her', able to handle her, manage her, get the best out of her – and though there was an element of delusion in this, it can't have been entirely wrong or I'm sure she would not have stayed with us as long as she did.

I believe I was the employer who lasted (who endured her, others would have said) longest. In the end she left, not to go to a rival firm offering more money for the same work, but to an organisation that helped people with (as they were described) 'mental issues' – people like Mahina herself, who'd had a period of hospitalisation and treatment and were out in the community again. They were such lovely people she said, hearts of gold every one; and she insisted on taking me to their office to meet them. It struck me as a scene out of Dickens. Just a normal office, but in which the jolly ones were jollier and noisier, the glum ones glummer and more withdrawn – normality, you could call it, but with a very broad brush. And it was clear they all loved Mahina, and she was happy there.

But the emails between us continued after she left, sometimes brief and infrequent, others (at least from her end) copious. Why did I keep it up – or allow her to? It was in part an addiction I suppose, because her messages could be very clever and original, and she got something out of me that no one else could. It was also a feeling of friendship and responsibility. So though I saw her seldom now I thought I could have told anyone who wanted to know – a doctor for example – pretty exactly how her inner landscape was looking.

Lately that landscape had been dark. She'd told me she was full of fears which had caused her to move some of the furniture in her bedroom against a door that opened on to a deck overlooking the garden. She said, too, that she suspected someone might be trying to poison her so she was being careful about what she ate.

I suggested she might want to report to the psychiatric ward that had treated her before, to receive some therapy and drugs. But she wouldn't do that. She said the rooms there were bugged and the bugs were bugged in turn by beings from outer space. She told me these things in a tone that made it clear they were jokes. But I knew by now there was a part of her mind that believed them – that's why she was scared. It was a question of which part of the brain was in charge at any one moment. If I'd known people she trusted out of her past I might have alerted them. I knew she'd been married and divorced, but to whom, and what their relations were now, I had no idea.

She told me she was hearing voices too; and that one she called the Bad Voice seemed sinister, sometimes threatening. This was where I persuaded myself I'd been useful. I adopted the calm, reasonable, unsurprised tone of the practical man. 'Use my name,' I told her. 'Tell the Bad Voice that Peter Preston says *it should go away*.'

That had been my last message, sent in fact from Medellin in Colombia, once the murder capital of the world and still a dangerous city, where my focus had been on staying close to our small party, taking care not be robbed, or kidnapped for ransom, and where the trauma hospital had a sign in Spanish which meant, 'We never close'. Paranoia seemed hardly possible in Medellin: any threat or danger might be real, and every fear reasonable. That, I suppose, might have been part of the reason for my taking Mahina's anxieties less seriously than I would have at home: I was in a state of anxiety myself.

But at this moment, waiting to taxi out for take-off at Santiago, there was nothing new from her. I skimmed other messages, then turned my attention to my fellow travellers and recognised the anxiety of a woman across the aisle from me. She might have been trying for some minutes to catch my eye. Could I just stand up, she asked me, and see if there were two engines on the wing on our side or just one. I stood up and could see only one. I thought probably there was a second, out of sight forward of, and below, the window – though there are plenty of these wide-bodied jetliners now that have only one on each wing. But since I could see she was anxious, and that it was important to her, I confirmed there were two out there on our side. 'And no doubt two on the other,' I joked.

'Oh yes, thank you,' she said. 'I'm such a bad traveller.' She was very handsome, of indeterminate age, plus or minus forty, a real estate agent in California, she told me, formerly married to a man from Transylvania – 'And please,' she added, 'don't make the usual joke.'

I assured her I wouldn't, though it's probable that only a hesitation about how to frame it ('Madame Nosferatu I presume?' or perhaps, 'Countess Dracula?') had prevented me from making that crass mistake.

'It's like names,' I said. 'You can't make a joke about a person's name that they haven't heard before a dozen times.'

I foresaw a lot of chatter as we crossed the vast unbroken reaches of the South Pacific between Chile and New Zealand, and took out the book, a thick thriller, behind which I planned a protective retreat.

My attention however was now drawn to a woman in late middle age who was telling a steward of uncommon Latin American good looks that she was somewhat breathless and would he bring her a glass of water so she could take her pills? He was back in a moment, leaning over her, attentive, producing such an effect that I felt it must be a game he liked playing, inducing in an older woman the illusion that he might be the devoted son she didn't have – or even the young lover, the man of her secret dreams. She was breathless now indeed, with the thrill of it. He exercised a practised, and even cynical, talent, full of charm and subtlety, while her husband sat stone-faced beside her, ignoring the game which he had no doubt seen before, but seldom, I'm sure, played by such an artist.

But it went on just too long. Now she was truly agitated, and complained of a pain in her chest. The steward's smile faded, he seemed to drift away from her, and a moment later was back with his senior, a commanding female who bent over asking questions I couldn't hear, to which the traveller, though still panting delicately, dismissed. She was fine, quite recovered. It had been just a momentary thing…

But it was too late. The mention of chest pain had been a mistake. Combined with breathlessness, and pills, it could not be ignored.

'She's quite alright,' her husband said, gruff, frowning, displeased. 'She gets angina – that's all. I assure you, there's nothing wrong with my wife.'

But already the call had gone over the intercom for a doctor – and soon two appeared, an Australian woman and a younger New Zealand man. They bent over the traveller who was now the unhappy centre of attention. After a few minutes they moved away, nearer to my seat, to talk out of earshot. I pretended to be absorbed in my book.

The Australian didn't believe there was anything seriously wrong. The New Zealander wasn't so sure. Probably not; but did they want to be responsible if they were five thousand miles out over the ocean, with nowhere for a landing, and the old girl's heart…

So it went back and forth, and in the end they agreed they should play safe.

They returned to her and explained that in the interests of her health and the welfare of all they'd decided she should have tests. There were very good hospitals in Santiago that would check her over and she would soon be on her way again.

This was no part of the poor woman's plan and she protested. She was soon in tears, insisting she was quite well, pleading. The senior cabin staff, then the captain, finally two security guards, were brought in to reason with her. When she flatly refused to budge she was told her luggage had already been removed from the hold. A wheelchair was brought and she was taken weeping away, followed by her husband whose rage was silent but unmistakable. He was white with it.

It had all taken time and our departure had been delayed. In the final minutes before we began to taxi out for takeoff I checked my laptop again. There was a new message from Mahina. It read:

'I told the Bad Voice that Peter Preston said it should go away. The Bad Voice said "I *am* Peter Preston".'

She had signed it 'Matariki.'

CK Stead is poet, novelist and critic. He received the New Zealand Prime Minister's Award for fiction in 2009 and won the UK *Sunday Times* short story prize in 2010. He is one of only two living New Zealand writers to hold the Order of New Zealand.

Hitching a ride

Nature knows no borders

Rebecca Priestley

IN the subtropical Pacific Ocean, 160 kilometres southwest of Raoul Island, Lieutenant Tim Oscar stared out of the window of the ship's bridge. Behind him were the heaving grey seas the ship had been battling all night. Before him, a vast white expanse glowed in the moonlight. Oscar braced himself, as if the ship was about to hit an ice shelf.

But there was no ice, not at this latitude. The ship's lights soon revealed a raft of pumice stretching out either side of the ship, further than Oscar could see. The ship ploughed through the metre-thick jumble of floating rock for half an hour, then sailed on.

It was midnight, 9 August 2012, and I was asleep downstairs, in a cabin shared with a geologist, two marine biologists, a journalist and a marine educator. We'd seen some pumice in the water the day before, floating towards us in long ribbons of white and grey, but nothing like this.

As we sailed north into the night, this giant floating pumice raft, the size of a small country, was heading for our home in New Zealand, and it was bringing visitors.

Next morning, as Tim Oscar tells us about his pumice encounter – 'it was one of the weirdest things I've seen in eighteen years at sea' – we weigh anchor next to Raoul Island, the northernmost of the remote and uninhabited

Kermadec Islands. We're one thousand kilometres north of Auckland, yet we're still in New Zealand. The seas are too rough for a boat to hazard the rocky landing platform so we transfer to the island by helicopter.

The island is young, the tip of an underwater volcano that emerged out of the ocean only one million years ago. The plants and animals that live on and around Raoul have all arrived from somewhere else – from Tonga or Aotearoa or Australia – and many are only subtly different from species found in my home islands. Pōhutukawa and nikāu forests cover the hills above the craters at the centre of Raoul Island. Kākāriki and tui flit about the trees and ungainly pūkeko strut through the grass around our tents.

On the sandy beach of Denham Bay, below the forest-covered cliffs, long streams of fresh pumice mark the high tide. Offshore, a sailor in an inflatable boat retrieves a soccer-balled sized rock of pumice from the water.

When we re-board the ship, Helen Bostock and I, both trained as geologists, are preoccupied with the rough texture and unexpected heaviness of this massive waterlogged chunk of pumice. We fail to notice what Libby Liggins, a marine biologist, spots and smells immediately. Minute goose barnacles, tiny little probes reaching up from the volcanic clast, adhere to one side of the rock.

After a week at Raoul we sail for home, the biggest lump of pumice bound for Auckland Museum, and smaller pieces kept by Helen for geochemical analysis. On our voyage south we're accompanied by migrating humpback whales, traveling from Tonga to their Antarctic feeding grounds. Other creatures – turtles, dolphins and sharks – island hop, travelling from Raoul, to Macaulay, to Curtis and Cheeseman, and on to the rocky stacks of L'Havre and L'Esperance. Some of them journey south of the Kermadecs to feed around the northern beaches of the North Island.

Our home is another group of remote islands in the middle of an ocean. In *Ghosts of Gondwana* (Craig Potton, 2006) entomologist and biogeographer George Gibbs refers to New Zealand's native fauna as the 'outlandish freaks' of the natural world. New Zealand's main islands, once part of the large continent of Gondwana, broke away eighty million years ago, when the Tasman Sea created a rift between what is now Australia and New Zealand. With so many years in isolation, our species followed distinctive, and often eccentric, evolutionary paths. In the absence of mammalian predators, our birds grew fat and flightless and our insects and snails gargantuan.

The weirdness of our biota, and the gaps in our ecology – we have no land mammals, snakes or turtles and are missing aggressive species of ants, wasps and termites – mean our ecosystem is particularly vulnerable to introduced species.

WHALES AND DOLPHINS occasionally surface alongside our ship, but we see only one other vessel on our return voyage. Far to the east, and identifiable only through binoculars, is a cargo freighter.

More than two thousand cargo ships arrive in New Zealand each year, bringing cars from Japan, clothes from China and electronics from Korea. Tourists come too, on cruise ships that berth in Auckland or private yachts that sail to the Bay of Islands. Another five million visitors arrive by air.

To protect both our unique biodiversity and our agricultural economy from overseas invaders, all international visitors are subject to vigorous pre-arrival checks and requirements. Some bioinvaders, though, sneak in and are intercepted at the border, like the fruit flies infesting a cargo of bananas from Queensland, the venomous snake hiding in a shipping container of washing machines from Thailand, and the eggs of the Asian gypsy moth found in the wheel of a Japanese car.

But it's not just the cargo that brings intruders. When ships fill their tanks with ballast water, used to maintain stability while they're sailing, they take on board whatever marine life is in that water – up to one thousand tiny marine organisms in every cubic metre. Some of the water-borne plankton species are microscopic, like dinoflagellates and copepods, but others are the larvae or young of larger species. Inside the enclosed ecosystem of the darkened ballast tank, some of these species can feed and grow and breed. If the water taken on in a distant port is discharged in New Zealand, it might bring with it exotic and unwanted fish, crabs, and algae.

Other unwanted arrivals ride on the outside of ships. Sessile plants and animals such as seaweeds, barnacles and mussels typically spend their lives in one place, affixed to a rock. But if they attach to the underwater parts of ships, to the hull or rudder or propeller, they can travel the world.

Anti-fouling paint and regulations around ballast water discharge stop some unwanted pests from arriving, but others still sneak through. Those interlopers that survive – if the temperature is right and they find food to eat – can displace native species, upset fisheries and clog waterways.

At passenger arrival halls trained beagles sniff out biological contraband that some people unwittingly – or furtively – try to bring into the country. European salamis that could harbour foot-and-mouth disease, wood products that could carry termites, and North American honey that could carry bacterial diseases, are confiscated and destroyed.

This 'offending', though, is nothing new. Humans have been assisting species to arrive in New Zealand since they first visited these islands. Radiocarbon dating of fossils suggests that early Polynesian voyagers brought the Polynesian rat, or kiore, here in the thirteenth century. When James Cook stopped here in 1769, he left pigs and potatoes as food for later voyagers, but may have also inadvertently added to the marine faunal assemblage. In 1769, while at anchor, he ordered his crew to scrub the hull of the *Endeavour* – twice – to remove the build-up of barnacles and seaweeds. Any plants or animals he introduced to New Zealand's coastal waters would now be indistinguishable from native species. In the nineteenth century, European settlers tried to create a sense of home, and provide food, by introducing fish to the rivers, fruit, vegetables and livestock to the land, and songbirds to the trees. Some species, like rabbits, got out of control, but the stoats that were introduced to control them preferred local lizards and the eggs of native birds.

TWO DAYS AFTER leaving Raoul Island, we arrive at Auckland, the busiest port in New Zealand. We don't need to declare our goose-barnacle infested pumice – despite our one-thousand-kilometre voyage we never left New Zealand waters. I hand it to Tom Trnski, from Auckland Museum, who will later give it pride of place in a new exhibition about the marine environment.

Helen gives the smaller pumice samples to volcanologist Richard Wysoczanski. Over the next few weeks, Richard and his students match the rocks' distinctive geochemical signature to the Havre volcano, a massive underwater caldera discovered only twenty years before and, until now, believed to be extinct.

Then, in November, Richard sails on the Niwa research vessel *Tangaroa* to Havre, where 3D mapping of the seafloor reveals the source of our pumice raft. A massive new volcanic cone, about the size of Auckland's Rangitoto Island, rises 240 metres above the previous crater rim. Inside the five-kilometre-wide caldera, the seafloor is covered in a layer of pumice ten metres deep.

In the ocean west of Havre, the *Tangaroa* sails through floating streams of pumice, more remnants of the several cubic kilometres of rock – basalt, ash and pumice – ejected in what Richard now realises was a massive underwater volcanic eruption.

Pumice rafts, while certainly not new to the oceans, are relatively new to science. In July 2012, University of Queensland volcanologist Scott Bryan published a paper about an enormous pumice raft created by an eruption at Home Reef Volcano in Tonga. Bryan tracked the journey of this 'temporary pumice island' more than five thousand kilometres over eight months. By the time it washed up on the beaches near where Bryan lives and works, the pumice was home to a complex ecosystem, with up to eighty different species of algae, bryozoans, corals, anemones, bivalves and gastropods.

Pumice is an excellent raft for oceanic mass transit because it can't be eaten by its host and does not decay in the sun and sea. But it's only one of many rafting methods. Masses of brown fibrous bull kelp found on Otago beaches have been found to carry tiny hitchhikers – goose barnacles, crustaceans, sea stars, snails and limpets – from their sub-Antarctic island homes. Driftwood carries burrowing insects or fouling organisms from Australia to our west coast beaches and plastic rubbish and nets abandoned by fishing vessels raft invasive species to our shores.

Above the waves, the dominant westerly winds bring a near constant steam of aerial invaders from across the Tasman Sea. Butterflies with names like 'blue moon' and 'painted lady' fly in from Australia's east coast, brightening the palette of New Zealand's Lepidoptera. Butterflies often intentionally fly long distances – like New Zealand's 'yellow admiral' whose local population is boosted by visitors from Australia – but other more hapless insects can just get caught up in the air flow. Tiny creatures like aphids and thrips, which don't usually fly far or high – or spiders, which have no wings at all – can find themselves airborne. Strong thermals, where heat from the ground pushes the air above it high into the atmosphere, can collect these tiny critters from their terrestrial habitats and take them thousands of metres into the atmosphere. If they reach a westerly airflow, they can be carried across the Tasman, a two thousand kilometre journey, in a matter of days. Those that aren't eaten by a sharp-eyed bird, plunged into the ocean by a rainstorm, or frozen at high altitude might make landfall in New Zealand.

But this aerial plankton raining down on us contains smaller invaders. In the otherwise pristine snow of the Southern Alps scientists have found pollen grains from Australian species, or patches of red dust that match the sun-scorched earths of the Australian interior. More worrying are the travelling plant pathogens, like the tiny fungal spores that can bring exotic diseases to our trees and crops.

The air is also filled with tiny spores of algae, mosses and liverworts, and bacteria, viruses and protozoa. Only a tiny percentage of these life forms could survive a journey across the Tasman, but some make the journey inside a raindrop or ice crystal protected by their watery cocoon.

Some of the most sinister airborne particles to arrive on our shores are too small to see, like the first radioactive fallout detected in Wellington, thirty hours after the 1953 British nuclear test at Woomera in South Australia. Longer lasting and more threatening radioactive isotopes came to be routine arrivals, as radioactive fallout – including particles of strontium-90 and caesium-137 – landed from the American, British and French hydrogen bomb tests in the Pacific islands north of New Zealand. These invisible particles rained down on our islands, where they got into the soil, then into the grass, then into the cows whose milk we drank. Babies born in the 1960s, like me, have radioactive strontium and caesium isotopes in our bodies in places where calcium and iodine should be.

MONTHS AFTER THE voyage, in February 2013, I get an email from Maggie de Graaw, who had first spotted the Havre volcano pumice raft from a plane heading to Auckland from Samoa, and with whom I'd started an email correspondence. She writes to me of some 'strange findings' on Opoutere beach in the Coromandel. Across the spit from a protected area where dotterels and oystercatchers patrol and feed, strange shell-encrusted masses have washed up along the shore. She recognises the substrate as pumice. I recognise the phallic-looking hitchhikers as adult goose barnacles. That same week, people in my Twitter stream start posting photos and tweeting about strange things washed up on Auckland beaches and on islands in the Hauraki Gulf. 'Found this rock at the beach today, with mystery shellfish attached to it by strong black feet. Baby pāua? Aliens?' tweets Jolissa Gracewood. 'Goose barnacles!' I say in reply. Jolissa found only one rock, but Maggie returns to the beach, puts some goose barnacle-encrusted pumice in a chilly bin filled with salt water, and sends it to Wellington. Geochemical analysis by Richard Wysoczanki confirms this was the same pumice we had encountered six months earlier – from the eruption of the Havre volcano – in the Kermadec Islands. Biologists study the critters on board; along with three species of goose barnacle, are a crab and some bryozoans, picked up somewhere along the journey. Not real aliens, but at least one of the species was alien to these waters – the subtropical goose neck barnacle *Lepas anserifera* is not usually seen this far south.

Over the weeks that follow more pumice washes up on North Island beaches, with biological cargo on board, but most is unseen and unstudied. More floats to Australia's east coast beaches. One massive raft, which hits the Great Barrier Reef, is laden with marine hitchhikers, including bristle worms and anemones as well as barnacles and bryozoans. Scott Bryan, the Queensland volcanologist who studied the Home Reef pumice raft, says this is the largest pumice raft the world has seen in the past fifty years.

OUR NEW ZEALAND biodiversity is bizarre, original, and precious, but it's constantly changing. Already, many of the species we think of as our own are recent arrivals. The large flightless takahe evolved from a pūkeko-like bird that flew here from Australia. Today's pūkeko – now found in the main islands of New Zealand and on Raoul Island – is a more recent Australian import. Our parakeets evolved from a parrot from New Caledonia. The silvereye, white-faced heron and welcome swallow, have all arrived in the past two centuries. Most of our dragonflies are Australian. The monarch butterfly is Californian. Almost all of our plants have arrived from somewhere else, through pollen blown on the wind, or seeds carried in the feathers and digestive tracts of birds. The Pacific oysters we harvest and the salmon we catch in our rivers are introduced species.

We need to try to keep out the worst invaders – the aggressive species that could displace native species or destroy our agriculture and aquaculture – but we won't keep things the same forever. New species will continue to arrive of their own accord, on the winds, on the waves and, just occasionally, on a raft of pumice. And, as the planet warms, more northern species will find the New Zealand environment habitable and will settle here, as part of the slow worldwide march of species towards the poles.

Maggie, who saw the pumice raft first from the air and again when it washed up on the beach beside her, is a jeweller and a fossicker who has always made jewellery out of the things she finds on the beach. I now wear a piece of pumice from the Havre volcano around my neck, a memento of my own voyage to the Kermadec islands, but also a reminder of longer voyages, and voyagers.

References at www.griffithreview.com

Rebecca Priestley is a senior lecturer at Victoria University of Wellington where she teaches history of science, science communication and creative science writing. Her most recent book is *Mad on Radium: New Zealand in the Atomic Age* (Auckland University Press, 2012). In August 2012 Rebecca sailed to the Kermadecs on the HMNZS *Canterbury* as part of a team of experts sponsored by Pew Environment Group.

Cliff Fell

L'Anima Verde

I ki paki waitara rā
I repa aitia Tunaroa
Nā Māui, ka haea ai ia
Mate ai ia, auē.

– I –

The green soul as Montale calls the eel,
a thread of water
that casts its stitches in the land,
or sister Longfin of the Pacific
who drills deep into hills and rivers,
slipping through the lowlands
with her tawny-black brother,
little muscle of the ocean, spawned
in God knows where
the sink-hole or trench, it may be
somewhere off Tonga,
or close by Sina's pool in Savai'i,
where it is said the princess swam
with an eel, the great Tunaroa,
whose violations provoked her brothers
into such a rage, they (like Māui)
killed and cut off its head, which they buried,
only to find that from the grave
there sprang the first coconut tree,
which is why, it is said,
the coconut has two eyes,
to gaze on Sina's flowing form
and see across the ocean

to where the eels are drawn
to the spawning holes
 – wherever they are –
by a trail of scents that emanate
on the currents and so return to mate
in a writhing tangled knot,
wild as Medusa's hair,
who was, or so we hear from Hesiod,
a creator of reefs, a sea-daemon
with gleaming unkempt coils
 – as much eel as serpent –
that now transmit
a hatch of transparent
leaf-shaped larvae, given to drift
on the steady currents of the old eel road,
no more than tooth and sensory intelligence,
a submarine mouth the swells will carry
across shipping lanes, the rusty churn
of freighters plying their trade,
war-ships heading north into the China Sea,
while the larvae pass from wave to wave,
shape-changing, thinning down
to form bone structure, until they gather
offshore awaiting moon and tide
to carry them into the estuary,
the glass eel, a shard of life,
elvers that swim into the inlet's fallopian waters,
swarming upstream to take on colour,
mottled browns and greens,
darkening, thicker, clambering up
waterfalls and dams, their teeth latching on
to stone and concrete,
making their way beneath the cold stare
of spring's full moon, and the great anchor
of the Southern Cross on which,
like a ship, the whole world turns,

and swimming into a labyrinth of creeks,
burrowing deep into the ovum,
the earth egg, as though to force open
the watertable, the mud runnels
and silent meadows, in a shudder
of fertility's engendering,
spermatozoid, a sexual emblem,
and yet unsexual in all their years
of freshwater life, of feeding on the land
they feed, *kīnaki, taonga kai,*
and slithering across pasture at dawn,
like the eel I found two mornings ago
(sunbeams at play on the heavy dew,
the moment's jewel flaring in the paddock)
a creature I drew
from the wet grass and swampy mud
of which Aristotle thought
the eel was sprung,
if only that I might look upon
the pulsing darkness of its form
and feel its cord of sinewy skin,
this curlicue scrolling through my hand.

— II —

And though the past should vanish
like a creature into water —
lost in the creek's subaqueous light,
a quiver on the surface, a last flicker
that leaves only weeds waving in the current,
there must yet be a trace of its wake,
a ripple echoing over the years
that remains at large, waiting for someone
to tune in to it again, to its testament
written in the sea's great volumes. For we read
the deep swells of the ocean,

or foam of rollers breaking on a shore,
or a small wave lapping in the lee of a reef
as if each were an image, a phrase
in which something else is happening.
Somewhere beneath its surface
an angelfish swims with the blue sea star,
giant clams close on the dugong,
barracuda gleam, a moon wrasse moves,
slow and sure among the fire dartfish.
There are some things, though, we'll never get,
that the sea only gives up with the unwilling
our nets haul from the depths.
In the reef off Ngemelis, in the Palau Islands,
scientists report a latest discovery,
a living fossil, old as the Mesozoic:
a species of primitive eel, *Protoanguilla palau*,
found in these islands where legends say
a woman was squatting one day
at work in the taro gardens
and felt an eel climbing
into the dark haven of her vagina.
It soon made itself at home in there
so that when her husband tried to enter,
it would bite at his penis.
These things can really happen.
Rectum. Colon.
We know of surgeons removing eels
from unexpected places.
Oh, and what do we learn from this? –
On *Peleliu*, in the same archipelago,
Japanese forces inflicted heavy losses
on US marines, late in '44,
by defending a warren of mountain caves.
The operation to remove them was not surgical.
My grandfather was there in May of '45,
the resistance all but mopped up.

'Tiny' Fell, a naval captain,
he was chasing the Americans for a mission,
his command, the secret Fourteenth Submarine Flotilla,
under orders in the Whitsundays.
Through Biak, New Guinea, Palau: he hitched a ride
on a Dakota loaded with sanitary towels.
In his memoir he writes of Wewak's
coral strip above a swamp,
smashed planes, bones and broken trees.
Jungle fires burned in the Owen Stanley Range,
where the fighting went on.
The ruins of Manila were miles of shambles
such as I had never seen, he says.
He took refuge on the one good floor
of a bombed out skyscraper.
A stand-pipe on the roadside and all night
the noise of bulldozers working on
the great hegemony of rubble. Their lights
like lost souls picking their way
through the circles of Hell, a world gone wrong.
We bury the past in lime pits and ashes,
as though it were one of the dead, who were, he says,
shovelled unceremoniously into communal graves.
The bulldozers would make it good again,
the next empire would reign. His gaze rested on
telegraph poles and bridges all going up,
pipelines and sewers down.

– III –

To know where the soul goes on its journey,
to be in on the inside of what we are
when all else is shucked away,
to go savage and naked
and not give a damn about the world on his mind:
the quest for this knowledge (the quest for sex)

the quest for the primitive —
these things propelled Paul Gauguin
on his voyage into the Pacific.
Go, Gauguin, the world might want to say,
though what the world should mean by this
is hard to know — a rallying cry, perhaps,
or, rather, Go home, Gauguin;
but go, you bad man with your gaggle of girls
and the doozie *douze* of your big colonial footprint,
go as you will — to listen
to the silence of the Tahitian night,
not even the cry of a bird,
though a falling leaf might rustle like
an idea tripping its way through the dark.
But, go — that we may go with you
to sit in the shade for days at a time,
gazing sadly at the sky's primal blue. And watching
for you to make your semiotics of heightened sensuality,
the blocks of primary colour
that proclaim the virtue of nakedness
and transaction of the gaze.
Go, even as though you are not you,
but she or he or me,
the third person implicit in the work,
the one who is we — for it's only in Tahiti
that Gauguin begins to realise
it's all in the eyes,
the gaze that will return his gaze,
but obliquely, glancing it away
into the eyes of the viewer, of the beholder,
and holding us there as witnesses,
actors in the life and death of the painting's deed.
This is what's new: the intensity achieved before
only in self-portraits, and one painting of his mother,
and the sly vulpine regard
of the conqueror in 'The Loss of Virginity',

the creature who is, of course, himself: –
the artist who will tell us now
that we can't live in these islands and not get to feel
the sleek muscle of the colonising eel,
the eel as it swims up into the land.
As in 1891, when Gauguin broke *tapu*
and wandered into the interior.
Through the valley of Punaru there is a huge fissure
which, as he tells us in *Noa Noa*,
divides Tahiti in two. From Tamanou,
you can see the diadem, Orofena and Aorai
which forms the center of the island
and is known as a place of miracles.
The people warned that he'd be tormented
by *tupapo*, the spirits of the mountain.
The riverbanks he walked were a confusion of trees –
breadfruit, ironwood, coconut, hibiscus,
guava, giant-ferns, what he calls
a mad vegetation, growing always wilder,
more entangled, until he entered the gorge.
There he made his way up the watercourse,
the river sometimes over his shoulders,
and the fissure so narrow, its walls so high,
the sun couldn't penetrate so that (as he tells us)
he was able to see the stars burning
in the brilliance of the sky at noon.
Where was he going? –
Did he know of Māui, trickster god,
who turned himself into something sleek,
a worm (read eel) so that he might climb into the vagina
of the sleeping goddess of the night,
and goddess of the underworld, Hine-nui-te-po,
into her great cavern, on a quest
to find the cure for death.
We know what happened: he looks so funny,

the fantail laughed, its shrill piping song –
and so he was lost in there,
which is why, the story goes, we people must die,
all on account of a waiata.
Gauguin camped that night in the bush,
troubled by a powdery luminous light
that flickered around his head,
making him half believe
the mountain was alive with ghosts.
In daylight the river was now a torrent,
now a brook, now a waterfall.
Sometimes, he says, it seemed to flow
back into itself, the green of the jungle
cascading in such depths around him,
he walked as though underwater.
Crayfish in the river regarded him curiously,
seeming to question why he was there.
Then, he says, at a narrow bend in the river
he came upon a young woman, standing nude.
She was caressing a great black rock
as she drank from a spring that flowed down
the smooth surface of the stone.
He watched her cup her hands to catch the water
and let it run over her breasts.
Sly old fox, Monsieur Gauguin:
the symbolism replete,
we gaze with him upon this scene
as she, his perennial subject,
senses his presence and plunges into the river,
though not before she utters a curse
– *Taehae* –
meaning 'cruel' or 'savage',
even as she glides among river pebbles,
a human no more, but in the form of an eel.

– IV –

The night I heard my father was dying,
that he'd fallen into a coma,
I thought of this:
we can only leave on an ebb-tide,
and this: that he was now half-man-half-eel
and setting his course for the sea.
And already that day the poem had called with an image,
with a way I'd thought to begin not end –
it was HMS *Bonaventure*, built as a cargo vessel
in Greenock, on the Clyde, in 1938,
but now fitted out as a naval depot ship:
the Fourteenth Submarine Flotilla.
Grandpa, my father's father, is on the bridge,
bringing her into Townsville.
It's May 1945. I could see her steaming
into Cleveland Bay, Magnetic Island
on the starboard bow. Early afternoon,
the sun still high and I, like a fool,
playing with this conceit, pressing
Messrs. Google and Co. into giving up
news of that grey ship,
and thinking I'd phone my father in the evening
for the stories he would tell.
But he had stumbled on a root in the woods,
out walking his dog, and would never speak again.
What could I say or do?
I only knew that I knew so little about the soul,
that other that maybe I have sensed at times,
gazing into the stillness of pool,
or in a child's cry on a winter evening,
or the great hook that holds us to the sky at night.
And I knew I'd make the journey
from the island of his birth to the city of my own,
crossing the ocean and land in a day,

and the shadow of my flight would fall upon
the course of eels returning to spawn
(so few of them, now we've drained their land)
and returning to the source of all,
for as Māori say:
Tēnā te puna kei Hawaiki
— the source is at Hawaiki —
fabled place to which the eels return,
as though they took the souls of those
who'd go with them, greening them
in the green of what they know.
But even as I saw that I must go
to my father, I found myself
listening as Townsville's citizens
welcomed *Bonaventure* to their streets.
In the scrub behind the beach
there arose the otherworldly calls
of the bush-stone curlew,
plaintive cries that locals believe
the ghost-keening of ancestors.
And now a muffled tread is coming
through the dunes, a rustle of chiffon:
a town-girl leads a young sailor
to a hollow in the sand,
where he will hoist her petticoats
as her fingers guide him in.

— V —

I flew to Hong Kong beside a monk
who wore the sky-blue robes of Shaolin,
the monastery of martial arts.
All the way across the Pacific
he played Angry Birds on his iPhone,
a beatific, childlike smile composing his face,
so that I wondered: who would have known,

at the end of that war,
the new world they were making
would be in thrall to a game?
Then, Frimley, near London: the flap
of yellow curtains in the summer breeze,
my father's panting breath.
You've made it in time, they said,
to say your farewells. Though it seemed to me,
he'd already slipped his mooring,
was making for open water.
His face thinned down by hunger,
craggy and translucent now,
but still the bushy riot on his brow.
And Grandpa's Townsville mission
was six midget submarines:
Bonaventure's secret cargo,
to enter stealthy into harbours.
Their operations in the last days of the war:
cutting communication cables, a ship in Singapore.
And some days among the Dyak in Borneo –
where he came bearing gifts: lipstick for the fighting women,
for, as he writes, *Bonaventure* was never defeated
for store articles. Half-smoked heads,
Japanese, dangled from their hips.
It was the day of Hiroshima.
He skippered *Bonaventure* for two more years,
plying the Pacific as a transport ship.
A love-boat, at times – or so Messrs. Google tell me.
The first ship's manifest: nurses from Sydney,
bound for Hong Kong's hospital.
The war was over. They'd survived. Almost all –
so many the women to climb into.
From the blog of Ric Ellam, ship's signaller:
VAD's, Voluntary Aid Detachment. (We nicknamed them Virgins Awaiting
Destruction.) They were housed in the officers' quarters, all fell for Fell, and other
officers too of course. The Radio Room had a porthole opening onto the promenade

deck just below the bridge. That deck became 'cuddles corner' and with lights
dimmed, porthole open, we sparkers inside the darkened office were privy to the
many chat up lines given by both sides of the sexes.
Submariners. (For the record, my father
was one, too. After the war,
partially blind, he was invalided out.
Earlier, aged eighteen in 1942, he took the helm
of the last launch to leave Tobruk.
The rat run, they called it. He wasn't brave,
he said, no, not brave, but lucky.)

– VI –

As for my grandfather, who would have made Admiral
– this was said by Hairy Brown –
if he'd had a decent suit –
in those months in the Pacific, like an Odysseus
glimpsing Ithaca, he was only days
from his home, from Wellington and Mahina Bay,
but didn't make it there.
Not for another fifteen years. And with another wife.

Full moon last night. Through the early hours,
I walked the creek, looking for eels.
Nothing but crayfish, who seemed to ask of me,
as of Monsieur Gauguin, what I was doing there.
But the soul is what we cannot see
or know, though there was a kingfisher today,
in the poplar, feeding its young.
And even as I write, in the way the past can play
upon the memory, the day comes back to me,
when my grandfather left –
1959. I was just four. Early morning.
He must have been off to Southampton,
to the P&O, was drying his flannel underpants
on the fireguard, when they caught.

A scorch-hole in the bum: I stood there
watching in childish wonder.
Liar, liar, pants on fire —
was that the last he said to me?
In the garden that night, under a big moon,
my father set up the telescope Grandpa had left.
The light seemed to pour into its tube,
the moon a fiery white,
the colour of those underpants,
but many more the holes in it.
Is that where Grandpa's gone? I asked.
No, my father must have laughed,
New Zealand isn't on the moon.
But I was off and bounding down the lawn,
and making the moon run away with me,
with its sparkle on the frost.
                                        And for those
who believe in Pure Land practice,
there is always this thought:
that among the most adept of monks
there are some who learn
to visualise the soul
so that in the moment before their death,
they will eject it through the skull.
I looked to my father when he died,
for something like a sign.
There was nothing on his head
but this: a strangely looping line
of freckles in a scrawl
upon the fontanelle, a curlicue —
the fountain and the source.

Cliff Fell's two collections of poems are *The Adulterer's Bible* (2003) and *Beauty of the Badlands* (2008), both from Victoria University Press. The first was awarded the Adam Prize and the Jessie Mackay Prize for Poetry. He lives near Motueka in the upper part of Te Waipounamu and teaches in the writing program at Nelson Marlborough Institute of Technology.

A Kiwi feast

Paua with wild silverbeet, samphire & sea grapes

David Burton

Ingredients

4 pāua
oil
butter
6 cloves garlic
large bunch wild silverbeet
16 stalks of samphire
4 miniature bunches of sea grapes

WORKING on the idea that the best rustic dishes convey a sense of place, this recipe speaks to the wider Pacific from Wellington's wild south coast.

Just ten minutes' drive from parliament, Wellington's south coast is a series of beaches and rocky outcrops winding around the fringes of suburbia from Ōwhiro Bay to Scorching Bay.

It's famous among recreational divers who forage for crayfish, abalone and sea urchins among the swaying underwater forest of seaweed.

The coast borders Cook Strait, where the cold ocean currents from the south meet warmer currents coming down from the north.

Species of seaweed overlap at their northern and southern limits, in a riot of diversity: almost half of New Zealand's 850 species are found here.

The rarest and most delicious of these belongs to the genus *Caulerpa*, commonly known as sea grapes, since their tiny caviar-sized beads do indeed resemble bunches of miniature grapes. Having a cucumber-like flavour and a satisfyingly crunchy texture, it's the only New Zealand seaweed palatable raw, straight from the rocks, without any processing or cooking. In fact, sea grapes shouldn't be cooked, or they begin to melt and lose their crunch.

A recognised delicacy throughout the Pacific, these sea grapes are cultivated in the Philippines and harvested from the wild in Fiji, Tonga and Samoa. At the Apia market, sea grapes are bundled into banana leaves and sold as *limu*, later to appear draped over fillets of fish at Apia restaurants, or mixed with fermented coconut as a domestic snack.

The New Zealand sea grape is even tinier than those found in the Pacific islands, arguably making it the most aesthetically pleasing, both in texture and appearance.

On Wellington's south coast, it can be found in isolated rockpools at low tide, near the masses of kelp that provide food for pāua, one of many species of the genus *Haliotis* found around the Pacific. It's a close relative of the Tasmanian black lipped abalone and distantly related to Japanese abalone and the eight species on the west coast of North America.

DESPITE THE PREDATIONS of poachers, legally sized pāua are still to be found in the crevices of rocks on the south coast, buried deep within the underwater forests of seaweed.

The remaining two ingredients for this dish are found struggling against the salt winds on the pebbly foreshore – wild silverbeet (Swiss chard, a hardy mainstay of every Kiwi backyard vegetable garden) and samphire (*Salicornia australis*), a knobbly succulent whose close relative is gathered from the wild in East Anglia for the smart seafood restaurants of London. Like the other main ingredients for the dish, both samphire and wild silverbeet come ready salted.

The challenge is to arrive at the beach armed only with butter, oil, garlic and a frying pan.

The fulfilment is to build a driftwood fire on the foreshore, using dried seaweed for kindling, then forage all the main ingredients for this recipe in the time it takes to reduce the flames to embers.

Having sent your companions to gather the greens, don your wetsuit, mask and snorkel (but not tanks, which are forbidden for pāua fishing).

Then, fighting the swirling swell, dive down and prise your daily quota of ten abalone from the rocks, using the pāua knife issued free of charge by the MAF fisheries inspector who may well be waiting for you as you emerge from the water with your catch. These knives are made of blunt plastic, so won't harm the pāua if it proves to be undersized and needs to be put back. Once cut or grazed, an abalone will haemmorhage and bleed to death.

Anybody who has single-handedly eaten a fully grown New Zealand pāua will concede it's a great fist-sized hunk of richness: if you were foolish enough to eat two, you might well begin to feel sick.

So for our party of four, I set aside four and put the remaining six pāua back in the bucket, covered with water to keep them alive, and intern them for special Japanese treatment back home.

At this stage, if I were a hearty Kiwi bloke, I'd wrench the beast from its beautiful mother-of-pearl shell, leaving its gut-bag behind.

Unsurprisingly, with the shock of disembowelment, the pāua seizes up and dies in an instant, after which no amount of beating will tenderise it.

That's why to this day, Kiwi blokes crank pāua through a hand mincer set up on the wooden fence of their weekend bach. The ensuing chips of car tyre go into a Kiwi national dish, pāua patties, which forever perpetuate the national myth that pāua are inherently rubbery. Everybody gets the cuisine they deserve.

Actually, abalone needn't be tough at all: here's how Chatham Islands paua fishermen shuck and tenderise their abundant resource.

Slide your thumb down into the shell behind the flesh and feel for the foot.

Using your thumbnail, very gently ease this thick stalk away from the shell and carefully remove the pāua with its gut-bag intact, so the animal remains alive outside its shell, and visibly squirms and quivers upon the clean tea towel which becomes its death shroud.

Wrap the pāua in this tea towel, deliver the last rites, then using a large wooden mallet or a length of four-by-two, whack it two or three times only.

Voila, tender pāua. Remove and discard the sac of semi-digested kelp, then feel for the beak and innards, and pull them out too.

Wash the pāua meat and slice thinly. Amateur cooks will find it easiest to slice vertically, into thin cross-sections, whereas a skilled chef might slice horizontally, into elegant oval-shaped fillets. Set the raw pāua aside.

Now take the silverbeet, wash it in sea water, cut the stalk away from the leaf in a V, and finely slice both stalk and leaf.

Put the frying pan on the fire, heat a little oil of your choice and gently sauté the chopped stalks for a few minutes. Cover the pan, place towards the outside of the fire, and leave them to braise in their own juices for fifteen minutes. Stir in a good knob of butter and two cloves of chopped garlic near the end. Transfer the stalks and their juice to a bowl and set aside.

Wipe out the frying pan and replace over the embers of the fire. Add more oil and four cloves of chopped garlic, sauté the silverbeet leaves for several minutes, then cover and leave to steam in their own juices until tender, about eight minutes. Stir in a knob of butter, remove these leaves and set aside in a bowl.

Place some water in the frying pan, cover and bring to the boil. Take off the heat and plunge in the stalks of samphire. Leave for thirty seconds only, or until they turn bright emerald green, then remove and plunge into cold sea water, to set the colour. Drain and set the samphire aside.

Place the frying pan back over the embers, add some more oil and fry the slices of pāua briefly, only a minute or two per side.

Now assemble the dish: on each of four plates, place a bed of silverbeet stalks and cover with the green leaves. Cover with the cooked pāua and strew four stalks of blanched samphire over each plate, topping it with a bunch of raw sea grapes.

Serves four.

Back in your kitchen at home, submit the remaining six pāua to the method recommended by the famous Sydney chef Tetsuya Wakuda. It's an adaptation of the technique used by his grandparents, who fished traditionally for abalone in Japan, using water glasses and long rods with special hooks.

Put the live pāua flesh side down in a large frying pan, preferably of heavy cast iron, without any oil or butter, and turn the element down to its lowest possible heat. Cover the frying pan with a lid and leave the pāua to their sauna. Don't disturb the pāua in the early stages, or you yourself may be disturbed by the sight of pāua writhing about in their death throes.

Leave the pāua for about thirty minutes, or until the shells are hot to the touch. Smaller species of abalone, such as those found in Japanese waters, will only need about ten minutes.

By now, the gut-bag will have cooked and shrunk, and can be conveniently removed and discarded, along with the pāua's beak and digestive tract. Best of all, the pāua meat will be fully cooked and tender, while the frilly lip, normally the toughest part of the beast, will have turned to jelly.

For more treasures from the deep, read 'The lobster's tail' by Chris Price, in the e-book *Pacific Highways: Volume 2*, available free at www.griffithreview.com

A forager from way back, David Burton is also a food journalist for *Cuisine* magazine and the *Dominion Post* and a culinary historian (*The Raj at Table*, Faber & Faber, 1994, *French Colonial Cookery*, Faber, 2000, *200 Years of New Zealand Food and Cookery*, Reed, 1983, *Biography of a Local Palate*, Four Winds Press, 2003). His twenty-eight literary prizes include six book awards and ten Qantas Media Awards.

Victoria University Press (VUP) is a leading New Zealand publisher of fiction, poetry and scholarly non-fiction.

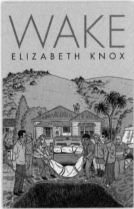

VUP authors include

Pip Adam, Vincent O'Sullivan, Bill Manhire, Jenny Bornholdt and Man Booker Prize 2013 winner Eleanor Catton.

For our full catalogue visit our online bookstore
vup.victoria.ac.nz

Gregory O'Brien

Whale Survey, Raoul Island, with Rosemary Dobson

Two poets on a headland, mid-survey
might pause suddenly and say
will this be your whale, or mine?

Moving, accordingly, from one observation area
to the next, a whale is 'handed over'.
Please take it. No, you first.

Early morning spent 'getting the eye in'
velocity of clouds, sea conditions noted.
Breaching, logging, travelling, the Pacific

divided between Coral Bay and Tropic Bird Face
Bomb Shed, Hutchies Bluff and Blindspot. Later
Rosemary observed to a friend

from the sharpest point of her triangulation:
If I stand still enough, I can see Wolverine Rock,
a water spout and, westerly, one cow and calf.

In memory of Rosemary Dobson (1920-2012)

Gregory O'Brien is a Wellington-based poet, essayist, painter and curator, whose recent publications include a collection of poems, *Beauties of the Octagonal Pool* (Auckland University Press, 2012), and a monograph on painter Euan MacLeod (Piper Press, Sydney, 2010). An earlier meditation on oceanic matters, *News of the swimmer reaches shore*, appeared from Carcanet (UK) and Victoria University Press in 2007.

When the swimmer reaches shore

Bruce Foster

I GREW up in the 'River City' – Whanganui. From the river mouth to the Aramaho railway bridge – about as far as a king tide pushes upstream – the city straddles the river. Beyond this bridge, for hundreds of years before Europeans showed up, Māori settlements flourished, a remarkable culture about which we were taught nothing. Between the port and the Victoria Avenue bridge, industries dotted the river bank; timber tanalising, wool scouring, car wreckers, soap, leather tannery, abattoir, the 'works' – a rambling, turn-of-the-century slaughter house and so on. A favourite parking spot after the movies was behind the bacon factory. Couples writhed on the back seats of Ford Zephyrs, Vauxhall Victors and Morris Minors while only a few meters away, the river slid by.

The waste from these factories– animal parts and chemicals – discharged straight into the river, as did the sewerage from the thirty thousand or so city residents. It drifted downstream on the ebb tide, passing beneath the wharves where we fished for herring and spotties, and out between the moles that poked into the sea either side of the river mouth. Depending on the weather, prevailing currents and winds, it was then sucked westward into the Tasman, or swept north, to flow parallel to the shore before being tossed up on Castle-cliff beach. The dominant colours of the beach were shades of grey – from pitch black at the water's edge to silver on the dunes where we would roam with bows and arrows, and where my sister once spied on a bikie piss-up and saw Blondie Saul, wrestling a man, half naked, wild, sweaty, their torsos caked with sand: iron sand, so concentrated you could lift it with a magnet.

In summer, swimmers coming ashore would scorch their feet within seconds. It was like fire walking. In winter, the beach was covered with driftwood, great hoary logs flushed downriver by floods – the legacy of generations of native forest clearance.

The beach was bleak and without shelter, but still we went there. The wind blew continuously. Cars got stuck. Then in the '70s, the council built a massive car park, spaces for several hundred vehicles, far more than what would ever be required. Decorated with a precise grid of straight white lines, a smooth bitumen pad reached towards the sea, its perimeter flanked by curved concrete slabs – bulwarks against the sand. But, like a cat, the sand crept in, innocuous at first, accumulating in little mounds topped with delicate rhythmic wave patterns. The mounds grew and became drifts: small dunes formed, and then, before the car park subsided from view, diggers arrived.

Structures built in a similar spirit to the car park at Castlecliff beach dot the coastline of New Zealand. At the water's edge these gestures in concrete, bitumen and steel mark a boundary between two worlds. One is solid and secure beneath our feet, the other is manifestly in flux. One, a place of familiarity and certainty, the other, mysterious, alluring, dangerous – an ocean in which our imagination knows no bounds.

Ototoko, 1983

Ohope, 2010

Tiphead, Greymouth,1989

Moa Point, 2009

Whanganui River, 1992

Opanake, 2010

Tiphead, Greymouth, 1990

North Mole, Whanganui, 1982

Since the 1970s, Bruce Foster's photography has documented and explored the
relationship between people, the acculturated environment and landscape.
Recent works record the despoliation of the near pristine marine environment of the
Kermadecs. Just published, *Citizen of Santiago* (Trapeze, 2013), is a collaboration
with poet Gregory O'Brien.

Thinking about waves

Knowing when to leave

Lynn Jenner

FROM *my research journal, August 2011:* Our sea is made up of certain blues. Sometimes, just before the weather changes, our sea is so pale it fades into the sky. At these times, the sea is almost silent. Sometimes our sea is bluer than a cornflower. These blues are inside us, enshrined beyond anything conscious, alongside the smell of hot sand and the sound of waves arriving from thousands of miles away.

By the time news from the rest of the world arrives here its voice is faint and barely audible above the noise of these waves.

September 4, 2013: This morning I went to an exhibition called *Refugee.* The heart of the exhibition, the reason for its existence, according to a reviewer, was a montage of hundreds of photographs of unnamed Afghani people, mostly in family groups. Murdoch Stephens, a young man from New Zealand, found the photographs several years ago on the floor in an abandoned refugee camp in Iran.

Visitors to the exhibition are invited to write their views on New Zealand's refugee policy on one of two white boards. The board on the left is for people who want New Zealand to do more for refugees and the one on the right for people who want things to stay the way they are. On the right-hand board, on the day of my first visit, someone had written that we have people here who need help, and we should look after our own people first.

On the left-hand board someone had written that we should share what we have in New Zealand.

September 5, 2013: I went back to *Refugee* today. This time I noticed that some of the men in the photographs from the Iranian desert camp had a rough cross in felt pen, drawn above or next to their heads. I am at a loss to explain how I could have spent time yesterday in the company of these photographs, understood the peoples' expressions as messages of grief and hunger and fear, but missed these crosses.

From the summer of 2011: People who live right beside the sea, as I do, think about waves. You might dream of a never-ending surge that lifts houses from their foundations and floats them out to sea. Or you might find you can imagine a single wave, thirteen storeys high, arriving as thunder that never stops. You ponder which fate you would prefer. You compare the odds of the giant wave with the odds of being hit by a bus while crossing Lambton Quay. You find reassurance in the fact that your house has stood in its seaside location for fifty years. You try to convince yourself that you accept your fate, that you are ready. As far as I know, everyone thinks about giant waves in these ways but I don't know anyone who has done anything practical as a result of those thoughts.

If a wave the height of my fence came and I did not have insurance on my house, a radio, a torch and enough medication, canned food and water for three days stored in the garage, prudent people would be shocked and disapproving. A wave the size of a fence is not only a known risk, it is an imaginable risk.

The lexicon of risk is mostly mathematical.

Statistical probabilities:	*Consequences:*
Almost certain	Negligible
Likely	Minor
Possible	Moderate
Unlikely	Severe
Rare	Ruinous

Your eye hardly stops as you take in the normal curve of probabilities. But then you get to 'ruinous'.

And this, from July 29, 2013: Over two days this winter, waves broke up and took away all the pieces of a fifty-year-old concrete boat ramp across the road from my house. Not that this process is really new. Beside the boat ramp, in the 1970s, there used to be a surf club and a house. And a few kilometres south, where, in 1942 the US Marines practised landings for the Pacific campaign, I am told the sea has taken three rows of dunes.

When I saw the damage to the boat ramp I was surprised that it had happened so quickly but did not really think about it much more until a few weeks later when I received a letter from the Kāpiti District Council forecasting changes in the coastline over the next hundred years. A diagram of 'Coastal Erosion Prediction Lines' showed the sea lapping, or clawing, at my letterbox in fifty years. By then the sea will have taken a hundred metres of sand dunes, a row of several hundred houses, gas and water pipes, electrical cables and a tar-sealed road.

The thinking all seems very scientific:

Coastal erosion prediction lines = LT + ST + SLR + DS + CU, where

LT= longer term historic shoreline change

ST= shorter term shoreline fluctuation

SLR= shoreline retreat associated with sea-level rise

DS= dune stability, and

CU= combined uncertainty.

Combined Uncertainty is scientific too, in its own way.

There continues to be much discussion among residents about whether this coastal erosion line is a likely scenario or only a possible scenario, this difference seen to have great significance for resale values.

When I read the council's letter, I remembered a man I used to work with in the insurance business, back in 2007. This man had spent the years since the Boxing Day tsunami in 2004 making mathematical models of the likely effects of tsunami of different sizes on Wellington's business district. When he talked at team meetings about his predictions, I used to picture us, leaning out the windows of our thirteenth floor offices, watching with interest as Hokusai's great blue and white wave rolled in from the harbour and up Featherston Street. Thirteen storeys, I thought, would be well above anything messy that might be happening at street level. From the vantage point of today, I have probably been wrong to worry about the threat of a single catastrophic wave. But, as it turns out, thousands of noisy brown waves, each just a little larger than they used to be, seem as though they might matter a lot.

January 18, 2012: Kāpiti Island, after which the Kāpiti Coast is named, is a Nature Reserve administered by the Department of Conservation. The island's regenerating native bush is a place for reintroduced native birds to breed, but these processes can only happen if the island is free of introduced pests and predators. After decades of hunting and trapping, there are no more cats or possums on Kāpiti Island but rats and stoats are still a worry. Rats climb into visitors' bags and travel to the island by ferry. Stoats do that too, and maybe they even swim across from the mainland. No one is quite sure exactly how they keep getting over there, but they do. Once rats or stoats are ashore, they breed furiously. That is the problem.

Official documents describe Kāpiti Island as five kilometres away from the mainland, but in fact, it moves towards the mainland and away, according to its own laws and designs. It may, if displeased, pull away and make the journey to the mainland impossible, as it did for a week last winter, trapping a young woman who had an abscessed tooth. Or it may decide to come close, as it does in spring, because of its sympathy for young birds.

In the dying hours of a nor'wester which had turned the sea brown and made waves as high as a fence, I crossed to the island with twenty other people, including a woman from Mexico who works as an environmental advisor to a German company trying to set up a coal mine on the West Coast, her mother who spoke only Spanish, a Māori chef from Otaki and two beautiful Japanese women who were on a summer holiday. Looking back from the island towards the mainland through binoculars mounted on a stand, we saw two men in a fishing dinghy in the distance, putting out crayfish pots.

Writing in a diary she kept between 1924 and 1942, Amy Wilkinson, wife of the custodian of what was then the Kapiti Island Bird Sanctuary, speaks of seeing smoke from summer fires on the mainland; bush clearances were a well-understood seasonal event in those years. I appreciate knowing that Amy Wilkinson witnessed all that burning. But, although I know this is unreasonable, I want more from her diary of these years than the date of sightings of the Shining Cuckoo and the Long-Tailed Cuckoo. I want to know if she saw a morepork in her kitchen on Kristallnacht or thought she heard the voices of women and girls singing, or anything else I could read as an omen. And what the sky looked like on 27 November, 1935, the night the first Labour government of New Zealand was elected. My father, aged nine, attended a party on that night, collecting signatures of men who would soon be cabinet ministers. 'Labour: the hope of the working man,' wrote one of these men.

ON KĀPITI ISLAND we had a guide who said that she could talk about animals or plants or history, whichever we requested. I chose history, which was a minority choice, so most of the time, as we walked around the north end of the island, she pointed to trees, named them, and helped us to spot birds in the branches, and skinks, which live inside boxes used to trap stoats, apparently undisturbed by blocks of blue poison several times larger than their bodies.

We walked downhill along a path into denser bush with a dark canopy overhead. It was a little like walking into a tunnel. As I entered this place, I felt something which I can only describe as a separate darkness. I walked on, saying nothing about this feeling.

A little further on the guide stopped and told us this story:

At dawn one day, spotters on the Island saw hundreds of canoes leave from Waikanae and Otaki and paddle towards them. The water was dark with canoes so they knew a battle was coming.

There had been warnings before this day came. The first was given by a party from Kāpiti fishing for hāpuku from canoes. Seeing another group on the water and mistaking this for a war party, they rushed back to Kāpiti to warn of an attack. After several days had passed, another food-gathering party crossed from Kāpiti to Paekakariki to gather shellfish and karaka berries. At night, while they were collecting mussels, a war party surprised them and killed three people before the survivors could escape back to Kāpiti. This killing was the second warning.

A week or two passed. One night two children climbed a tall tree, looked out towards the mainland and saw hundreds of flickering campfires. Those fires were the third warning. It is said that later that same night a man from the war party crossed to Kāpiti and told the people on the island when and how the attack would be launched. That was the fourth warning. That man crossed back and joined the canoes in their early morning attack.

Both the guide on the island in January 2012 and Wakahuia Carkeek, writing in 1967, say that Te Rauparaha and his men defeated this army of perhaps two thousand men on flat land near the lagoon at the northern end of the island. One by one, captured men of the Ngāti Apa tribe were duly consigned to the ovens, Carkeek says, making it clear that no other end was imaginable.

Undated – early in 2011: This morning I found, somewhat to my surprise, that I was talking with a woman of my own age, from my own country, but whom I don't know very well, about the Holocaust. Any conversation about the Holocaust is a bit uncomfortable. Sometimes silences occur in these conversations which no one knows how to end. One of these silences grew between me and a German friend in 2002 and it has not been broken yet. Increasingly these days I try to *avoid* these conversations, finding that my views on the topic are too Jewish for non-Jewish company but not Jewish enough for my Jewish friends.

This particular conversation started when the woman asked me about my upcoming trip to visit museums in Australia and New Zealand which have Holocaust exhibits, as background for my latest writing project. The conversation went quickly to a bus tour this woman had been on which included Auschwitz as part of the package. After a few minutes of descriptions of heritage sites and monuments, she stopped talking and looked away, downwards and to the right. After just a minute, the woman raised her eyes, looked at me again and told me how shocked and surprised she had been when, in the 1970s, she met two middle aged people in Lower Hutt who had been in the camps.

Around the same time as the conversation about monuments, a Jewish friend, who speaks five languages and reads several more, told me it would not be possible to write about the Holocaust from New Zealand. There's so little to say here, she said. You should go to Europe.

But this is where I am, I said. That is the problem. This is where I am from, this is who I am, and this is where I am.

MY GREAT-GRANDFATHER ARRIVED in New Zealand in 1878, probably from what is now Poland or Russia. He said different things about where he was from, according to the audience. We do not know the names of his relatives in Europe or the villages they lived in – there is no one left now who knows these things.

On arrival in Wellington, an official wrote 'Cardiff' for his departure point and 'Hebrew' for his religion, and that was enough to get him off the docks and into town. We know he started his new life in New Zealand quickly, marrying a Jewish woman from the same ship, and making a large family. For whatever reasons, Isaac (that was his English name) did not apply for New Zealand citizenship, which meant that in the 1930s, when Jews everywhere worried about their safety, he was not a New Zealand citizen. Bed-ridden, Isaac banged his walking stick on the wooden floor of his upstairs bedroom to call attention to his needs. This noise terrorised his children and was still spoken of during my childhood.

I sometimes imagine Isaac listening to the radio in his living room in Aro Valley, hearing about Kristallnacht or the Nuremberg laws. Once I went as far as to imagine him receiving a letter, in Yiddish, from a sister, telling him how and when his parents died, where they are buried, and asking for him to sponsor her son and his family to come to New Zealand. She doesn't care about herself, his sister says, but he should help the children if he can. He rages and cries and bangs his walking stick on the wooden floor and tells no one about the letter, not his children and not his wife. Perhaps he is ashamed of not having money to help them, or perhaps he is angry because he thought he had left them all far enough behind that no claims could ever be made. In my teens, when I was first starting to learn about the Holocaust, I remember being preoccupied with the problem of how *I* would know when it was time to leave New Zealand. I would read about people whose lives were deeply rooted in a certain place in Europe – more deeply rooted than mine felt here in New Zealand. I saw pictures taken of these people in 1932 or 1936, as they walked in pairs along a street they knew well. This is *Before*.

I looked and looked at *Before* photographs of Jewish people, trying to see if *they* knew it was time to leave. I thought there would be something obvious, a darkening in people's faces, or perhaps a solemnity that said they knew it was already too late. But there wasn't. Or maybe there was, but I didn't recognise their expression. 'Backshadowing', or reading the past backwards, is one word for what I was doing.

As far as I can see, nothing answers the question of how Jews were supposed to know when it was time to leave Europe. I think this unanswerable question is the reason that I have inherited a sensitivity, common among Jewish people, to suitcases.

November 2011: I visited four museum exhibits related to the Holocaust, two in Australia, two in New Zealand. On my return, my sceptical friend asks gently whether my visit was satisfying. I think for a while and then I say yes. She asks me what exactly I saw. I tell her that I met six people who had survived the Holocaust, and that until then no survivors had ever looked me straight in the eye and told me their story. She looks at me for a moment without speaking.

I tell her that they all said I could ask questions. One man said 'you can ask me *any* questions'.

Why do you do this? I asked. 'To warn everyone', the man replied. His answer has a different quality from the rest of what he says. It is very direct. His voice is in a low register.

'What do you think Australia should do about the boatloads of illegal immigrants arriving every week?' I ask.

He says it is a difficult matter. He has great sympathy for them, coming with their families and risking their lives. His eyes water as he says this. But the state has to do what it needs to, he says. If the government did nothing, millions of immigrants would come from Asia. The government should do what is necessary he says, but they shouldn't be cruel. That is the important thing.

September 10, 2013: Waves keep arriving. No need to say any more about that.

The sound of waves is like the sound inside a shell – meaningless, and strangely consoling. I learned that from six years of walking by the sea.

Through the sound of the waves, you can hear voices. I thought that was the case but now I am sure.

Books, museums, art galleries and taxis help us detect faint signals. Think of a trumpet, narrow at your ear, and opening wide towards the world.

Lynn Jenner's first book *Dear Sweet Harry* (Auckland University Press, 2009), a mixed-genre work starring Harry Houdini, Mata Hari and Jenner's grandfather, won the New Zealand Society of Authors prize for Best First Book of Poetry in 2010. 'Thinking about waves' contains excerpts from the manuscript of her forthcoming second book, *Everyday Life in the Ancient World*.

Dinah Hawken

The uprising

2013

1.
Here we are a skinny country
in the largest ocean on earth
spell-bound, windswept, lashed.

The land is like a canoe heading south
to an icy continent or heading north to equatorial islands.
No one seems to know.

On Tuvalu the ocean is rising, in San Francisco
the ocean is rising, in Sydney the ocean is
rising, in Nagoya the ocean is rising

while here, in Paekakariki, outside my window
the Tasman Sea, moon-bound, rises and falls.
It breaks up on the sea wall and falls.

2.
The land is like a sea-bird but where
are its wings? The land is like a fish.
The fish of Māui, hauled up from the sea floor, writhing.

The ocean is a road, a table and a bed.
It takes our bodies up to air and floats them.
The ocean is an open question.

The ocean is an open sewer. So far
it takes what it gets: toxins, dead zones,
blooms, blasts, oil, waste, radiation…

Our country is asleep – dreaming of a gull
that circles the Pacific, and circles every island.
Our country has forgotten where it lies.

3.
On Antarctica the Pacific is rising,
in Majuro the Pacific is rising:
people leave when they cannot stay.

In Lima the Pacific is rising,
on Nukunonu the Pacific is rising,
in Paekakariki the Pacific is rising.

Around the rim it calms, feeds and livens
human beings while we, its offspring – resourceful
and distracted – give back plastic and acid.

Today the sea came gently to the sea wall
and pulled back into itself
in the overall global uprising.

4.
The whole indivisible ocean,
that has no motive and no name,
fits over the earth like a blessing

and slips around, between and over
the territories and nations we have made.
Currents, drifts and creatures come and go.

It shows up outside my window and,
though spell-bound and moon-bound, is unbound
with a swell and momentum of its own.

Because we have emerged from it perhaps
we have a mind for its envelopment and treachery;
its weight, sheen, depth, saltiness and flow?

5.
Our country is a park. We have the high
ground and the low ground. Our mountains
are peace flags and we're free

to break out of bush, flax, pingao
or any dead-end ideology
onto a charged and open-ended coast.

The land is like a knife, out
of its sheath and glinting in the sun.
I'd like to hold that pointed knife.

I'd like to speak with that knife.
I'd like to save a home, a tribe
and a heritage with that knife.

6.
And all I can do is rise:
both before and after I fall.
All I can do is rally,

all I can do is write.
I can try to see, and mark,
both where, and how, we are.

All I can do is plant,
all I can do is vote
for the fish, the canoe, the ocean

to survive the rise and fall.
All I can do is plead,
all I can do is call...

Dinah Hawken lives in Paekakariki on the Kāpiti coast, north of Wellington. Of her six collections of poetry, published by Victoria University Press, four have been finalists in the New Zealand book awards. Her most recent book is *The leaf-ride*, published in 2011.

MEMOIR

The beach

States of transition

Leilani Tamu

A sweep of reef, two dashing freshwater rivers and a towering mountain, the bay of Apia, on the north coast of the island of Upolu, Samoa, has seduced many a traveller. As a young New Zealand-born Samoan I used to dream of Apia. I would listen to my grandparents and their stories of Lelata (our family land); they spoke of picnics, the shop on the waterfront, the picture theatre; and I would try to envisage this faraway place.

In the songs and stories shared by my handsome, blue-eyed grandfather, I imagined Apia as a place in-between. A place that had given birth to him and his sense of identity as an *'afakasi*.

In my youth, I took the term 'afakasi for granted. I knew it loosely translated to half-caste. For my grandfather, the term 'afakasi went hand-in-hand with his identity as a Samoan, by the way he carried himself, and danced a Samoan *siva* and the emotion in his voice when he spoke about his heritage. It was a part of his *being* as a Pacific Islander that he celebrated. His identity could not be cut in half.

The term half-caste was never used in our home. It was a term I heard outsiders use, but I never regarded it as having any practical or tangible relevance to my life. Then, as I entered my teenage years, I came to resent the use of the term half-caste — not because it was ever used in an overtly derogatory way towards me but because it didn't capture the complexity and beauty of being 'afakasi.

The difficulty for me, though, as a New Zealand-born Samoan, was that I didn't grow up with those cultural reference points that validated my mother and grandfather's identity as 'afakasi. I had never been to Samoa and growing up in urban Auckland made the islands of my mother's birth seem distant and removed. On top of this, the Samoan kids at school asserted their identity through shared skin colour. Having brown skin was considered essential. My own skin is white (a trait shared by my grandfather and mother), so I didn't qualify for entry in to this group. It was around this time that I started to realise that some of my Pacific peers resented — even detested — 'afakasi. We were considered to be privileged, to be 'up ourselves' and not truly Samoan.

Yet, at home, I was expected to behave like a proper 'Samoan girl' with strict rules and expectations determining my behaviour. The contradiction was frustrating: why should I behave like a Samoan when I wasn't accepted as a Samoan by others? At times I wanted to deny my cultural heritage and just blend in. But given the cultural values and pride instilled in me by my grandparents I could never fully let go of that part of myself.

By the time I was thirteen this sense of insecurity led me to seek out experiences, people and places that existed on the periphery. I turned to the streets, I slept in school playgrounds, I smoked drugs with strangers. Auckland's streets offered a transient space where I could be free to define my own sense of self.

But over time this freedom began to overwhelm me. One day I woke up in a stranger's house in South Auckland and made a decision to go home. I walked the train tracks from Manurewa to Morningside, made my way home and knocked on the door. As punishment, a male relative beat me and cut off my hair.

I was told that this punishment was light compared to what I would have received if I lived in Samoa. There, I was told, a woman's hair would be shaved off in front of the whole village. Again, this place I had never been to was shaping my identity.

VISITING SAMOA FOR the first time I was amazed at the beauty of the islands. I found it difficult to recognise the place described to me by my grandfather. Most of the historic buildings in Apia had been demolished and it was only in the physical landscape of the wide shoe-horn bay that I caught glimpses of the place I had travelled to in my childhood dreams.

Soon I would enrol in a Masters in Pacific history and focus on the beach community resident in Apia during the nineteenth century, and there I was to glimpse the place that had shaped my identity as an 'afakasi long before my birth. And it had a name. It was called 'the beach'.

In the early years the political nature of the beach was of little importance in comparison to the greater heartlands of the Samoan world. The epicentres of Samoa were ancient places such as Leulumoega, Safotulafai, Manono and Lufilufi. But this would change irrevocably with the arrival of foreigners.

Within the Samoan archipelago there were only two anchorages with the capacity to cater to a large number of visiting ships at any one time. To this day Pago Pago on the island of Tutuila is renowned for its beautiful harbour, ideal for deep draught vessels. By contrast, Apia, on the island of Upolu, sits in a more exposed position (particularly during the cyclone season of December to March) although it has a natural break in the reef, which allows access between the open sea and the lagoon.

During the early years of the nineteenth century the popularity of these two anchorages was largely determined by the influx of whaling ships that began to frequent Samoan waters from the 1820s on. The greatest number were American, from Nantucket and New Bedford. Initially larger numbers of ships called in at Pago Pago, but from the 1840s onwards this began to shift to Apia because of its greater potential to draw on resource supply links from the islands of Upolu and Savai'i.

Slowly the port settlement began to take on a character of its own, with a distinction emerging between the eastern side of the bay at Matautu and the western side at Matafele, Savalalo and Sogi. To the east of the township were the British and American consulates, while to the west was the Hamburg (later German) Consulate, and referred to as 'the German part of town'; a reputation further cemented by the establishment of the Pacific headquarters of the Hamburg mercantile house of JC Godeffroy & Sohn (in 1857 subsumed by the Deutsche Handels und Plantagen-Gesellschaft), with the English trading company William McArthur & Co settling on the other side of town.

In the 1820s an eclectic ramshackle assemblage of tin huts, stone houses, adobe churches and *fale* (traditional houses) began to spring up from one horn of Apia bay to the other. This township was named after the village upon which it was the most dependent, Apia.

As in other Pacific port towns – Honolulu, Kororareka, Pape'ete and Levuka – the beach was a place of cross-cultural meshing. These port communities were connected to and separated from the beach that fronted their harbours. It was a place of transaction and exchange that brought together fragments and memories and stories – of these the tale of the beachcomber was the most prominent.

The term 'beachcombers' was first given popular currency by Herman Melville when his rugged character Salem said to the Consul at Tahiti, 'I'm nothing more than a bloody beach-comber.'

Through the experiences of the first group of foreign residents in the Pacific the beach came to represent more than the space upon which their survival was dependent; these were also spaces that reshaped their identity.

For some the beach offered a means of escape – from the cramped and often poor conditions aboard ships, from imprisonment in New South Wales (in the case of runaway convicts) and perhaps, most importantly, from the social mores and constraints that shaped the home societies they had left behind. In the Pacific references to the beach evolved, according to Stevenson, 'as a South Seas' expression for which there [is] no equivalent elsewhere'.

In the literature the beachcombers were both celebrated and reviled. They were recognised for the essential roles they played in establishing the port town community but at the same time were type-cast as degenerative, disreputable and dishonest. Similarly, half-castes who were acknowledged as playing important roles in the day-to-day cross-cultural functioning of the community were considered to be meddlesome, untrustworthy and cunning.

Writers such as Robert Louis Stevenson, Louis Becke, and later, Somerset Maugham, established a literary tradition whereby the half-caste would come to subsume the space previously occupied by the beachcombers.

Negative connotations associated with 'the beach' and 'beachcombing' were put about by missionaries, consuls and naval officials. From them there was little tolerance for white men who had 'gone troppo' in the South Pacific. In a visit to Tonga in 1832 the missionary John Williams wrote in his diary: '...I was astonished to find so great a number of runaway sailors here. They are a noisome pestilence in the South Seas. They were I believe all bound to the Navigator Islands [Samoa] where at present there are enough to paralyse the effects of the most zealous missionary labours.'

Similarly, in 1856, Apia was described by a visiting US Commodore Mervine: 'A state of society that beggars all description; composed of a heterogeneous mass of the most immoral and dissolute Foreigners that ever disgraced humanity: principally composed of Americans and Englishmen, several of whom have been Sidney [sic] convicts'.

By the 1850s, the whole community at Apia was seen to share the qualities previously attributed to its first migrant settlers, the beachcombers.

Their circumstances were to improve, and by the 1890s Stevenson assessed them as a 'fairly respectable population.' Stevenson as the most internationally recognised writer resident in the Pacific would play an active role in redefining 'the beach'. In his writing, the beach is only ever mentioned with reference to disreputable characters living out a state of wretchedness inimical to any efforts to bring order and civility to Samoa.

To Stevenson the urban settlement of Apia was a physical manifestation of the squalor found on the beach. Writing from his residence at Vailima (about a day's journey on horse-back from Apia) he wrote about the various misdeeds of the beach community. In his efforts to redefine the reputation of the community, he was also active in attending and organising fancy dress balls, theatricals and picnics. The Stevenson family even took a lead role in establishing the 'Half-Caste Club' at the request of local resident Laulii Willis.

In the narratives of Melville, William Mariner and Becke the beachcomber survives and seeks reintegration back in to the home society. The tale was always told from the viewpoint of the European who returned 'home', if indeed they made it home. In Becke's 1897 story 'In a Samoan Village' a beachcomber, Bill, has this to say: '...What are we in our own minds? What would any of your or my countrymen think of us but that we are a pair of shameless, degraded beings, unfit to associate with; sunk too low to even think of returning to civilisation again?'

PONDERING THE EVOLUTION of 'afakasi identity and the transient nature of the beachcombers I recognised tensions in the narratives that resonated with me as an 'afakasi growing up in New Zealand.

As one walks along the seawall of modern-day Apia there are few remnants of the old beach. Gone are the sand and the shingle, and in the middle of the wide curve of the bay sits a mass of reclaimed land, which marks the place upon which the rusted hull of the German naval ship, the *Adler*, sat for nigh on fifty years. Any remaining urban evidence of the beach of the nineteenth century is slowly being eroded.

But, as a historian turned poet, I have become interested in the ways in which the past can be excavated through alternative forms of story-telling. On this journey I have dug out the sense of space that connects me to my ancestors. And like those that came before me, I refer to it, simply, as 'the beach'. Whether I am sitting on a beach in Samoa, on an island in Tongatapu, or at home in Aotearoa or in Hawai'i where I am currently resident the beach is always within me –

Where that last shard
Of light is broken
And the word is no longer spoken

Where I
Walk the cusp of history untold
To pay homage to deeds
Best forgotten

It is the place that I have excavated for myself
That exists at the edge of all things defined

For more on the power of place, read 'On matters of national significance' by Patricia Grace, in the e-book *Pacific Highways: Volume 2*, available free at www.griffithreview.com

Leilani Tamu is a poet, social commentator, Pacific historian and former New Zealand diplomat. In 2013 she was the Fulbright/Creative New Zealand Writer in Residence at the Center for Pacific Studies at the University of Hawai'i in Mānoa.

Born to run

The remarkable tale of Steve Adams

John Saker

THE loincloth-clad figure who stood on the deck of the frigate HMS *Tagus* clearly impressed its skipper. '(He was) about twenty-five years of age, a tall fine young man about six feet high, with dark black hair, and a countenance extremely open and interesting,' Captain Philip Pipon RN wrote.

Pipon was the second caller to Pitcairn Island after it had been outed as the *Bounty* mutineers' bolthole in 1807, nearly twenty years after the mutiny. Following the early years of murder and mishap on the isolated molehill of volcanic rock, by the time of Pipon's arrival most of its small population was made up of a second, blended generation, the offspring of the naval miscreants and their Tahitian sweethearts. The youth described by Pipon was Thursday October Christian, son of mutineer-in-chief Fletcher Christian and his wife Mauatua. Pipon's admiring tone was echoed by many of the island's other fascinated early tourists. The young Pitcairn Islanders' size – at six feet, Thursday October Christian would have towered over the nineteenth century Jack Tars – and physical dexterity were a source of wonder. These earliest Euronesians took to 'Davey' (their name for the sea) from their canoes, swimming like eels around visiting ships, and hared up and down riggings when they came on board. For sport, they had invented their own hazardous form of surfing, which they called 'sliding'. Using three-foot-long boards, they would leap from rocks on to passing waves, ride them and pull out moments before the surging water broke over rocks, sandy beaches being non-existent on Pitcairn.

Just one mutineer remained at the time of Pipon's visit, John Adams. A wily old survivor, by then Adams was on to his fifth Tahitian partner. I mention this only because of the coincidence provided by the name and the marital record.

Sailors and other Old World escapees washing up on antipodean shores, falling in with local females, spawning handsome children, settling into simple lifestyles on beautiful unpopulated islands, largely free of the constraints of their former lives…it was to become an often-reprised theme in the historical score of the South Pacific. It gave us New Zealand's first European settlers, the assorted salts who became the so-called 'Pākehā Māori'.

A RINGING CONTEMPORARY riff in New Zealand comes through in a story with many remarkable scenes, one of the most recent taking place in Brooklyn, New York in June 2013.

National Basketball Association commissioner David Stern is onstage at the Barclays Centre, presiding over the final draft of his long career heading the world's premier professional basketball league. The draft, where the league's teams take turns to pluck their chosen blooms from the current crop of available college talent and other eligible players, is an annual event watched by millions worldwide.

The 2013 draft has the pundits guessing. There are no Magics or Shaqs out there to be pounced on immediately; it's a year characterised by a perceived paucity of blue-chip talent. No one is taken aback when surprises start being hatched. Teams are taking punts all over the place, especially with players of international origin. A Canadian is picked number one for the first time; an Iranian (yes, Iranian) behemoth gets taken in the second round, another first. New Zealand does its bit to widen this circle when twenty-year-old Steven Adams is the twelfth name called out by Stern.

Up to the stage strides 'a tall fine young man…with dark black hair, and a countenance extremely open and interesting.' All that's missing from Pipon's appraisal is the height reference. Being seven feet 'high', Steven Adams has a good twelve inches on Thursday October Christian.

STEVEN ADAMS IS not an unknown, but nor is he any kind of name. He has only been playing the game for six years and has completed just one year at the University of Pittsburgh. There he posted stats that did not evoke visions of NBA greatness. But his height, mobility and general athleticism (particularly what basketball insiders like to call his 'foot speed'; for his size he has a quicksilver first step) has given teams pause when assessing him. Beyond his abilities, his bio has also piqued interest. Everyone loves a good back story – America especially – and Steve Adams' backstory is up there with the best.

It began when his father Sid Adams fetched up in New Zealand as a young man around 1960. Adams was born and raised in Bristol, England, and prior to making landfall in the Bay of Plenty his working life had been spent in the Merchant Navy. Powerfully built, forearms clouded by the mandatory tattoos, he was your typical able seaman but for the fact he was so tall, somewhere between six feet eight and seven feet. It has been reported that back in the old country he was mocked about his height. From what I have come to learn, taking the mickey out of Sid Adams would have been foolhardy at best. Even so, those early barbs apparently contributed to his decision to start a new life on the far side of the world.

According to family lore he jumped ship, for which he did jail time soon after arriving in New Zealand. Like many before and since, he solved the problem of his irregular immigration status by marrying a local. There followed a life mostly spent in the Bay of Plenty town of Rotorua.

Rotorua became the cradle of New Zealand tourism in the mid-nineteenth century, when the pink and white terraces caught the world's imagination. These glorious oversized staircases of silica, one of each hue and dubbed by some the eighth wonder of the world, vanished under the fallout of volcanic eruption in 1886. The visitor traffic did not die with them. Rotorua still had enough geysers, belching mud pools and Māori cultural attractions to continue reeling in a steady conga line of tourists. Tourism remains one of the town's major earners.

Beneath the daily turnover of dazed happy snappers lies another, darker Rotorua. The district as a whole is ranked in the bottom third on New Zealand's deprivation scale and its crime rates are well above national totals. It is a place of rough neighbourhoods and hard lives. Māori author Alan Duff was born and raised in Rotorua, witnessing the brutality and sadness of its booze barns and public housing ghettos first hand. His best-known work, *Once Were Warriors* (University of Queensland Press, 1990), is sheeted to that experience.

SID ADAMS WAS never going to lead a tour party on a gavotte through geyserland. All his life he worked in jobs where a pair of hands and a strong back were the only prerequisites, and he believed in working hard. He took a job in forestry, Rotorua's other big industry, driving logging trucks. Finding work boots big enough was a constant problem and his huge, callused hands bore witness to the fact that early on he'd abandoned all hope when it came to gloves.

In 2007, at seventy-six years of age, Adams breathed his last lying on a couch in his small Rotorua home. He'd refused hospice care during the later stages of his stomach cancer. Hovering medicos, drips…that sort of carry-on had never been his style. Sid Adams died poor, and largely unnoticed outside his family and a few mates.

In many ways it was a small life, but in another it was voluminous.

Adams' fecundity was astonishing. The most often quoted tally of his offspring is eighteen, though you also hear twenty-one, sometimes more. At his funeral, some of these children were discovering each other for the first time. The number of female partners who bore him children is also open to conjecture – some say five, some six. What most of these women had in common (besides their connection to Sid Adams) was Polynesian ancestry. Daughter Valerie says two of her father's partners were Tongan, another Tokelauan, another two Māori, and one Pākehā.

The year before his death, when asked by a local reporter to explain this rich conjugal diversity, Adams intimated he had trouble maintaining relationships because he was 'a lousy bugger' to live with. He added: 'I'm old fashioned. I tell them it's your job to stay at home and cook and they don't seem to like that too much.'

Some of these women he married, some he didn't. When his extended brood gets together, the Adams kids joke that the 'small lots', where there were one or two siblings from a single mother, were 'stress release' punctuation marks between the larger lots Sid Adams conceived with his married partners.

These family gatherings might also be the scene of some terrific sporting contests. Sid Adams may have scattered his seed with reckless abandon, but in doing so he made a remarkable, unwitting contribution to his adopted nation's obsession with sport. Adams himself was apparently never that interested in playing games, yet he and his partners created a cadre of super athletes.

Running through the family is a combination of size, rare athletic talent and a strong work ethic. The average height of an Adams male is six feet nine and for females it is six feet. Before the emergence of Steven, the youngest as well as the tallest, it was his sister Valerie whom the world knew for her accomplishments with the shot-put. She has won gold at two Olympics, two Commonwealth Games and four World Championships. Six other Adams children have played basketball for New Zealand.

I WAS PERSONALLY introduced to the Adams DNA towards the end of my own basketball career in 1990. Ralph Adams, one of the clan's eldest children, was in his early twenties and had come to Wellington to play for the national league side from which I had just retired. Three of us – Ralph, a veteran guard on that team and myself – convened at Newtown Stadium to shoot around and play an abbreviated form of the game where three players all play half court against each other. Ralph Adams calmly drilled threes over us, blew right by us, dunked on us…pretty much owned us. 'This guy's awful,' I muttered as I sat with the other vet in a post-demolition daze. 'Did you have to ask him along?' Height (six feet six), quickness, balance, shooting touch – Ralph was the embodiment of the complete basketball player. Over the next few years Ralph, and another brother (Warren, who was six feet eleven), were not just among the best players in the New Zealand national league, they were widely considered NBA material. In those days, the US was a more distant shore than it is now and there were fewer navigation aids available, especially for a couple of kids from a tough background in Rotorua.

A sense of missed opportunity hangs over some of this. The Adams offspring to have achieved the most in sport are Valerie and Steven, both of whom found themselves away from Rotorua in their early teens, living in larger cities and under the wing of excellent coaches. In Steven's case, after his father's death a broken education and life on the street looked to be his lot were it not for swift action by an older brother. Warren plucked him out of Rotorua when he was fourteen and brought him to Wellington. There he received daily basketball tuition from a former national league great, American Kenny McFadden, who also made sure his protégé was performing in the classroom.

Warren Adams would have seen the great potential in his younger brother. But he also would have viewed it through the filter of his own career, which perhaps carries the tint of a strong sense of what might have been.

It's no surprise basketball became the family's chosen sport (it was also Valerie's main game before putting the shot took over). Their vertical blessings would have made it a logical choice. But it is also a game of their colour and class. The arrival of the national league and the American imports in the 1980s saw basketball and its attendant hip-hop culture take hold in New Zealand's Polynesian communities. Along Rotorua's Te Ngae Road, where Steven Adams and many of his siblings grew up, kids dribble balls and spend weekend afternoons at the school playground hoops. Kobe Bryant and LeBron tops are prized currency; young dudes walking past those wearing them snap to mock salutes. Basketball has become part of the landscape.

Sid Adams may not have had much time for sport. But he would have approved of one thing it gave some of his children, particularly Steven, as it was something mutinous Sid himself valued: a means of escape.

John Saker was born in Wellington in 1955 and educated at Victoria University of Wellington and Carroll College (USA). He was New Zealand's first professional basketball player and captain of the NZ national team, the Tall Blacks. He is the author of three books, the most recent *Pinot Noir: The New Zealand Story* (Random House, 2010).

Fitting into the Pacific

Some things you ought to know

Peter Swain

I MET her mother first. Emi was head of the typing pool in a government department where I worked and, in those days, before everyone had a PC on their desks, the senior typist determined the order that work was completed. Emi was the most powerful woman at head office. She was someone that you needed to get alongside if you wanted to get your typing done promptly. As a junior staff member, my strategy was to start work early, take my handwritten correspondence up to the typing pool first thing, and ingratiate myself with the senior typist.

Emi was an early starter. Her first order of the day was a cup of tea and completing the *Dominion Post* crossword puzzle. By the time I arrived with my typing, only a few clues remained unsolved. Sometimes Emi would ask me to help her with a word or two. Our friendship grew, and my typing was completed in good time.

I had not realised that English was not Emi's first language. She looked to solving crossword puzzles as a daily discipline for building vocabulary. While Emi was boss of the typing pool, she had many other roles, including matriarch to her Samoan family and the voice of New Zealand to her homeland. Each week she would prepare a bulletin of local news in the Samoan language to broadcast it to Samoa over the short-wave service of Radio New Zealand. She did this for twenty-five years. Emi lived in two worlds: Samoa and New

Zealand. She was a bridge between the two, and eventually she would invite me to cross that bridge.

My family were South Island farming people of Scottish stock. I had moved to Wellington after my marriage had failed, working full-time and caring for my three children by myself. Times were tough and I had lost my bearings. It must have shown because later on I learned that Emi and the typing pool had given me the nickname 'Tragic'.

In later years Emi would claim that she was the matchmaker who brought her daughter Winnie and I together. Arranged marriages are a Samoan tradition. At the heart of the *fa'asamoa*, the Samoan way of life, are lands and titles – and they offer places of belonging and identity. In the old days, parents would work to build political alliances between families and villages through strategic marriages. Perhaps Emi thought that the tragic *palagi* who helped her with her crossword puzzles would be a suitable match for her daughter?

Winnie worked on the same floor as me. I sat up and really noticed her when she arrived one afternoon dressed for a Samoan meeting. The community worker's jeans and denim jacket had been discarded for an elegant *puletasi* and a flower in her hair. A vision of the Pacific in a dreary office.

Soon after, I was asked to talk about accountability at a staff training workshop. I was hoping to impress Winnie. I outlined the theory and practices that managers could use, and I thought that I had done all right. But after the session Winnie took me aside and gently told me that I could choose to be accountable. Whereas for her, accountability was not a choice. She said that she was accountable to her family and the Samoan community for everything she did or said.

I was deflated that my presentation had been shot down with a smile by the woman I fancied, but relieved that Winnie had not embarrassed me publicly. Later I would learn more about the importance of relationships and reciprocity in the Pacific, the sacred space between people that must be respected, and accountability. I had started my voyage into the Pacific.

A DECADE AFTER we met and had married, Winnie was bestowed the *matai* title Luamanuvao. Samoan chiefly titles are bestowed at a *saofa'i* (a titling ceremony) on individuals chosen by the elders of the family. As the eldest daughter of the eldest daughter of her line, Winnie had the bloodline for this high title in Emi's village, Vaiala. But Samoan chiefly titles are not determined solely through inheritance and birthright, as in the primogeniture of the British Royal family. *O le ala i le pule le tautua*, (The way to authority is through service) guides selection. Potential matai must have the requisite genealogy, but must also have served their families well and have demonstrated leadership and wisdom in village and family affairs.

There are two kinds of matai titles: *ali'i* and *tulafale*. *Ali'i*, are known as sitting chiefs, deriving their authority from sacred origins and aristocratic lineages. Tulafale are talking chiefs or orators, holding the genealogy of the *aiga*, and acting as the voice of their ali'i at ceremonial occasions. While the tulafale may be doing all the talking the ali'i calls the shots. Raised eyebrows and other subtle non-verbal signals determine the direction and outcome of meetings. Under the surface of oratory a subtle discourse of power is often at play.

I soon came to understand that Samoan society is a complex hierarchy with a place for everyone, and everyone in their place.

On first meetings Samoans do not ask your name. They inquire of strangers: *'O ai lou aiga?'* (Who is your family?), *'O fea lou nu'u?'* (Where is your village?). People are identified according to their place of belonging and links with aiga, ancestors, titles, and place, rather than with personal status or achievements.

Winnie, Emi and her husband, Ta'atofa, had gently introduced me to the Samoan world. The orator, Ma'ilo, would deepen my learning about identity and place of belonging, and help me find my place.

Nu'uiali'i Mulipola Ma'ilo Saipele, the senior orator of Vaimauga, told me that knowing who you are and where you belong may be the difference between life and death. These are his words:

'Tupua Mataafa ia Sina o lologo ma fa'atausala o le Ifi tele. That's the joining together of the connections of the country of Chiefs and Orators. *Tuiluluma ia faatausala o le Ifi tele, o la ta nono'a ma la ta soa'a, Tui Manu'a le ia tama ia la talanoa o lana fetaupea'i po'o va i lagi, nofo si aitu ia va i lagi, o manu, tui tau ia manu, o fainu'ulasi ma ua le galu, Tuitele ia Uale galu, o folo o le La, Sina atalaga ia Folo o le La, o le Ia Manaia ma le teine o Le tutu'u, Galumaifele ia Letutu'u, o Gauifaleai, Malietoa Laauli ia Gauifaleai o Lenatoitele, Manua o le Sagalele ia Lenatotele o Vaetamasoali'i ma Atomauga o le Tuitoga. Tuiae selenato ia Vaetamasoali'i o Tui a le tama alelagi.*

Tuitamaalelagi ia Vaetoifana, o Salamasina, le Tupu o Samoa mai Saua e o'o i Falealupo.
That's our Queen, Salamasina is the Samoan Queen from Manu'a to Falealupo.
She held the four titles: Tuiatua, Tuiaana, Malietoa, ma Vaetamasoali'i.

'That is the genealogy of the whole body of our country. I give it to you
for your information. If you know those addresses, you know the in and out
of the *fa'asamoa*. If there is anything happens somewhere... For instance; if
you come over there and are driving a car that hits someone, then the only
thing they must do is try to kill you. But once you know these things, then
you say: "How about spare me for a few minutes? I come from..." Then you
say where you come from, then you repeat those things I told you, once you
mention Malietoa... Patu is the one who comes from the Malietoa line, once
you mention Malietoa Laauli, then Patu will be there too and that is your
safe side. People will stand up and say: "If it was without that, we would kill
you." But now it's finished, thank you very much. Quite safe. That's why I
determined to give it to you for your information.'

IN MA'ILO'S BILINGUAL recitation of *gafa* (genealogy), as in many utter-
ances by skilled orators, the sub-text carries the intended message. Winnie
is Patu's niece. Luamanuvao is the *matua* (parent) of the Patu title. As I am
married to Luamanuvao I am also connected to Patu, and through that link
to the gafa that connects all Samoans.

As I look back now, and ask myself what have I learned over the past
two and a half decades of living and working in the Pacific, I keep coming
back to Ma'ilo's words. *'You are not a stranger, you too are connected, you have a
place of belonging.'*

Ma'ilo's words jolted me. I had always felt an outsider, coming from those
cold islands in the south. I knew my family history but for years struggled to
understand where I fitted into the Pacific.

Ma'ilo posed an existential question – a question of belonging. He was
telling me that I could not stand apart as an outsider. Everyone has a part to
play – we are all connected.

The structure of Samoan society is set out in a *fa'alupega,* the list of matai
titles and ceremonial greetings, recited when chiefs meet. Formal greetings
acknowledge the title, rank, village and connection between those present

linking them with their mutual ancestors. The fa'alupega has been committed to print but is still principally an oral record, held in the memories of tulafale, and subject to debate and revision. Political boundaries between the independent nation of Samoa and the United States Territory of American Samoa are ignored in fa'alupega. These recent political divisions are seen as ephemera when compared to a record that links living people with Tagaloa and the other Polynesian Gods of creation.

Luamanuvao's village, Vaiala, is one of several villages of the sub-district of Vaimauga, part of the principal district Tuamasaga, on the island of Upolu. Most villagers live in a communal household unit (*aiga,* extended family) of three or four generations. The village does more than provide its residents with a place to live; it provides a place of belonging for resident and non-resident aiga. And *palagi* (Europeans) married to aiga have a place too.

Emi and Ta'atofa were part of the Samoan diaspora. Many from the village have migrated to New Zealand, Australia, and the US. While a Samoan family may be dispersed globally it remains connected to its village – the place of belonging.

Emi was the eldest of her line. Patu, the high chief of Vaiala, her younger brother. They were always on the phone to each other. Although she lived in New Zealand, Patu would consult with Emi about lands, titles, and important matters relating to the Aiga Sa Patu. In important decisions, a high chief must consult with and defer to the views of his sisters.

One thing that it took a long time for me to understand was that the brother-sister relationship is the primary relationship in Samoan society. It is stronger than the bond between husband and wife. The girls and young women belong to the *aualuma* – the honour of the village. *O le teine o le 'i'oimata o lona tuagane* (a girl is the pupil of her brother's eye), describes the closeness of the relationship between brother and sister. It is a brother's lifelong responsibility to protect his sister and he must do what she asks.

I saw this played out in my own family. Luamanuvao's first responsibility would always be to her parents, brother and his children. Her brother would always look out for her. She would care for her brother and his children. When we married Luamanuvao warned me: 'You are not just marrying me. You also marry my family, my village, and Samoa.'

For Samoans, the fa'asamoa is all pervasive, part of everyday life, high occasions, life and death, the centre of their being. The fa'asamoa is used as noun, verb and adjective. Metaphorical expressions are frequently used to explain the nature of the fa'asamoa.

MA'ILO DESCRIBED THE fa'asamoa, the Samoan way of life, to me in an extended bilingual monologue:

Ona e fa'apea lea, susu lava tamali'i ma failauga. You cover the whole thing in one word.

Ia o a mai oe? How are you?

O loo manuia lava fa'afetai. I am very well thank you.

O anafea na e sau ai, when did you arrive?

Na ou sau ananafi, I arrived yesterday.

Ia o fea e te sau ai nei? Where were you from?

Sa ou i Niusila.

Na e taunu'u mai anafea i le atunu'u? And when did you arrive in the country?

Na ou sau talaatu ananafi. I arrived here the day before yesterday.

Ua fa'afia ona e sau i Samoa? How many times have you come to Samoa?

Ua fa'avalu ona ou sau i Samoa. My eighth trip to Samoa.

Aisea e te fia sau ai i Samoa? Why do you always like to come to Samoa?

Ou te fia iloa lava le gagana a Samoa. I very much like to learn the Samoan language.

Ete silafia la ni nai upu mai ia gagana Samoa? Do you know some of that language?

Ioe ua ou iloa. Yes I know some words.

O ana upu? What are those words.

Ua e sau. I come, you come, yes I come.

O ai na lua o mai? Who came with you? Well, I came alone.

Ete iloa nisi o lenei aiga? Do you know anyone in this family?

Ioe ou te iloa uma lava tagata o lenei aiga, o tagata matutua ma tagata laiti. I know all of them, old and young.

Ou te iloa lelei a latou. I know them well.

Ou te iloa lelei mea uma ma vaega eseese o le aiga, ma le fa'asamoa, ma le gagana

Samoa. I know all the ins and outs of the family, the culture, and the Samoan language.

Ou te iloa lelei vaega eseese. Those are the things you ought to know.

I'VE NOTICED THAT the discourse on the fa'asamoa in the village of Vaiala appears to operate on two levels. A cover story, subscribed to by all villagers, represents the fa'asamoa as an unchanging, traditional way of life existing today with unbroken links through the ancestors to the ancient gods of Polynesia. A second story speaks of the changing role and adaptations that the fa'asamoa had made since the coming of the papalagi and the major changes occurring today including the Samoan diaspora.

Our branch of the family is based in New Zealand and Luamanuvao has the responsibility of leading and maintaining the fa'asamoa. We regularly return to Samoa for important events: funerals, weddings, saofa'i, maintaining our links to both worlds.

Emi and Ta'atofa left their villages and made their home in Wainuiomata, a dormitory suburb of Wellington. They retained their village links throughout their lives, contributing to village projects, providing remittances to village-based *aiga*, and maintaining relationships with Samoa-based family. When they retired, we built a family home in Vailima on the hill above Apia and they spent their last New Zealand winters in the warmth of Samoa.

When Emi died the chiefs and orators from Samoa came to New Zealand and the wider family gathered to farewell her. As we celebrated her life, many stories were told of her journey from Samoa to New Zealand and her contributions to both. Emi, Ta'atofa, and Ma'ilo, who told me 'the things I ought to know', have passed on.

The cyclone early in 2013 knocked down the large mango tree that shaded the house we built for Emi and Ta'atofa. It's cleared the view. These days I sit on the deck, gaze out across the Pacific, and solve crossword puzzles with Luamanuvao.

Peter Swain recently retired from the position of International Programme Manager with Volunteer Service Abroad, New Zealand. For the past twenty-five years he has worked throughout the island nations of the Pacific. His doctoral dissertation was on the role of civil society in economic and social development in the Pacific.

Walking meditations

Fingernails, feet and fossils

Hinemoana Baker

MY MOTHER'S FINGERNAILS

The fumes were acid and sugary at the same time. The polish seemed to melt under the remover-soaked cotton ball. There were many stages to this ritual. The nail file, that strange shape of hash-cut metal, a surgical instrument, hook at one end, blade at the other. Cuticle-bullying blade. My own cuticles were so sensitive, I flinched as if she were cutting herself. Sometimes she would skip this stage and go straight to the shaping.

Her nails were almond-shaped, rounded at the edges and filed to an almost-point. Like almonds, there were also striations on the surface – vertical grooves, the result of some nutritional deficiency or other, or perhaps just years of polish and remover. Nowadays the girls wear them square.

When she was finished there'd be a pile of cotton wool in the blue glass ashtray. By the next day the middle of each cotton ball would be almost solid, a hard, pink wad, and the edges would still be puffy and white. The smell was sweet and faint.

She would walk her fingernails up my arm. It was part of putting me to sleep. Perhaps I was an anxious child, she would read to me, sing to me, teach me harmonies, and how to harmonise – the one, three and five of it. Then I would say to her *Tickle my arm, mum.* She would shuffle a bit closer and push up the sleeve of my nightie. She'd sing an old-timey song about dancing. Left, right, left, her fingernails tapping and stroking the inside of my elbow, the top of my hand, my wrist.

LION PARK TARTAN

Australia. It was a place that people went when they left home, it was where my Uncle Gary lived. It was hot and had lots of awesome stuff to buy, in places known as shopping malls. I was twelve when we went there, me and my mother, and we stayed with my Uncle Gary and Aunty Edie, who had a pool and lots of large indoor plants. My older sister was already staying there. We were visiting her. She said *Mork and Mindy* was on every night over there. She said there was chewing gum with liquid inside and it was called *Spurt*. She said the spiders were the size of dinner plates and they could kill you.

I had brought all the wrong clothes because I liked to wear them at home. Mum tried to explain that different fabrics had different properties, and I wouldn't need wool in Brisbane, but the colours pleased me. The brown and yellow tartan of the trousers and the plain yellow of the hand-knitted, short-sleeved shirt with its large collar made me feel like a small work of art. Occasionally I did a cartwheel.

The Lion Park was where it all really came home to me. The lions themselves seemed okay with their outfits of fur, though they moved very slowly on their heavy, hinged paws. It was 40 degrees outside the car. It was the first time I realised what it meant to be able to open a window, and what it meant to not be able to open a window. I had never breathed air that was warmer than the inside of my body.

I held a koala that holiday. It sat, huge and stinking on my two flat palms, which I had placed in front of me face up, one on top of the other. Onto this sweaty seat the attendant lowered the koala. It was much heavier than I was expecting. It seemed to be only half-awake. I smiled at it, and my inside upper lip caught on my braces, as it always did. The tiny, pink rubber bands that stretched between my upper and lower jaw are visible in the Polaroid photograph. My long, wet hair is plastered to my neck, and the gold ribbon which holds it off my face is flat against my head. I am red-cheeked and my head is leaning slightly away from the koala.

HEAD OF STEAM

We're swaying along beside the Bremer River – on the banks of which, Ian the Conductor tells us, the first trains were constructed. We're in first class: black leather upholstered into diamond shapes with black buttons. The wood is a bronze colour, the fittings are heavy and dark. The lightshades are off-white, scallop-edged glass with large, loopy, eco-bulbs poking out of them like stamens.

All along the line there have been pockets of people with sound equipment and cameras on tripods, flags and hoisted children, cheering the train and our blurry, waving hands as we steam past. I walk out through our 1920s Pullman Sleeper Car, soot crunching underfoot, to stand on the small verandah between carriages for a while, taking in the view. Cattle, pale green long grass, a few train-racing, or train-startled, kangaroos.

This is the Q150 steam train, also known as 'The Writers' Train'. The train's journey is part of many events celebrating the sesquicentenary of Queensland becoming a state, separate from New South Wales. There really isn't an equivalent of this kind of thing back home, not even the Treaty of Waitangi sesqui 'celebrations' in 1990. I wonder what mana whenua think about this 150-year thing. I don't really have to wonder long.

There's a truck following us that normally sprays weedkiller along the sides of the tracks. Today its job is to spray the tracks with water to quell any risk of sparks starting fires.

As we hit the base of the Toowoomba Ranges the train slows to a stop and the temperature starts to climb. I wonder for a moment if we are waiting for another train coming the other way. I thought perhaps we were building up a head of steam to make the haul to the summit. Out here, lots of things seemed to become non-metaphorical. I'd just got back from a visit to the actual Black Stump, for example. Soon it becomes clear that we're waiting for another steam engine to come and help haul us up the hill. As we start to move again, clouds of steam drift past me, changing from white to grey to black to mustardy brown. A swallow-shaped bird flies through it, looping back and forth.

The welcome at Toowoomba is spectacular – the platform's swarming with flag-waving locals and a small brass band is playing *The Girl from*

Ipanema. There are many baked goods, most of which are being given away for free.

Later that evening, I write what might pass for the beginnings of a poem:

> *Add galloping to the horse.*
> *Add holding back to decay.*
> *Add watermelon to the soap and some*
> *kind of moth, essence of,*
>
> *to the Prickly Pear. Add 'sh'*
> *to the upholstery*
> *soot to Toowoomba*
> *citrus to the railway*
>
> *tracks, the juice in waiting*
> *on the huge percussive press.*

NICK WILLIAMS

Walking along the Maiwar River yesterday and a guy asked me about my tā moko, wanted to know if it was Tahitian. Turns out he's Māori too, his name's Nuku-mai-ngā-iwi-ki-te-motu-take-nui. He calls himself Nick.

'Nick Williams,' he says. 'I live on that boat there.'

Sixty bucks a week, he says. Not glamorous. He was brought up a Mormon but he came back from overseas drinking and smoking. Tells me about his mate rowing a dinghy up in Darwin, looks over the side and sees a shadow in the water, three times the length of the dinghy. Sees the croc's eyes.

'No such thing as rollbars on a dinghy,' says Nick, cracking up.

Dave has a band of shark's teeth around his Akubra. He's a Kiwi who worked in the mines near Kalgoorlie. Forty-five degrees, he tells me, is the angle of the seam gold grows in, and he owns the world's largest mobile train setup.

Fortitude Valley is the kind of suburb my Uncle Gary calls 'colourful'. The view out my window is cranes and visiting ibis birds that perch on the roof. There's a Queers Welcome rainbow sticker on the Westpac Bank door. But even here, the Brisbane equivalent of Cuba Street, everyone's shoes look new. The punk-rock dykes wear brand new jackets and their dye-jobs are faultless. All the fruit is sweeter, especially the bananas. At the reading, the woman I have dubbed 'Gold Coast Jane' has flecks of gold in her eyes. Last night I had dreams of blue and gold butterflies that became peacocks. The pillow sings in my ear all night about mountains, cops, poisons. I am planning exercises for our young writing students: *Ruin This Poem! Writer's Tennis! Poetry Skeleton! Welcome Ghosts!*

BEING SPAT AT

I walk a lot with our dog. His name is Tai, he's a farm-dog, an eye dog, black and white, border collie-huntaway cross. The beach that we prefer is the beach at Queen Elizabeth II Park, which spans the kilometres between the township of Paekakariki and Raumati. It's a series of rolling hills, the occasional pocket of cattle, the odd lightning-struck tree, lots of fencing, and beautiful sand cliffs. Off the coast about five kilometres is Kāpiti Island, looking for all the world like a dark, long reptile with a blunt snout, sleeping in the weather.

The island is big enough to create its own weather. It's a Department of Conservation reserve, and it's Māori land. Ancestrally, through my father and his mother and her mother, I connect to that island in several different ways, some of which I understand, many of which I don't. To me, looking at the island is like looking Te Rauparaha in the face. Because I'm from the Ngāti Toa tribe, I love our chief Te Rauparaha, and I am grateful to him for providing for his people. Because I'm from the tribe Ngāi Tahu, I'm terrified of him.

There isn't much beach today, and what's there is soft, the sand sucking at each step. On the sand there's the odd pile of ankle-turning driftwood, large spreads of white pipi shells. Everything is several shades of black, white and grey.

Because it's a Monday and it's early morning, we are alone here, me and the farmdog Tai, son of Lucky and an anonymous huntaway bitch, Tai whose two brothers and a sister all succumbed to the parvo.

It wasn't until we got Tai that I learned how the parvovirus takes a few years to die in the soil. I heard recently that the reason there are so many parks and green spaces in London is that there are plague victims buried under them. Any time there's an idea to dig them up and build something, someone quietly points out that the plague wasn't so great first time around.

The counsellor I have been seeing for post-earthquake anxiety tells me that grounding is the most important thing I can do. Grounding involves walking on the beach, or it can mean using a small, solidish, foam ball, the likes of which you can buy from a two-dollar shop. These usually come in very bright colours with patterns of stars or polkadots. Lime green with black stars. Bright fluorescent orange with black polkadots.

The technique involves taking off one's shoes and breathing, shifting the consciousness from the head down through the body and into the feet. Then you drop the foam ball under the sole of one foot, rolling the foot over it. The amount of pain I feel when I do this is extraordinary, but I continue because I can sense the wisdom in what she is saying. Grounding, yes, the opposite of what happens to me when my upper chest starts to rise faster with my breath, my jaw aches, the tendons in my neck begin to feel like bungee cords at full stretch. What are they holding down? What will fly off if they are loosened?

The white shells used to have creatures inside them, of course, which the birds have dug out. Maybe they picked them up in their beaks and flew to a height, then dropped the pipi on rocks to smash out their tasty, animal contents. The drifts of shells seem very interesting to the nose of the dog, as well as being a relatively reliable non-ankle-turning pathway for me this morning. Occasionally, even though I'm far from the tide's edge, I feel a cold splash of water on my ankle or shin, and I realise I've stood on a half-shell full of sea-water.

ALIVE VS DEAD

A feeling of visceral dread came over me as I looked out over the landscape from the top of the jump-up near Winton. We'd just been through the Australian Age of Dinosaurs Museum. I'd met the bones of Banjo and Matilda, two very large creatures who were being slowly put back together with the help of the museum volunteers, staff and an impressive array of drills and chisels. The one I remember was a pneumatic chisel called an 'Air Scribe'. The walk around the exhibits was longer than I'd expected, and I was feeling tired and hungry by the end of it.

When I stepped outside into the bright, and looked out across the vast landscape – our guide, Trish, called it a 'gondwanavista' – I found I was having trouble breathing for a moment. My heart started to pound and I felt a bit sick.

When my father was teaching me to scuba dive, he started by taking me and the other students to a shallow lagoon near the Rurima Islands, just off the coast of where he lives in Matata, in the Eastern Bay of Plenty. We had done descents, ascents, hand signals, underwater navigation. I knew about atmospheres and nitrogen narcosis. We'd got to the stage where I had to take my mask off under the water. This is done to train us for any instance in which something or someone, the current or a fish or a colleague, might knock our mask off accidentally, and you have to know how to calmly retrieve it, put it back on your face, clear the seawater out of it, and continue with your dive – all while under the water.

I wasn't prepared for the feeling of panic that rose in me. I couldn't under-stand why I was so scared. My breathing apparatus was completely intact, my regulator was still in my mouth, I was still breathing air in and out, so by defini-tion I wasn't drowning. But something about the ocean making contact with a previously dry part of my face, and my eyes in particular, when I was deeper than I had ever been, was terrifying beyond all expectation. It was a feeling of being completely at the mercy of something huge and indifferent. It was irrel-evant that I could still breathe, because I now understood, on a purely physical level, exactly how fragile, almost accidental, that fact was.

Dad told me later he has more trouble with this part of the training than with any other. Many times he has had to grab a student's weight-belt and hold them down, to stop them from tearing back up to the surface too fast and risking the bends – 'getting bent', as he would say. It's the point where students pull out and decide not to finish the course.

My father says that when he dies, he wants to have a traditional Māori funeral, where there is no embalming, and where the tūpāpaku is wrapped in a specially woven whāriki in a plain wooden coffin. He saw one of these tangihanga on Māori TV, where the family of Parihaka kaumatua (elder) Rū Wharehoka carried out his last wishes by reviving these ancient practices.

'That'll do me, too,' he said.

'Oh dear,' I thought. 'My weaving sucks.'

The other morning, I was in bed with my partner watching a YouTube channel called 'Ask a Mortician'. This is what we sometimes do during the odd couple of hours that pass for leisure time in our house, but which are more often just me and Christine trying to stay awake long enough to talk to each other about things other than what time the alarm is set for. We have big plans for these rare occasions when we can spend time together, but instead we tend to collapse into the internet, or telly, or just fall asleep.

We had just finished watching a video called 'Dangerous Dead Bodies', which talked about how toxic (or not) the dead are to the living. At the end of it, YouTube offered us, as it does, a digital patchwork quilt of other videos we might be interested in watching. One of them was simply called 'Cadaver Dissection'. Fortunately neither of us had our glasses on, so we weren't quite sure exactly what the still picture advertising the video showed. But it looked a lot like a dead body, quite heavily discoloured with what looked like concentric rings of bruising at the shoulders and other joints, lying face down (unusual?) on a dissection table, with a man in whites standing beside it.

I am convinced that one day I will be the person who finds a body on the beach. Especially now that I have a dog. It's just a matter of time. I feel ill when I think of it. The way I did at the First Aid Course I attended recently, whenever I thought of having to put into practice any of the things we were learning.

Acknowledgments are available at www.griffithreview.com

Hinemoana Baker is a poet, sound enthusiast and teacher of creative writing. She has produced several albums, published two collections of poetry and edited several anthologies of New Zealand writing, including *Kaupapa: New Zealand Poets, World Issues* (Wellington DRC, 2007). She is the 2014 writer in residence at Victoria University of Wellington.

WAIHEKE ISLAND

EMILY PERKINS

THEY were worried about the boy so they sent him to me. I needed a job done. You'd think he was eighteen from the way they talked but he was twenty-seven. He turned up with combat boots, shorts, a hard bare chest, those earrings that stretch your lobes into some kind of saucer, and his soft voice. Good teeth; I've always treated family for free. His emails had come with exclamation marks and 'lots of love' – what is *this* I thought – this is my grandson? Ha. His dad harbours something against me, but the mother – my daughter-in-law – arranged the deal. She's a communicator. After she left the island I saw her Xeroxed image up in a café, tear-off strips with her phone number underneath. Her bleached pineapple leaf haircut, her clenched fist. How to communicate effectively.

They came on the ferry and we crossed the lawn towards the cliff, holding our take-out coffees. My daughter-in-law saw the flying birds as a sign of an earthquake coming – I said they were a sign of spring. Kākā, four of them, in one of those tight, fast groups – birds that seem too big to fly so swiftly and so close to one another. Boom, incredible, jostling across my arc of sky. She admired the pohutukawa. I hadn't told them the plan. Lew was silent, seemed to be happy to go along.

My grandson, same name as me. When I asked what it was that worried his parents he shrugged, smiled a cracker of a smile. Perhaps he is a bit simple. Chronic unemployment, a bad crowd, who knows. He had a mate on the island with an excavator and a loader. We'd get the glyphosate from the hardware store. It would be a long job, taking these trees out, a few weeks, and I wanted to get it done before they flowered again and those scribbles of red gave me second thoughts. I promised myself to landscape after, no row of unsightly stumps, not when the whole point was that glorious view. The thought of stumps disturbed me. Root systems spreading below the ground, abrupt vanishings above. He'd live in the shed halfway down to the beach. Called it a boat house but it was too far to drag the kayak, so I had another little lock-up down by the water. He brought a camp bed, a pillow, his sleeping bag, backpack, chessboard. I gave him citronella candles. We ate together on my deck.

AT THE ISLAND get togethers, when they still invited me, women in long dresses the colours of a sunset, straw-hatted men, those people used to say, a *dentist* – how interesting? All day in the mouths of others? We've all got a mouth, I'd say, which shut them up. Early retirement: I got lucky with the markets, although the investment thing was just a hobby and I don't know why it went so well. 'When everybody's leaving the burning building, that's when you have to walk in.' But I wasn't brave. It was timing, not mine but the decade, and once I had that haul I got out, the flames licking my ankles. Moved to this place, where people come to connect with something they have lost.

The only thing I miss, aside from my hygienist, the kindest woman I've ever met, is touching the frightened patients. Not in that way. (*!!!! lol xxxxx*, Lew would say.) There was something farm-like about it. I'd be close enough, working over a molar or tamping down a filling, that my belly would press, evenly, against the side of the patient's head or shoulder. Just human contact – you could feel their heart rates drop. Eyes drift closed.

Some on this island are for the marine reserve but as many are against it. The optimists believe in saving fish. The pessimists warn of overflowing car parks, the ferry queues, the – what? Hard to know why they mind. They think the island will be repopulated, like some alien invasion movie, by space-takers waddling down the central road with snorkels, flippers slapping from their feet. It won't be ours any more. 'Ours,' they say.

And these same ladies stopped me, shaking, in the service station forecourt and said, 'Those trees! Our privacy!' because Lew let slip somewhere on his amorous kayak trips with the local maidens – I've seen candles burning yellow outside the boat shed at night, I've heard the music floating up the cliff – what the excavator was for. 'They're eucalypts,' I told them, which was not a lie if they knew half as much about botany as they should. 'They house possums and mar the view.' It's true, the pōhutukawa were pest-damaged. Possums hissing as they stalked the grass at night. Not that I needed a reason, I just wanted my horizon. When I bought this place the first thing I got rid of was the old turning clothesline that would creak in the wind. That noise interrupted the sound of the sea like those scraggy branches blocked the sight of it. People had opinions then too: there's a sort of nostalgia built up around white sheets stretched out on the breeze. The concrete pour at the base was rough to get out, like a skin lesion on the lawn. With the trees gone, if anyone forfeits privacy it's me – yachts in the bay see straight to my house now, I can't stop them. I'm prepared for the council fine. It's worth every cent. There'll be money for an upgrade to the art gallery but the shaking ladies won't think to thank me then.

WE COULDN'T GET hold of a stump grinder – the golf club wouldn't lend theirs, I've never been in with that crowd – so young Lew was grubbing out the stumps by hand. His strong shoulders, brown in the sun, a streak of red across the tops. I chucked him sunscreen and he squinted up at me with a grin. He was having a ball here with the girls, the water, taking the dinghy out for fish a few times a week. It was a bonding time, I told his mother when she rang. We worked together on our devilish task. I'd thought he might resist, with his earrings and tattoos, his greenie stance. Another man would have tried to talk me out of it but there was something passive about Lew. We were different animals, but I like to think he enjoyed it as I did, the spree in slow motion, two of us wielding blades in our protective goggles, earmuffs, boots, gloves – a pile of broken up tree wherever there had been a growing one, the same matter, different form. The council man came and shouted at me and I let him watch as the buzz saw took the last amputee trunk down. Tell me that wasn't a thrill, the righteousness I handed him.

Oh the grief I got about birds and erosion. The possums were more danger to those tui than the loss of a few feeding spots. And if you've ever walked below a beach cliff you'll see hanging roots, the dry clay crumbling around them, the pale system greedy for space, pushing the earth away – maybe trees prevent collapse but boy they cause it too.

Anyway they're gone. Seven trees, chopped into bits and burning long and hot. The stumps are a problem. Poison isn't working, the hand grubbing is a bastard, we're going to have to wait for rain and get some diesel in there to burn them out. I patrol them for new shoots, and as I walk amongst the stumps I breathe it all in – the perfection of that ocean beyond the frame of the rocks, the haze over its lip, the low sweep of cloud. When the sun comes down shadowed ruffles will form on the water, the skin of the sea will swell and come closer, solidify, it will seem to look at me with its million invisible eyes. Lew is out there, in the orange kayak, a tiny figure on its surface. I stand beyond the place where the trees were, watching him. As I walk right to the edge of the slope to get closer a few loose stones skitter down the beach path, there's a fast trickle of dust. I wonder if he'll look back.

Emily Perkins is the author of several novels, including *The Forrests* (Bloomsbury, 2012) and *Novel About My Wife* (Bloomsbury, 2008), and a short story collection, *Not Her Real Name* (Picador, 1996). She lives in Wellington, and teaches creative writing at Victoria University's International Institute of Modern Letters.

Sea of trees

The road not taken

Ashleigh Young

*An experience of remoteness, space, natural quiet and solitude is
gained standing amongst the extensive dunes against
the vastness of the Southern Ocean.*
NZ Department of Conservation

It will be a long tunnel for us.
Masahisa Okuyama, father of a hikikomori

IN the photograph the young man is sitting crosslegged on a bed, holding
a sword across his knees, almost like an offering. In another photograph he
holds it loosely across one shoulder. On a table in the room are a clutter of soft
drink bottles, food packets and cigarettes; in one corner is a pile of bulging
garbage bags. The young man looks directly at the camera, his eyes clear. He
is a *hikikomori* – a young Japanese person, usually a man, who has shut himself
into a bedroom or flat for six months or more, sometimes years, sometimes
decades. (The Japanese word hikikomori combines the words *hiku* or 'pull'
and *komoru* or 'retire'; literally it means 'pulling in and retiring'.) In other
photographs of hikikomori I have seen, the young person turns his back, or
he is pictured in profile staring into the middle distance. His face is usually
obscured, his posture suggests shame. But there is an openness in this young
man's face which is at odds with his cloistered surroundings. He could be
looking forward to something. He could be about to stand up, heft a pack
onto his shoulder, and open the door.

There is another, more disturbing photograph of a hikikomori, wearing a hooded sweatshirt with a kind of elongated balaclava, almost like a trunk, that stretches from his face to the computer screen. He doesn't trust his own eyes – they might stray to the bedroom around him, crowding him in – so this clunky portal keeps his focus trained. His body looks like an encumbrance to him, something to be blanked out or wished away. On a hikikomori support website, members are asked how they kill time. The replies advise the internet, music, sleep: 'I sleep until my eyes are about to rot. I see dreams.' Immersion is the desired state – it is an escape from physical surroundings, from the passing of time, from worried parents, from the world outside. These replies echo the idea of renouncing or throwing away the self, a state that Buddhist monks are trained to achieve. To be free of the self is to be free from worldly attachments, from uncertainty, from confusion.

THE URGE TO understand or to at least describe makes us liken hikikomori, or 'shut-ins', to islands – remote, generating their own weather, enclosed by an inhospitable environment against which they barricade themselves: pulling down blinds, covering windows with black paper and duct tape. If not likened to islands, they are peninsulae, or 'almost islands', because many hikikomori do maintain a thread of connection with the world beyond their bedrooms. They live in the homes of their parents, who bring them meals each day, who worry about them, who worry about what others will think, who wonder what they could have done to stop their child from shutting themselves in. Inside their rooms, hikikomori play video games, read, listen to music, drink, pace, or do nothing. Or they surf the internet, latching on to online communities and forums, the networks through which they can connect with others who have withdrawn. In one online support community run through Daizenji Temple near Kōshū City, Yamanashi, hikikomori can meditate with a Buddhist priest who instructs them through an online camera. Some keep their identities hidden by putting on masks, and those who are afraid to be seen at all meditate without using the camera.

The internet is also a place to pool knowledge about a state that is not often openly discussed. 'It's important to make them not frightened,' writes a member of the Q&A website Quora in reply to the question *Any advice or ideas on how to deal with a hikikomori*? 'If there's something terrifying, make it nothing. And then try to let him know what the outside world is.' The member himself is a hikikomori, he says, or 'soon to become one'.

Hikikomori seem to vanish from the world, so it's hard to know their true numbers. A 2010 survey for the Japanese Cabinet Office came up with an estimate of nearly 700,000, but some psychiatrists – including Tamaki Saitō, who gave the condition its name in 1998 with the publication of *Hikikomori: Adolescence Without End* – believe that the figure is well over one million. We know that cities can be places of profound loneliness and social disconnection. We know that in dense communities, when commuting, when working, when trying to sleep, people withdraw into themselves to cope. But the reality of so many people hidden away, as if in a forest, puts a sharper, more unnerving edge on that understanding. It threatens our broad understanding of what it is to be a human being living in the world, what it is to be one of the numbers who inform the present and the history of a place. (We can warp what we see, too: one fashion blog portrays hikikomori as if it were a clever kind of solution: 'In times of recession, many young Japanese simply stay home. They personalise little rooms at the top of milquetoast suburban houses in exaggeratedly eccentric ways.') Last year I was struck by the photographer Michael Wolf's depictions of people compressed into Tokyo trains at rush hour – beautiful but ghostly images of faces behind streaked glass – which showed the ways in which people tend to endure agitating conditions: by retreating into themselves, eyes squeezed shut, bodies stiffened against walls or windows.

My own experience of self-imposed isolation is brief, but vivid. At high school, deeply shy, I tried to make myself disappear at morning breaks and lunchtimes. For some months I would go to a dressing room behind the stage in the assembly hall, where my art class was stretching, and later painting, some canvases. To get to the room you had to clamber up onto the stage and duck behind the curtains into the left wing, past reams of moth-smelling gym mats and a clutter of music stands, then jam the key into the lock before someone saw you. There was a long narrow window, where I could see people's feet as they walked past outside. I would lie on the wooden bench in the room and watch the feet, or stare at the blank stretching canvases. I was unable to read or write because of a constant low-level anxiety that I would be found, and the anxiety produced a focus that was somehow too acute to translate words into sense – but pictures and sounds stretched and shimmered like blown glass. As the months went on and the canvases grew thick with my classmates' paintings, my mind seemed to drift farther and farther away from my body, in its lumpy green uniform.

Neither the metaphor of an island nor a peninsula helps us to imagine the inner world of the isolated. At their heart these metaphors have only their remoteness; they don't provide a path into or out of the state. In their abstraction, they echo, too, an unwillingness to talk openly about the condition of hikikomori. 'In polite company, the subject of hikikomori is seldom brought up,' Michael Zielenziger writes in *Shutting Out the Sun* (Random House, 2006). '*Shikata ga nai*, the Japanese say, or "It can't be helped".' In Japanese, *mori* is a homonym for 'forest', and I find myself going back to the image of a forest as a way of trying to understand what happens when a person shuts themselves in; how their world, so narrowed, might fill and grow so densely that a person becomes lost in it. It is a forest, too, that has become Japan's most well-known site for suicide. Aokigahara forest, also known as the Sea of Trees, lies at the foot of Mt Fuji, four thousand hectares wide. Its trees grow closely together, blocking the wind, and it is home to few animals and birds, so it is quiet. Each year, volunteers who patrol the forest manage to talk people out of taking their own lives there.

WHEN I THINK of a pathway out of the forest, I think of the path that the Japanese woman Keiko Agatsuma constructed between the cave where she lived and the beach. She built her path out of pieces of driftwood and covered it in washed-up fishnet to stop herself from slipping as she walked down onto the sand. A simple, cursory path made from the materials at her feet.

Agatsuma had arrived in Christchurch with a three-month tourist visa in August 1978. After travelling around the lower South Island, she took a boat to Stewart Island, a heavy backpack on her shoulders. She arrived at Freshwater Landing, where the launchmaster warned her of dangerously changeable conditions and a boggy wetland track to walk across. But she set off alone; I imagine that she didn't look back. The launchmaster later described her as 'wiry, tough-looking'. It took her two days to reach the Forest Service hut. She began to explore the island, foraging for food as her supply of groceries dwindled, and soon – in Doughboy Bay, just south of Mason Bay – she came across a cave with a high ceiling and overhanging rātā trees that sheltered the entrance from rain. She set down her pack at the back of the cave, where it was dry. She constructed a bed from driftwood and fishing net. She hung colourful buoys in the trees around the entrance.

It's impossible to know for sure why Agatsuma came to such a remote place. Those who spoke to her on Stewart Island – park rangers, fisher-men – said she had mentioned an abusive husband, and a feeling that she did not belong back home; perhaps that she felt *barra-barra*, 'broken apart from others', as hikikomori do. We can assume that she wanted not only to be by herself, but to feel the relief of placing a great distance between herself and her home country, the opposite of homesickness. The cave was a dwelling only: it offered no particular culture or history, asked no questions of her. However, Agatsuma was to live there for only one week. Her overstayer status was quickly discovered by authorities, and she was deported back to Japan, travelling with her brother who had come to Christchurch to take her back. The story of her isolation rippled outwards. International media were fascinated by the tale of the 'Japanese woman cave dweller', and she fell into Southland urban myth. She later inspired a short story ('Of Memory and Desire' [1991] by Peter Wells), a film based on that short story (*Memory and Desire* [1998] by Niki Caro), and a Noh play (*Rakiura* [1993], written by Eileen Philipp) – and perhaps all of these works are testament to the symbolic power of that image of a woman far from home, living inside a cave, as if in exile. It seems so far removed from the young man with his blinds pulled down in a bedroom in suburban Japan, but this is a story, too, that ripples outwards, that remains unsolved.

In her essay 'Last call' (*New Yorker*, 2013), Larissa MacFarquhar gives a brief account of a hikikomori leaving a room from which he had not ventured for many years. To receive help from the Buddhist priest Ittetsu Nemoto, the young man has to leave his room and walk to a remote temple, where he will be expected to articulate his feelings to this stranger. Nemoto's theory is that people have to want his counsel enough to make the journey to see him, otherwise he probably won't be able to help them. The man has been living as a hikikomori for a long time, and now he not only has to leave his room but also his city, and walk for five hours. It is the promise of Nemoto's help at the end of this unimaginable journey that pushes him on. As he walks, he thinks about what he might say to the priest. The account of his journey ends when he reaches the temple – because after all that time walking, and thinking, he feels that he has reached some kind of understanding. What that understanding is, it's impossible to say. But the man feels sure enough of himself that he is able to turn around and walk back the way he came.

How can a person in isolation make their way back? The paths the isolated must build are yet so modest, using whatever tools they can find – some left by others, some scattered, almost forgotten, within the walls – to help them walk, howsoever briefly, into the world outside.

Ashleigh Young is a writer and editor currently living in Wellington, New Zealand. Her first book of poems, *Magnificent Moon* (Victoria University Press) was published in 2012. Her essays and poems have appeared in *Sport*, *Landfall*, *Turbine*, *Booknotes*, and *Hue & Cry*. She blogs at eyelashroaming.com.

ESSAY

O Salutaris

Between here and there

Ian Wedde

O sa–a–lu–ta–a–ris * *ho–o–sti–i–a*
Quae cae–ae–li pa–an–dis * *o–sti–um*
Be–lla–a praemunt * *hosti–i–li–a*
Da ro * *bur fe–er au–xi–li–um*

Uni–i tri–no–o–que * *Do–o–mi–i–no*
Sit se–em–pi–ter–r–na * *glo–ri–a*
Qui vi–i–tam si * *ne ter–r–mi–no*
Nobis * *do–ne–et* * *in pa–tri–a*

PA Henare Tate, the elderly Catholic priest who conducted the requiem mass for the artist Ralph Hotere, did so in Māori, Latin and English, with a bit of French thrown in here and there for good measure. At one point he referred to Ralph as a 'Latinist' as well as an artist. Because of the large crowd assembled on Mātihetihe *marae* at the end of a gravel road on the North Island's remote west coast north of the Hokianga Harbour, the mass was held in the *whare hui* or meeting house called Tu Moana (At the Ocean) rather than in the small church, called Hato Hēmi (St James). The meeting house had room for about a hundred and fifty mourners, and at least that number spilled out across the marae next to the adjacent church and the *whare kai* or dining room called Nga Ringa Rau o Te Akau (The Hundred Hands of Te Akau).

Ralph was famous, a recipient of New Zealand's highest civil honour, the Order of New Zealand, his work sought after by private collectors and public museums, and so the crowd included many from the art world where he was held in high esteem. But the majority of those paying their respects were Māori. The nearby car park was jammed with vehicles and children played among them. A large marquee had been erected next to the dining room; visitors had slept there and in the whare hui over the four days of the *tangi* or funeral. It was Monday, the last day. Many people had been up all night in the whare hui telling stories and singing. After the mass, Ralph was carried up the hill to Maunga Hione (Hill of Zion), the *urupā* or graveyard of Te Tau Maui, a *hapū* or subtribe of Te Rarawa. Ralph's own family was from another affiliated hapū of Te Rarawa, Te Aupōuri. His mother Ana Maria is buried down by the church, but his father Tangirau and some siblings are buried up there in what locals call 'Hotere Lane'. After lengthy debate on the marae, his grave was dug right out on the promontory affording what his brother Moss described as a million-dollar view; the best seat in the house.

Ralph's coffin arrived in a black Air Force NH90 helicopter on Friday afternoon, after what was effectively a state funeral in the Catholic Cathedral in Dunedin. But the tangi at Mitimiti was the real one as far as most people there were concerned. The Air Force helicopter, a black New Zealand Army Humvee that conveyed his coffin from the landing pad to the marae, and the large catering tent with army supply trucks and staff, had all been requisitioned by senior Māori politicians. No one, least of all the Minister of Defence, the Chief of the New Zealand Defence Force, or the Governor-General Lieutenant General The Right Honourable Sir Jerry Mateparae, himself a former Chief of Defence, had apparently thought twice about turning the request down. The landing pad for the helicopter was in a paddock near the car park. It had been marked out with a large black cross of scorched diesel. Next to Ralph's open coffin in the whare hui were a number of objects associated with him, placed there by members of his family and by friends. They included a customised number-plate: HOTERE – as the black Humvee suggested, he'd loved flash cars as well as the colour black.

However, the first vehicle of Ralph's that I remember was a battered Land Rover in which we used to rattle over the hill to Purakanui in Otago to get mussels. I also remember a red Mercedes-Benz and an elegant E-Type Jag. Among the objects next to the coffin in Tu Moana were some of Ralph's favourite golf clubs, including his number one wood, Big Bertha. After the burial rites up on Maunga Hione, mourners descending to the marae were invited to take one of Ralph's drivers and belt a golf ball out across the black sand of the beach. Several elderly *kuia* hitched their black skirts up and confirmed what most people knew already, that Ralph's extended family offered mean odds on the golf course. They'd mowed a nice driving strip just below the urupā, and one after another the white balls arced across the black sand or the oxidised glitter of the creek. A couple of Ralph's hard-case nieces had jacked this up, and they'd got it just right – people were laughing as they went on down the hill, but the flights of the golf balls also drew gestures that, along with the black-cross landing strip, seemed to come from Ralph's own hand.

The last time I saw Ralph alive was a couple of days after his eightieth birthday, in the Sacred Heart Home run by the Little Sisters of the Poor high up on Brockville in Dunedin. We had a glass of very good Twin Paddocks Pinot Noir from Sam Neill's vineyard and a slice of birthday cake. Ralph had never said all that much but now the stroke he'd suffered some years previously meant he said even less. Then it began to snow heavily but slowly outside his window. It was late in the afternoon; the snow fell in thick arcs and loops across the dark foliage of the garden. Ralph put his glass down and began to trace the movement of the falling snow. 'White,' he said. I remembered his smile a year later as the white golf balls drew parabolas across the black sand at Mitimiti.

PA TATE MADE the requiem mass congregation in Tu Moana titter with a slightly risqué play on what he called 'Sixty-Niners' – those familiar with the pre-1970 Tridentine Mass. Then he took the children of Mitimiti School and Te Kura Taumata o Panguru through the Latin phrasing of 'O Salutaris', for which he'd handed out copies marked with the intervals and stresses for us all to follow.

'Again!' he said, rolling his eyes in mock frustration. 'Again!' The Sixty-Niners inside knew their stuff and sang along; they also knew the Latin responses in the liturgy. At one point, Pa Tate suggested that he probably deserved a salary hike on the strength of offering a Latin mass. After a well-judged comedic pause, he added that one of Ralph's paintings would do instead. The congregation laughed – jokes about the market value of Ralph's work had been a feature of the tangi. They laughed again when Pa Tate added, 'So long as I can tell which way up it goes.'

Northland in New Zealand is poor country: unemployment figures are high, the unacknowledged cash crop is marijuana whose 'social harm' costs were estimated at NZ$100 million in 2012, but methamphetamine labs are also causing enormous harm. Unemployment figures are the highest in the country at about 10 per cent. So the running gags about works of art worth tens or hundreds of thousands of dollars have an edge up there. The edge has been sharpened by a few well-publicised disputes over ownership of Ralph's work, and during the tangi there were mutterings about the Hotere Trust's rumoured intention to dragnet 'gifted' art works. Ralph was famous not only for his alleged wealth, but also for the reasons why he wasn't all that wealthy in the end – he gave a lot of work away, he paid for members of his family to visit his brother's grave at the Sangro River in Italy where Jack had been killed in action during World War II, he gave away cars, he sometimes paid his lawyers, former landlord, dentist and occasional tradesmen with works, he gave works to friends to help with their kids' educations… During the dusk-to-dawn story-telling session in the whare hui the night before the funeral mass, one person after another got up and told a story about Ralph's generosity.

These were real stories, not just sentimental wake yarns. The sculptor Chris Booth told the story of leaving Port Chalmers in Otago where he'd had an artist's residency and had built a large work on the promontory where Ralph's studio was situated. Chris and his family were trying and failing to fit everything into their car. Ralph chucked him the keys to his ute and said, 'Take it.' Chris thought he meant borrow it, but he didn't mean that. He considered it a fair swap for the work Chris had made. Or not even an adequate swap – as Chris and his family were leaving, Ralph and his wife then, the poet Cilla McQueen, ran out with paper parcels which they stuffed into the ute. Chris thought these were food, but back home in Northland they discovered the parcels were rolled-up artworks.

Ralph and Cilla's daughter Andrea, who'd sat to one side of the open coffin in the whare hui for three days while Ralph's wife Mary sat on the other, told a story (as I remember it) about the time she and her husband were struggling to make sense of things, and Ralph tossed the keys of the red Mercedes on their kitchen table and told them to keep it, the car would make it easier for them to visit. But, she said, the real reason was that Ralph knew how much she loved the Merc, and that it would cheer her up – it did.

When my son Carlos was about four years old he drew a circle with squiggly bits coming off it, called it 'A Sun With Legs', and gave it to Ralph. A while later, Ralph gave him a painting called 'A Sun With No Legs' – one of his immaculately drawn circles on a mottled ground of black and amber lacquer. Ralph and I collaborated a couple of times, and he always considered an exchange of works was fair enough in return for whatever I'd written. There are hundreds of these stories. There are also many stories about Ralph's survivalist savvy. Once, after we'd collected a feed of mussels from chilly water at Purakanui, he took his soaking pants off, rolled them in the dry sand, and shook them out. It's the kind of thing you'd get used to doing if you'd only had one pair at some time in your life. He helped me to lay a tongue-and-groove floor once. He knew how to do it without fancy tools, just a couple of nails and a four-by-two lever. He stared down the powers-that-be on the Otago Harbour Board and parleyed owner-ship of a fine old two-storey bluestone bank building on the main street of Port Chalmers when his studio up on the hill was demolished to increase wharf space.

He was an implacable leader of protests at the proposed siting of an aluminium smelter at Aramoana near the Otago Harbour heads. He seldom spoke out, but the works of art he made on that theme became the well-known speaking-objects of the protests. They made use of recycled sheets of rusty corrugated iron with beautifully scumbled and dripped surfaces, the lead-head nails he loved, bits and pieces of scrounged timber, and laconic, stencilled phrases such as 'Aramoana pathway to the sea'. These works were both vernacular and sophisticated – recycled frugally from the kinds of useful stuff you'd hoard in remote, under-resourced places; and at the same time reminiscent of Mark Tobey's white calligraphy, and in particular the *pintura matérica* of the Catalan artist Antoni Tàpies, whose work Ralph knew well even before spending time in Barcelona in 1988.

ON SUNDAY, WHILE some of those attending the tangi were at mass in Hato Hēmi, I went up the Moetangi Valley with Ralph's brother Robin Hotere (one of five surviving siblings – there were fifteen in all), his niece

Debbie Martin (Robin's daughter) and the cinematographer Fred Rēnata. Debbie was recovering from a loud, boozy party on Saturday night. It's a good hour-and-a-bit's hike up the creek to Moetangi where the Hotere house used to be. Ralph and the other kids used to walk to school at Mitimiti and back every day. But first, once they were about eight years old, they'd have to round up the cows and milk them. They'd start about four in the morning, in the dark; they milked by hand, in the open. The milk can went down to the road on a sledge behind a horse. The horse had to be rounded up in the scrub too.

Ralph's mother Ana Maria, named for St Anne, was a devout Catholic. His father, Tangirau, was a *katikīta* or catechist; he was also a poet. Robin said there used to be a rosary garden by the house, and that the roses had run wild over the scrub. When we got to the little plateau above the creek where the house used to be there was nothing to see but a clump of self-propagating arum lilies. The severe summer drought of 2012 had killed the roses. Robin pointed out where the vegetable gardens used to be – you could see how the plateau retained the contour of cleared land. There were a couple of lichened, rotting fence posts still sticking up. There's a spring that runs from a cleft in the hillside down to the creek. Once, there had been an orchard of peach trees above the spring's gulley. They had apples and pears as well. They grew corn, kumara, potatoes and greens; they had chickens and sometimes a pig.

The house had one room and a hard earth floor. There was a lean-to for cooking. Another room was added as the family grew larger. There was no lavatory at first – you did your business up in the bush. Later, the Department of Health provided materials for a long-drop. Sometimes Tangirau and Ana would be away at tangi for weeks at a time. The kids knew how to look after themselves. Further up the valley, said Robin, there's a cave with some old canoes, feather cloaks, and other *taonga* or treasures in it; there were probably human bones. Robin pointed out an old karaka tree where bodies used to be placed until the flesh had gone and the bones could be interred. When heavy rain caused a slip to expose the entrance to the cave and to what was inside it, members of the whānau dynamited it and sealed it off. Now the markers that vectored the entrance are gone, along with most of the big forest trees.

On the way back down the valley we came to a bend in the creek where a natural pool formed. Robin looked at it a bit misty-eyed. This used to be the family's bath. We could all see what he was thinking. We stripped to our undies and hopped in. Fred took a photo of Robin and his daughter Debbie up to their necks in the pond. They have their arms around each other's shoulders and are grinning broadly. It looks like a kind of conjoint baptism, into memory, perhaps – the kind of memory that can never be erased from a place if you know how to read the signs, however minimal.

THERE'S A QUESTION that begins to form around the circumstances, memories, and symbols of Ralph Hotere's tangi. He was one of the most esteemed, successful and celebrated New Zealand artists yet. In the late 1960s, after four years in London and in France, he began to paint what would come to be known generally as 'Hotere's black paintings' – austerely minimal works in which, in three seven-part series from 1968, impeccably black lacquered rectangles were marked by finely drawn crosses, each panel's cross in one of the seven subtractive primary or spectrum colours. At the time they were first exhibited, most critics drew parallels with the black paintings of Ad Reinhardt; Hotere himself was on record as having expressed regret at missing a lecture by Reinhardt at the Institute of Contemporary Art in London in 1964.

In 1997, after visiting America to watch Tiger Woods play at the US Masters Tournament at the Augusta National Golf Club, Ralph gave his dealer Sue Crockford a copy of the 1991 MOMA *Ad Reinhardt* catalogue. Having skipped fifty pages of plates, he annotated the eighteen plates of Reinhardt's 1956–66 black paintings with the names of the Augusta Club's eighteen holes, granting each a par of given yards, beginning at 'Amen Corner' with the overall attribution, 'This is Tiger Country' – also the title of one of his own works from 1983. This elegant homage links Hotere's 1968 black paintings to what is in effect a book-end late series of works including large, black lacquered sheets of corrugated aluminium in 1999, again marked by variations on a cross, this time cut out of the metal or formed in part by vertical space between the corrugated sheets.

Ralph managed to combine his love of black with his love of fine cars: the late works were made in collaboration with an artisan car-painter in Dunedin who laid their impeccable mirror-black grounds. A major collaboration with his friend the artist Bill Culbert, *Blackwater* (1999), commissioned by René

Block for the Fridericianum museum in Kassel, Germany, is said to have had its sheets of sleekly reflective corrugated iron painted by Mercedes-Benz at Ralph's request. Here, a certain kind of content – a narrative about cars, friendship, and a political claim to pleasure – becomes a kind of deadpan subversion.

The minimalism, elegance and sophistication of these works made them favourites with critics and curators wary of narrative content, traces of regionalism, or, god forbid, affective hooks into the kind of cultural memory that might have been laid down in the artist's childhood in tough, self-sufficient conditions in the remotest part of Northland, imbued with Catholic ritual and symbols and Māori *mōteatea* or poetry. Nor were the works' enigmatic subversions noted. They were seen to be aligned with formalist international benchmarks of the time, not with some kind of narrative thick description or backblocks art semiotics. Ralph himself contributed to the laconic austerity associated with his work by famously refusing to talk about it. It was this aura of detachment and coolness that guaranteed the Mitimiti congregation's knowing response to Pa Tate's joke about 'which way up'.

MANY IN THE congregation also knew that Ralph had chosen to live in Otago, a long way from the place of his birth near Mitimiti – a long way from them, his *whānau*, and a long way from Northland, for that matter. They knew about the time he'd spent in Europe, especially in France, including time at Avignon with Cilla McQueen from 1978, the year Pope Paul VI died; and in Minorca the following year when John Paul I died (a well-known series, *The Pope is Dead*, came from these events). Along with jokes about the value of artworks they might have stashed under the bed in the sleep-out, or whether a collector might now want to fork out a couple of hundred thou' for the corrugated-iron shed down the back, the congregation joked about how they'd got Ralph at last – how he'd 'come home'. The hidden narrative here, of course, is that there was a gap between where Ralph had gone and what he'd come back to in the end.

It's the nature of this gap or the tension between here and there (there and here) that shapes the question that has kept emerging hesitantly over the years in critical discussions of Ralph's work. Sometimes the question has been repressed in exhibitions that privileged the minimal black works and their apparent occlusion of content by form (with much explaining-away of the cross motifs). It's made frequent, dithering appearances in discussions over what to do about the fact that Ralph was Māori but refused to be character-ised as a 'Māori artist'. It's associated with Ralph's own annoyance with the reappearance at auctions of his early, genre works including still-lifes. The question has sometimes appeared as a full-blown revision, answered when the cross motifs in Ralph's work are sheeted back unambiguously to the religious traditions of the Hāhi Katorika, the syncretic Catholic-Māori devolution of French Society of Mary missionaries via Mill Hill Brothers in the Hokianga; or in which the white-scumbled, rivulet-and-splatter surfaces of corrugated-iron works in the 1980s are read as transliterations of the mudflat landscapes of the Otago harbour; or in which 'black', both the colour and the metonym, is invariably read as political. But neither formalist avoidance of content, nor modernist squeamishness about the ethnographic, nor their contraries in literal narrative content match-ups, understand the question about the gap between here and there, let alone come up with good enough answers.

All of these options want to answer the question, What's to be done with the apparently contradictory co-presence in Ralph's work of austere understate-ment and rich content? And by implication: Does urbanity trump provincial narrativity, or can rich content be attributed to even the most minimal forms?

The space between the backblocks and the metropolis is easily – even usually – characterised as one between a simple, probably uneducated, cultur-ally unsophisticated place, and the cultural complexity and sophistication of cities. The urban sophisticate appreciates refinement, including the aesthetic refinements of minimal abstraction. The provincial likes stories. This, at least, was the modernist diagram of progress towards hegemonic art 'centres'. Though the diagram has been contested and redrawn since Ralph first made 'black paintings' in the late 1960s, it still exerts influence, and it still asks the wrong question. Development remains a one-way traffic, apparently. Anything going in the reverse direction from the city to the provinces is on a sentimental trip into the never-never – the jaded sophisticate in search of traditional authenticity, the urbanite looking for the naively exotic.

BUT AT MITIMITI for Ralph Hotere's extended requiem, we were reminded of some simple facts. He was brought up and educated in a tri-lingual culture

– Māori, English and Latin. His father, Tangirau, was a noted poet. Ralph himself was well versed in the poetic traditions of Ngāti Ruanui and Te Aupōuri, and could quote at length from memory. The place he grew up in was in the vicinity of old, buried treasures. Baptised Hone Papita Hotere by the successors of Bishop Jean-Baptiste Pompellier, the French Society of Mary missionary who came to the Hokianga in the 1830s, his name was both a reference to John the Baptist (described by Pa Tate as 'a stirrer') and to the French bishop. I got the impression his French was okay and he read poetry in it, and in Spanish. He was aesthetically at home both with the dark austerities of Reinhardtian minimalism and the poetics of Spanish tenebrists.

Often, however, the character of his work is defined by the radically simple anti-aesthetic of political outrage. His sociability – the extent of his friendships and associations, his legendary hospitality – was equally well described by the French word *gentillesse* and the Māori *manaakitanga*. In his garden at Carey's Bay, he used to grow fierce, reddish Provençal garlic. His house contained an astonishing collection of art works, most of them by friends. And when he travelled, he liked to do so in style – as in the black Air Force NH90 helicopter that brought him back to the marae at Mitimiti, over the hill from Moetangi, the place he'd left in 1946, sponsored by the church to go to school at St Peter's Māori College in the city, Auckland.

The cultural complexity of this metropolis in the 1940s may even have seemed thin by comparison with where he'd come from up north – or, at best, not likely to overawe Hone Papita Hotere, a kid 'from the sticks'. He went where art took him, which was often a long way from Mitimiti, but it would be a mistake to see that journey as an improving trajectory from the benighted to the accomplished, or his 'return' as a vindication of roots. It's not a question of how he managed to juggle 'there' and 'here', periphery and centre. He closed the gap – he shut the question down.

Ian Wedde is a poet, novelist, curator and essayist. He was New Zealand's poet laureate 2011–2013. His most recent books are a monograph, *Bill Culbert: Making Light Work* (Auckland University Press, 2009), a novel, *The Catastrophe* (Victoria University Press, 2011) and a collection of poems, *The Lifeguard* (Auckland University Press, 2013).

Pure brightness

Conversations with ghosts

Alison Wong

EACH April at Pure Brightness Festival (Ching Ming) Chinese families sweep the graves and perform traditional rites to honour their ancestors. On 4–5 April 2013, a hundred people gathered in the remote far north of New Zealand to commemorate those lost when the SS *Ventnor* sank off the coast of the Hokianga on 28 October 1902.

The *Ventnor* was carrying the exhumed bones of 499 Chinese for reburial in their villages in China as well as impoverished elderly Chinese men whose fares home had been paid by fellow Chinese New Zealanders. Some crew and most of the Chinese and bones were lost at sea. Some bones washed up along the coast and were recovered and cared for by Te Roroa and Te Rarawa.

The trip was soon after the death of artist Hone Papita Raukura (Ralph) Hotere, who is buried amongst his Te Rarawa *whānau* at Mitimiti.

Day 1 Trans-Tasman: On the plane *auē* I break bread the colour of old bone. Bubbles break the surface. I cross time borders, move from emergency number 000 to 111.

Day 2 Te Roroa – Waipoua, Kawerua: Our old people told us, Don't forget to look after the Chinese – they are buried there also. This rain, it is the tears of our ancestors. The fog is filled with *aroha*, with *wairua*. Your ancestors are probably saying, It's about time you fellas came.

We open striped golf umbrellas and sing:

E hara i te mea
Nō nāianei te aroha
Nō nga tūpuna
I tuku iho i tuku iho

Our oldest and youngest unveil the plaque. A new grove of kauri planted in remembrance. *Tāne Mahuta* – kauri born before Christ. When He returns, how many will remain?

At Chinaman's Hill, bones lie buried. We set up the altar overlooking the water where the ship went down. Three sticks of incense. We bow three times before apples, mandarins, almond biscuits, roast pork, *baak jaam gai* with feet and legs and head, red paper folded in the beak. We scatter rice tea wine; burn paper money gold; eat pork and *baak jaam gai*, an unwrapped sweet on the tongue. Electric fire crackers bang bang bang over the sand.

Day 3 Te Rarawa – Rawene, Mitimiti, Kohukohu: A blue day. We cross blue water. Everywhere drooping plumes of *toetoe*. The bus slips and slips on the metal road.

You're late – we must be related. What is Chinese time? Somewhere close to 111 years. Uncle Mingo heard from the signal station master's lips about the ship that went down. Uncle Mingo, we must be related – my name's Meng, my wife is Ying and this is Charlie Ding.

A red gate wrapped in white calico stands high on the hill over the breakers, over the beach where bones washed up wrapped in white calico. A red and gold gate stands unwrapped amidst the *urupā* HOTERE HOTERE HOTERE. A white wooden cross, yellow roses, brightly painted stones – your grave still fresh, Hone Papita Raukura.

We find a worn headstone without its Chinese name, an empty red jar. Once outside the *urupā*; now inside the *urupā*.

Down on the beach where bones washed ashore, our quattro sinks in the sand; our Māori *whānau* give us a tow. Kia ora Toyota. Kia ora bro.

We set up the altar. Three six nine sticks of incense. Together we bow three times before apples, mandarins, almond biscuits, roast pork, *baak jaam gai*... Electric fire crackers bang bang bang over the sand.

At Blackspace Gallery we gather before porcelain bones, photographs and paintings of journeys, headlands surrounded by water...our own stations of the cross… places where we wait as we move from one world to another. We wear black these days, Hone Papita, not the white of our ancestors. I know *whānau* in my bones, but not the word in Cantonese… Sing the dark chapel of water. Look up, the stars they are calling us home.

Day 4 Arai-te-uru, Opononi, North Head: We cannot go back to where the ship went down. We cannot cross the bar. At Arai-te-uru we look out like the signal station master over where she lies in deep water, over the bar and the white-edged breakers, over the coast where lifeboats came ashore, over the coastline north and south where bones washed ashore.

We cross water, walk past dunes, over sand, over stones, around the head. On a smooth round boulder we set up the altar…

> KOTAHI MANU
> I TAU KI TE TAHUNA
>   TAU ATU
>   TAU ATU
>   KUA TAU MAI

> One bird
> Has settled on the sand bank
> It has settled over there
> It has settled over there
> They have settled here

> Āmene A mun Amen

WE ARE ONE hundred from the Hokianga, Auckland, Hamilton, Gisborne, Wellington, Dunedin; from Sydney, Melbourne, Geelong; from Hong Kong and Singapore. We are Chinese, Māori, Pākehā.

We come with home baking. We make mango pudding, (gluten-free) soba seaweed salad and kūmera noodle salad, more salad. We eat roast pork and *baak jaam gai*. We raffle roast pork and *baak jaam gai*. We eat *marae* food, barbecue food, *hāngī*. We eat leftover sausages from Liu Shueng's own organic beef for breakfast, lunch and breakfast. We make sandwiches together and tell each other off because we don't know how to make sandwiches. Why is the bus driving away? Isn't the bus taking us to the beach? We walk through the little stream or help our elders up and around and along the narrow track. We walk to the closest beach. But look – isn't that the bus back again? We walk back through the little stream or help our elders along and around and down the narrow track. We ride to a spot further away. We massage each other when we have a headache. We give each other headaches.

Who are your mother and father? Doris Hing and Henry Wong? From Napier, Wairoa. Your grandfather was True Light. Oh, your mother grew up in Ohakune, in Auckland. Your grandfather was Yoi Hing. I played basketball with your uncle. My daughter married your cousin. Your uncle who married your mother's younger sister, he is my brother. Your grandmother was the cousin of my grandfather. My mother was the sister of your grandmother. I am friends with your niece. I looked after your nephew – the Wong boys, they all competed against each other in Dunedin you know…

Thanks for letting me tag along, says Glenn. Some of you, your ancestors were on the ship; some of you, your ancestors recovered the bones; ahmmm… my ancestors only sank the ship. And so he sings a sea shanty…

DISINTERRED FROM FORTY cemeteries, you were cleaned and wrapped in calico, arranged in wooden boxes marked with your names and villages. You were placed onboard in Dunedin, Greymouth, twenty-six other ports. Ten of my Jung Seng county kinsmen joined you in Wellington.

Now we do not know who you are. Only one – Choie Sew Hoy, whose grandchildren and great-grandchildren and great-great-grandchildren came. Were your families all left in China? Waiting.

You were lost on the spirit highway, lost in deep blue water. You believed to be lost in water was to die a second death, to wander forever a hungry ghost. What is time? Are you now beyond time like God? Even in our long absence we honoured you. We lived and worked; we did not die out. We came that you might find rest in the land we now call home.

Did you know my family? Wong Sik She – my mother's mother's uncle? He arrived in Wellington in 1879 from the village of Melon Ridge. The

Evening Post in 1889 describes an incident at one of his shops. A European man mocked then assaulted the Chinese shop attendant while his companion 'amused himself by throwing the stores about the place.' Were you there? Were you the one assaulted? One of those who ran to help?

In 1892 Sik She brought out two younger brothers, including my great-grandfather Wong Sik Hum. The newly arrived brothers managed a shop in Greymouth. The town's finest ladies bought groceries, fancy goods, a wide variety of fruit – 'some never before seen in Greymouth.' Chinese shops enabled even the poor to buy fruit. In 1893 the *Grey River Argus* reported: 'One of the most dangerous places…in the town is in the vicinity of the Chinese store' because of 'those careless members of the public who scatter banana peels and orange rinds promiscuously about the pavements'. I see the silent movie. It provides light relief from the usual stories – YELLOW PERIL, public denouncements that we are the most debased people on the face of the earth in our 'immoral, wretched…and diabolical habits', warnings that children wandering down Haining Street are kidnapped, boiled in a copper and turned into preserved ginger.

WE HAVE SO many names, so many ways of writing our names. Wong Sik Hum changed his name to Wong Kwok Min – Citizen of the Republic – to express his support for Sun Yat Sen and the first Republic of China. Authorities did not understand that our surname came first and then our two character given name, and so my mother's father, Ng Yoi Hing, ended up with the surname Hing instead of Ng. Police documents, newspapers spell my father's father's father's name as Wong Way Ching. Sometimes a character escapes and he becomes Wong Ching. In poll tax records he is Wong Wai Tsun; in family histories, Wong Wei Jung. Names were anglicised. Wong (surname) Ah Poo (infant name) Hoc Ting (adult name) became Appo Hocton; his descendents are Hoctons. But how did Chinese become Thackerays? Wong Way Ching arrived in Wellington from Melon Ridge in 1896 just before the poll tax was raised to £100. This tax – a full life's savings – on every foreign-born, non-naturalised Chinese entering New Zealand applied even to those born in Australia or the UK. He arrived just before the required cargo per Chinese was doubled from

100 to 200 tons. Were any of you on the ship turned away after tonnage requirements changed en route?

Way Ching did not earn enough to visit his family or return to China. He paid for his only child, True Light or James, to have a Chinese scholar's education. In 1908, twenty-two years after he had left home, he had at last saved enough for True Light to join him in Wellington.

A police file describes Wong Way Ching as quiet and harmless. On 12 September 1914 he was murdered in his fruit shop, 100 Adelaide Road, Wellington. It looked like robbery, but he didn't have the money to pay the lease. There was probably less than a pound's worth of silver in the till. The *robber* used a heavy iron bar to smash his head seven times until his skull completely collapsed. One blow was enough to kill him. The case was never solved. In 1930 True Light exhumed, cleaned and shipped his father's bones back to China for reburial. The skull disintegrated in his hands. But great-granddad's bones did make it home.

True Light helped new arrivals in Wellington. His father's police file records him as secretary of a New Zealand Chinese association. He attended the Chinese Anglican Mission. A European woman chased him – he tripped over his basket of vegetables and broke his arm.

You were lonely without your families. Many of my generation had great-grandfathers, grandfathers who spent much of their lives in New Zealand, yet their parents were born in China because wives were left behind.

NINE YEARS AFTER Wong Kwok Min's arrival he sent for his wife, Ah Loo, with her half-bound feet. My grandma, Lily, her sister and brother were all born in Greymouth on the west coast of the South Island. The family moved back to China where two more sisters were born. Lily remained in Melon Ridge while her father and brother returned to New Zealand. At twenty-two she came back to marry Ng Yoi Hing. He came from Tile Kiln, the neighbouring Ng village. His sister and brother-in-law had brought him out to New Zealand when he was seventeen. Lily spent her earliest years, almost all of her life, in New Zealand, yet she spoke little English.

I grew up speaking English. Whenever our parents spoke to us in Chinese, the Pākehā lady who worked in their fruit shop thought they were talking about her. She shut our Cantonese mouths. New Zealand refused our Chinese teachers entry permits to make us *bananas* – white on the inside. My grandma and I tried to speak with each other. It was mime, it was art house cinema without the subtitles, it was drinking sips of water from a sieve.

True Light married Dorcas (Ng Yuen Tai) before he left for New Zealand. My grandmother was named after a New Testament woman who was always doing good, a woman who was raised from the dead. Dorcas moved from Tile Kiln (the same village as Yoi Hing's) to her husband's village, Melon Ridge. She was lonely. She would ask my other grandma, Lily, to keep her company. Sometimes they'd have a tiff and Lily would grab her quilt to go back home. Dorcas would grab the quilt back. She'd beg her to stay. Twelve years after he left, True Light had at last saved enough for Dorcas to join him. It was late 1919, just before New Zealand implemented a permit system to control immigration from everywhere except Britain and Ireland.

Because True Light was Christian, my family did not follow all the old Chinese traditions. The females of our family were treated more fairly. When True Light died, the inheritance was divided equally between his six children, including his two daughters. We did not have a family altar, and although we tended the graves, we did not make offerings to ancestors… Yet I lit incense for you, offered pork and *baak jam gai*…

My father, Henry, was four when True Light took the family back to Canton for a Chinese education. They visited Melon Ridge often. At school they were teased for being *gweilo*, foreign devils. Perhaps they should have lived in the village where money from New Zealand had developed amenities, including a very good school. New Zealand was the main destination for those leaving Melon Ridge – a father was followed by a son, a brother, a nephew, a brother-in-law, a cousin. Now there are more descendants in New Zealand than in the village itself.

The family could not afford all the fares to return to New Zealand – a youngest brother was born in China and they would have had to pay his poll tax – and so the three oldest boys including my father were left behind at Church of England boarding school. My father was seven when the brothers came back third class, eating only rice, noodles and rice porridge during the three-week journey. An elderly Chinese man looked after them and when he left the ship at Sydney my father cried. He wanted to go with this kindly old man. My father could not remember his parents, just as True Light would not have remembered his own father when he eventually arrived in Wellington.

True Light chose the small Hawke's Bay town of Wairoa because of its large Māori population. Māori also had limited English and suffered racism. They were the main purchasers of mutton-birds, dried shrimp and roasted peanuts; elders would sit chatting for long hours outside the shop. True Light was popularly known as the *mayor* of Wairoa. At the end of World War II, a big dance was organised to celebrate. The first dance was taken by True Light with the mayoress, my grandmother Dorcas with the mayor.

DID SOME OF you meet Thomas Bracken in Dunedin? He wrote *Chinee Johnny* ridiculing us; he wrote the lyrics of *God Defend New Zealand*. What did he mean by 'God of Nations' and 'Men of every creed and race'? Where were his 'bonds of love'? It's the Māori version that makes me tearful, and Tīmoti Karetu's back-translation, 'O Lord, God, of all people, Listen to us, Cherish us, May good flourish, May your blessings flow…' Does not *all people* include every ethnicity, faith, political persuasion, immigration or refugee status, socio-economic group, gender, sexuality, ability, disability…

In 1905 Englishman Lionel Terry, who had not been in the country long, murdered Joe Kum Yung, an elderly and penniless Chinese who had lived in New Zealand much of his life. Joe had been injured in a mining accident and walked with a limp. Perhaps some of you knew him. Terry shot Joe in the head to protest Chinese immigration. Terry's defence was: Chinese are not human, therefore he could not be tried for murder. Is this how all prejudice works? To see the other as *not like us*, as not fully human? Terry dined with Members of Parliament. He was six foot five; he wrote (appalling) poetry. He was *the perfect British gentleman*. After the murder he became a folk hero, helped by the public on his many escapes from asylums.

In 1904 Terry had published a pamphlet, *The Shadow*, where he described the Chinese as 'drug-besotten, sin-begotten fiends of filth'.

Yet it was Britain that had forced opium on China. We tried to stop and destroy it, but were met by gunboats and military occupation. New Zealand mothers sedated their crying babies with laudanum (opium), but for the few of us who smoked, it was illegal. Horse-racing was and remains celebrated, poker and two-up were openly played, but from 1881 to 1974 all Chinese games of chance were illegal. Our *pakapoo* (white pigeon lottery) was hugely popular with people of all ethnicities and walks of life because everyone knew it was run honestly. Lotto and Keno are not dissimilar, except that the chances of winning *pakapoo* were much better, but whereas the modern-day lotteries are government-sanctioned and nationally televised, ours were raided and resulted in fines. You would be surprised at the proliferation, the glamorisation of gambling now – casinos, sports betting, pokies...

The 1920 census showed 2,349 males born in China and only twenty-seven females, yet from 1925 all Chinese females were denied permanent entry. Then for twenty-five years, adult Chinese males were denied permanent entry. From 1935, ten New Zealand-born Chinese men a year were allowed to bring over a Chinese wife. Five naturalised Chinese a year were allowed to bring over their wives and unmarried minor children, though given we were denied naturalisation from 1908 few are likely to have come. Until 1939, females were never more than 21 per cent of the Chinese New Zealand population. Why assume lonely men were immoral? Do we judge according to the character of our own hearts?

Is hell knowing the suffering of loved ones left behind? We were photographed and thumb-printed; we had to pass the English reading test. Even those of us born or naturalised in New Zealand could not receive the old age or widow's pension or family allowances. There were so few Chinese women yet for many years if we married a New Zealander, she automatically lost her citizenship. We could not be naturalised for her sake.

In 1939 China and New Zealand were allies and Canton Province, where almost all Chinese New Zealanders came from, had been invaded by Japan. A one-off concession allowed 249 wives and 244 minor children to enter New Zealand. The men had to pay a £200 deposit and £500 bond to guarantee that after two years their wives and children, *including any subsequently born in New Zealand*, would be sent back. The War and continued civil war prevented repatriation. Eventually they were given permanent residence.

But sixteen hundred Chinese men still remained separated from their wives in civil war-torn China. From 1948 fifty permits a year were given for the wives and minor children of men who had lived in New Zealand for at least twenty years and who were deemed of suitable character for naturalisation – even though naturalisation rights were not re-established until 1951. (I grew up knowing the first Chinese to be naturalised that year.) At this rate it would have taken another thirty years for the men to be reunited with their families. The idea was to only allow entry to wives who would be past child-bearing age. Naturalised or local-born Chinese women were refused permits for their Chinese fiancés.

True Light's cousin's wife died in 2012 aged 107. I am uncertain when she came out from China. Many of our elders did not speak of the past. (No one told me of great-granddad's murder until 1995 when we were preparing for the centenary of his arrival in New Zealand.) Our families were too busy working. Was it too painful? Were they worried the bad luck would spread? This great-aunt may not have arrived until 1948 under this permit system. Children were born, in 1950 and 1952, to replace two who died in China. Can you hear me cheering? She was good-natured, dutiful, born into a wealthy family, highly educated. Yet she ended up married to a New Gold Mountain man, separated from him for many years, living in modest circumstances, having to work grindingly hard. I interviewed her as research for my novel, *As the Earth Turns Silver*. Some of her story was fictionalised for the good wife left behind in China. She told her daughter it was better not to be born than to be born a woman. True Light and his father cared for the family. Where True Light went they followed.

My mother, Doris, was born in Wellington where her mother's extended family worked in fruit shops. She was a toddler when her father decided to take the family back to China for a visit. On the way they went to see his sister in the small saw-milling town of Horopito. Back then Chinese were allowed to use the cleared land to grow vegetables, as long as they removed the tree stumps. Yoi Hing's brother-in-law persuaded him to stay to grow vegetables in nearby Ohakune. Yoi Hing never made the expected quick money. He was never able to return to China. And so my mother grew up in a cold, isolated central North Island town. At age twelve she left school to run the new family grocery store with her thirteen-year-old sister. The two girls managed the shop completely on their own as well as working in the market garden and looking after their nine younger siblings.

My parents had the same loyalty to family, to community, as those before them. This is how the Chinese gold miners made a living from claims abandoned by European miners, why in 1865 the Otago Chamber of Commerce first invited Chinese miners from Victoria. When others gave up, we persisted. We worked hard. Together. This is how many of us survived.

MY PARENTS WERE the first generation to choose their own spouse. Yet even before they met at a wedding, my mother had already heard about my father from her grandmother Ah Loo, who had returned to New Zealand in 1939 because of the Japanese invasion. Until the 1970s very few Chinese arrived except on the grounds of family reunification. We were a small inter-connected Cantonese community. Then Britain joined the European Union. New Zealand had to diversify its trading partners. Some Chinese with profes-sional qualifications were finally allowed permanent entry.

My parents opened the first supermarket in Hawke's Bay. Beforehand we moved to Auckland for a year so my father could learn the trade from my mother's brothers. Dad was president of his Rotary club and the Hawke's Bay Chinese Association. My parents had friends of all ethnicities. And yet my father told me there were people who did not like his achievements because he was Chinese. Even in the 1960s, some customers would be pleasant in the fruit shop but ignore my mother in the street. One neighbour castigated another for giving us a lift into town – after all, we were Chinese.

When I was born in 1960, there were about 8,500 Chinese – 0.3 per cent of the population. More than half were born in New Zealand, yet there were still more males than females.

My parents worked hard to give us the education they never had. We grew up with unspoken expectation. Just about every Chinese of my genera-tion who could manage Bs at school surely ended up at university. We were meant to make our parents proud by becoming successful professionals, academics, business people. We had no artistic or literary role models – art was too precarious, too irresponsible. Our families had suffered enough poverty.

My parents wanted me to marry another Chinese New Zealander. We would be culturally similar. I would not suffer racism from my husband or his family and friends. But I liked reading, scribbling poems. I wasn't interested in money or playing basketball. I didn't feel Chinese. It wasn't until my early twenties that I started learning Mandarin, then spent a couple of years first on a scholarship at Xiamen University, and a decade later, a year in Shanghai.

My parents came to Xiamen to visit me. It was the first time my mother had visited China, the first time my father had been back since he was a boy. They visited the villages, now a common experience for Chinese New Zealanders of all ages, including young people who go on organised trips to study Chinese together and visit the ancestral homes. My nephew and his future wife met as fellow students, much to the delight of my sister.

On that first trip to China, my mother met her mother's sister. She had been born after the family returned to China and had never come back to New Zealand like her own mother or her older New Zealand-born siblings. My mother cried. She looked so much like my grandmother. Years later when my parents went back, they couldn't find her. In recognition of her father, Wong Kwok Min, who is regarded as a patriot by both mainland China and Taiwan, the government had moved her to improved housing.

When I was a child my mother would sing: *Danny Boy*, *Loch Lomond*, *A World of Our Own*. She sang a few Cantonese songs. I never knew what she was singing, apart from the first two words of one which she sang with particular gusto – a tiny, twinkly-eyed Chinese woman with the pluck of a dozen fighting fit men. In Xiamen I heard this song again and again, sung in Mandarin. When I told my mother, her eyes opened wide in surprise. It was now the Chinese national anthem.

COMEDIAN RAYBON KAN wrote in the *Dominion Post*, 'The absence of Asians in media meant my first Asian role model was Mr Spock.' We were always alien. The *other*. In the stories of Katherine Mansfield we were either the exotic celestials of chinoiserie and dreams of adventures along the rivers of China, or we were Chinamen, Chinks, John. In *Ole Underwood*, our faces were 'yellow as lemons'. Only once, in *Prelude*, were we named and then only because our paintings were 'awful hideous'.

People always remember the luminous Audrey Hepburn in her little black dress in *Breakfast at Tiffany's* (1961). They do not notice Mickey Rooney – heavily made-up, bucktoothed, myopic – as the sleazy Mr Yunioshi.

In the 1970s the TV series *Kung Fu* aired and every Chinese family in New Zealand gathered round the box. But I kept wondering why the lead character was played by a half-asleep white guy. We went to every Bruce Lee movie. When Chuck Norris appeared – Chuck, who looked like a lumbering hairy elephant compared to our Bruce – we all booed.

In 1986 there were 26,541 Chinese in New Zealand – 0.8 per cent of the population. By 2006 there were 147,567 – 3.6 per cent of the population. Asians have the lowest fertility rates. What happened?

In 1987 for the first time in more than a century New Zealand introduced an immigration policy based on merit. The unexpected influx of wealthy and/or professional or business immigrants from Hong Kong, Taiwan and Korea, especially to certain suburbs of Auckland, resulted in a backlash against *Asians*. The suburb of Howick became *Chowick*. Some immigrants found the unfamiliar business environment difficult and returned to their home countries to work, leaving their wives and children in New Zealand. Some moved to Australia. Now the largest number of immigrants come from China, closely followed by the UK and India. China provides our greatest number of fee-paying students, a number that has been decreasing, but which New Zealand desperately wants to increase. China is New Zealand's largest trading partner followed by Australia, the US and Japan. Korea is our fifth largest export destination.

It wasn't until 1991 that finally there were as many Chinese females as males. Now there are more Asian women than men. More overseas-born Asian women than men immigrate to New Zealand. The gender imbalance is especially noticeable with Thais, Filipinos, Japanese and Koreans, but also with the Chinese. Within these ethnicities females are much more likely to form inter-ethnic partnerships or marriages than their male counterparts. A number of years ago a friend told me that at social events people often assumed she was a 'mail-order bride'. She is also descended from the original Chinese families and is married to a Pākehā. She is at the top of a highly respected profession. Not long afterward, walking in downtown Wellington on a Friday night, a man lurched towards my Pākehā boyfriend and asked, 'Where do you get one of those?'

We lived quietly for generations – the *model minority*. Newer immigrants came with a confidence we never had. They often came from countries where they were the dominant ethnic group. Most spoke a different dialect: Mandarin. We are no longer a homogeneous people. Yet our newer brothers and sisters have revitalised Chinese food, festivals, language and culture. They have given us courage to find our voice. We have many voices.

Some New Zealanders are afraid again. *Asian Invasion*, they say. We had never thought of ourselves as *Asian*. The Statistics New Zealand categorisation is so diverse as to seem almost meaningless – Chinese, Indian, Korean, Indonesian, Filipino, Afghani… *New Zealand for New Zealanders*, people say. But who decides who is a New Zealander? A few years ago I was driving out of my own street when a man yelled at me to go fucking home. I don't think he was asking me to turn around and go back into my driveway.

One hundred years ago, anti-Chinese organisations counted among their members chief justices and prime ministers; racism was institutionalised, a societal norm. In 2006, *North & South* published a highly misleading article linking Asian immigration and crime. The Press Council slammed the article for discrimination and breaching standards of accuracy. New Zealand First leader, Winston Peters, continues to shamelessly scapegoat the Chinese. His allegations of Chinese transforming Auckland into a 'supercity of sin' are almost as sensationalist as the *New Zealand Times* reporters of 1896 who after accompanying an Inspector of Nuisances in Taranaki Street, Wellington, and expressing disappointment at the cleanliness of Chinese bachelor accommodation, then fabricated a story of 'Plague Spots of Asiatic Vice in Our Midst' and 'Dirt, Opium Smoke and Vegetables'.

Surveys indicate Asians are perceived to be the most discriminated against group in New Zealand, yet racism is no longer socially acceptable. Just as Edward Gibbon Wakefield, architect of the planned colonisation of New Zealand, considered Chinese ideal immigrants, so too 160 years later the *National Business Review* refuted Peters' claims, quoting Statistics New Zealand figures of low Asian crime rates, expounding the virtues of Asians.

In 2002 prime minister Helen Clark apologised for the poll tax and the way our families were separated. About 4,500 of us paid the poll tax, over £300,000 (in 2001 terms: $28 million). The Chinese Poll Tax Heritage Trust was set up with $5 million seed money to help fund publication of Chinese

New Zealand histories, staging of performances and festivals, continuation of Cantonese language schools, upkeep of historic graves…

IN 2010, I was introduced at a New Zealand literary festival as someone who didn't look like a New Zealander. People might ask where I'm from. But in Australia I am not Chinese. Aussies recognise my accent. They're friendly. Either that or they haven't a clue what I'm saying. At a petrol station a young Aussie-born Māori heard my accent and asked if I was Māori. Everywhere I go Kiwis come out of the brickwork and unreinforced masonry. They tell me they're from Wainuiomata, Invercargill, Christchurch or Auckland. At the Australian Prime Minister's Literary Awards shortlisting, David Malouf said to me, 'Ah, so you're the New Zealander.' He did not say, 'Ah, so you're the Chinese,' or, 'Ah, so you're the Chinese New Zealander.'

My son does not have a Chinese name. He has brown hair. In New Zealand, people might wonder whether he has Māori or Polynesian blood; in Australia, anything. He does not see himself as Chinese or Pākehā.

WE NEVER FORGET the land where we were raised; it is deep within our bones. The Hokianga is not the resting place you longed for. Yet Māori *whānau* have cared for you. Our red memorial gate stands high on the cliffs overlooking water. May our kauri live ten thousand years.

Grandfathers, great-grandfathers, great-great-grandfathers – we bow before you. Peace be with you.

A fuller version, notes and translations available at www.griffithreview.com

Alison Wong's novel, *As the Earth Turns Silver* (Pan Macmillan, 2009), won the 2010 *New Zealand Post* Book Award for Fiction and was shortlisted for the 2010 Australian Prime Minister's Literary Award. She currently lives in Geelong, Australia.

Postcard from Beijing

Artistic villages and empty mansions

Kate Woods

I'M living at Three Shadows Photography Art Centre, in an extraordinary brick building designed by the artist Ai Weiwei, who lives down the road. The centre was founded by the artists RongRong and Inri, well-known for their individual and collaborative photography. This art space is dedicated to contemporary photography and video art – one of the first of its kind in China; and I'm here as a recipient of an Asia New Zealand Foundation artist residency.

Caochangdi, where I am, forty minutes from central Beijing, is a vibrant mix of village life and art elite creating an eclectic mix of buildings, art galleries and happenings.

One recent morning I woke to what sounded like gunshots outside. Looking through my narrow bathroom window I saw plumes of mysterious pastel pink smoke rising from the street. Later, on a walk, I spied a giant pink blow up archway covered in images of hearts and cupids and leftover pink streamers covered the ground – I assume the morning fireworks were part of a wedding.

This side of Caochangdi where Three Shadows is based has tree-lined roads. At night everyone comes out to eat together and gossip. The narrow lanes become full of happy gangs of miniature dogs.

At the moment driving toddlers around the streets in large remote-controlled vehicles seems to be a fad. The first one I saw was a small baby being driven in a plastic red convertible down the road, via remote, by its father. Last night I saw another small child being remote-driven in a replica police jeep.

I've been to a few other artist villages in the past week. One visit was to return artwork from a friend to a local artist. I was awarded, for my journey, with an hour-long tea ceremony. This involved Lao Xiang soaking the beautiful clay teapots and cups in tea – the tea was eventually poured into tiny, low circular vessels. Xiang trained as a sculptor but now works primarily as a photographer and assists Western artists, on residencies, to create large-scale sculptural works. We are close in age; and note that much is similar, such as our generation of artists training in one art form but working in another.

Although since the 1990s the contemporary art scene in China has moved away from the collective, to individual exploration of ideas, artists seem to still band together in terms of how art is shown. Some groups of artists have tried to normalise avant-garde art so that it is not politically interfered with. There still seems to be some invisible rules about what is okay to exhibit in public. New types of exhibition spaces help the cause and so do independent curators who are often themselves artists. This is where the villages really come in to play – a singular place where the artist lives and exhibits too. Many villages have galleries amongst their houses and studios, providing space for artists to experiment – sometimes with no commercial or political agenda.

CLOSER TO HOME, near the outskirts of Caochangdi, I came across a small sign announcing the 'Juangita art complex'. Led by curiosity I walked down a dirt road until I came to a clump of half-finished buildings. Greek in style, and so incongruous of their surroundings they seemed surreal. Hidden behind them was the artist village. Hardly any galleries were open, but still, its utopian structures were impressive; a huge cubist form of rusted metal and an immense hulk of grey minimalist brick formed another gallery, with a peep hole for a window.

A giant spider sculpture swung eerily from the power lines, a left over from the village's more active past. Residents still live there and the experimental architecture of their homes is fascinating.

So many things in China are built on a monumental scale. It's rumoured that a new art gallery is to be built with the sole aim of making it bigger than any other gallery in the world. Still, I wonder why so much of the art is built on such a large scale. Is it paralleling the impressive historical and architectural history of Beijing? I bought a book on Wang Qingsong's work the other day, after a visit to his studio and immense constructed photographs. The writer, a Western curator Jeremie Thircuir, was asking similar questions in the book about the scale of Qingsong's pieces. He compares their size to Chinese scrolls, 'bigger than what the mind can capture in one glance'.

I travelled in China ten years ago but hardly recognise Beijing this time around. Cranes loom everywhere. The sheer amount of construction is incredible. Demolition takes place in view of many blocks of new foundations and real estate hoardings.

On my way back in to Beijing via an outer subway line I noticed new communities of identical, souped-up, stone mansions being built amongst the dusty mist of rural land. I couldn't document them from the subway and there were no formal roads to come back along. The infrastructure had still to be built, and so the mansions were, for the time-being, husks of stone within rural fields.

Kate Woods was born in Auckland in 1981. She holds a BFA from Elam School of Fine Arts, Auckland University. Kate has exhibited widely in artist-run spaces, dealer and public galleries including Te Tuhi Centre for the Arts, Auckland; XYZ Gallery, Tokyo and City Gallery Wellington.

School report

Cracking the literacy code

Bernard Beckett

LAST weekend, in a bid to compress a wet Sunday, I drove my two young boys out to the seaside suburb where I'd lived a decade earlier. At the fish and chip shop a familiar face greeted us from behind the counter; his smile as wide as ever, his English as faltering.

'How are your boys?' I asked. 'Must be at college now.' I remembered them just starting primary school, already working the cash register, or off to the side, bent over their homework.

The proud father shook his head. 'Otago.'

I had seen this look on his face once before. Some years ago I had been the judge at a writing competition, a sort of literary theatresports, and his eldest son had been competing. The father had sat at the back of the room alone, surely understanding little of it, just happy to watch his son moving effortlessly through the rituals of a foreign culture.

'Medicine?' I asked.

The father shook his head, and tapped his front teeth with his finger. Dentistry.

Such is the power of education. The immigrant child, brought up in a home where very little English is spoken, the family working long hours for meagre rewards, the son heading off each day to a school where everything is foreign, and coming out the other end as a dentist. Or a lawyer, or an artist, or an actor or the owner of a trucking company. When education works, it delivers opportunity. In social policy, there are precious few silver bullets. A well-resourced, inclusive education system might just be one of them.

Yet, talk to any teacher, and the counter-examples flow. The fifteen-year-old, for whom truancy is a well-established habit, whose flashes of charm and enthusiasm are swamped by long stretches of surliness and disengagement. Despite ten years in one of the world's leading education systems, he (and more often than not, it is a he) struggles to read; a fact he expends great time and energy hiding from the world. He senses his teachers expect little of him and would rather he wasn't there. He will leave early, bereft of qualifications, low in confidence and easily sold on the proposition that the world is against him. If the dentist-to-be is our success story, this boy, and thousands like him, is the face of our failure.

Between these two extremes sit the great bulk of the student population. Those who are developed by the experience, but not transformed. They acquire the basic skills they need to function in the modern world, and along the way, hopefully, find the chance to develop their curiosity and their passion. Their days are held together with the things we remember from our own school years: the sport, the musicals, the film making, friendships, camps, dances and social intrigues. Most of the time they are happy enough to be at school and then, when the time comes, they are happy enough to leave.

The challenge of the modern education system is simply expressed. How to serve the dentist and save the delinquent, and do it in a way that doesn't compromise the quality of the experience for the other three quarters? For most of our students, we are doing a remarkable job. A world-beating job, in fact, and far too little is made of this. For a significant minority of our students, we are doing something even more important. We are providing the means by which they can break the constraints of circumstance, and that too must be celebrated.

But the rest, we fail. Disproportionately Māori and Pasifika, disproportionately the victims of poverty, disproportionately male and disproportionately the children of parents with low levels of formal education, these students are, academically speaking, untouched by the system.

They leave without work habits, drive or qualifications, and for the rest of their lives, they pay the price. So will their children, their communities and, by extension, all of us.

Somehow, the same schools and teachers that year in, year out produce success in a hundred flavours, also produce the most abject failure. Something is going wrong. What exactly that something is, and what we might be able to do to reverse it, is no easy question. If it were, we wouldn't have the problem, and nor would any of the other countries that battle it. It turns out that across the developed world, educating most students is a fairly straightforward task, while educating a small portion of them is exceptionally difficult. Difficult here, difficult in the US, difficult in the UK, difficult in France, difficult pretty much anywhere you care to look.

THE MOST EXTENSIVE snapshot we have of student attainment is the Programme for International Student Assessment (PISA): surveying more than seventy countries which between them account for 85 per cent of the world's GDP. The latest data available at time of writing is from the 2009 survey, although the 2012 survey is due soon. In the accompanying report on inequality, which focuses on the reading ability of fifteen-year-olds, New Zealand stands out for all the wrong reasons.

Three particular statistics demand explanation. In the gap between top and bottom New Zealand is very close to being the country with the highest overall spread of grades (France, Belgium and Israel have similar profiles). To be fair, this is in part due to how very well our top students do. Only students in Shanghai, China, outperform them, and that's the population of a single city compared to our much broader social profile. So our teaching of the very able is not just good, it's outstanding. Still, that's the not the whole story, and the ability gap between our top and bottom students cannot be dismissed.

Second, when individual results are plotted against socio-economic background, New Zealand has the steepest gradient of all the countries surveyed (narrowly pipping France for this dubious honour). This means that our education system is particularly poor at overcoming economic disadvantage or, in reverse, social disadvantage in New Zealand is particularly good at resisting education's attempt to mitigate it. Either way, the educational price a student pays for being poor is greater in New Zealand than in any other surveyed nation. If one of the noblest goals of an education system is to break the cycle of intergenerational deprivation, then not only is New Zealand failing, but failing spectacularly.

Third, and most intriguingly, the survey asked students whether they were read to in the home as children. And again, New Zealand is an outlier. Not being read to made a more marked impact on academic aptitude for New Zealand fifteen-year-olds than their peers in any other country. This appears to reinforce the previous statistic. For the child who starts off a step behind, be it in terms of material wealth or exposure to books in the home, the chances of catching up are slimmer in New Zealand than in any other surveyed country.

Taken in isolation, these three figures probably overstate the case for the prosecution. If we focus on the proportion of students who fall below what the PISA survey considers the minimum literacy level for fifteen-year-olds, New Zealand doesn't look so bad. The OECD average is 25 per cent for boys and 13 per cent for girls respectively. New Zealand's numbers are 21 per cent and 8 per cent. By this measure, our ability to educate bottom end students is above average. In fact, only a handful of countries do significantly better with their real strugglers.

The PISA survey considers the percentage of what it terms 'resilient' students, those classified as coming from low socio-economic backgrounds, but nevertheless doing well academically. Escaping, if you like, their educational fate. And here, despite poverty having a greater overall effect in New Zealand, resilience levels are slightly better than average. This is a statistic that demands explanation. Although relative poverty has a significant effect on educational achievement, a great number of those from poorer backgrounds do very well.

Finally, New Zealand is notable for having much of its variance in achievement occurring within, rather than between, schools. In other words, it is not that there is a large split between schools with a lot of top achieving students, and schools with a lot of strugglers. Rather, a great many of our strugglers are working within the same institutions, and with the same teachers, as their world-beating peers.

As the principal of Wellington College, Roger Moses, recently noted, it's hard to believe that the same teachers who function so well when teaching the best students, turn into instructional also-rans when confronted with less able or motivated students.

A study of Pasifika achievement in primary, secondary and tertiary sectors sought to identify the characteristics of those teachers noted for their success with Pasifika students. The final list of attributes will come as no surprise to those familiar with general teacher effectiveness research. Pasifika students do best when there are strong positive relationships between teacher and student, when they sense the teacher cares for them, when the teacher is enthusiastic, and passionate about their subject. Which is to say these students, whose overall achievement profile is significantly below the national average, do best when exposed to exactly the same sort of teaching that works with every type of student. Good teaching is good teaching, and that too needs to be borne in mind when considering the nature of our failure.

WHAT STORY SHOULD we tell, then? Why, in such a high-performing education system, do roughly 15 per cent of students fail to reach the minimum standard? Part of the answer might lie with those very few countries that manage to do better with their bottom end students. Consider the list of over-achievers: South Korea, Finland and two Chinese cities, Shanghai and Hong Kong. Canada, although not quite in the elite group, significantly outperforms New Zealand. So, what do they have that we don't? It is very hard to look past remarkably homogenous populations. Which is to say the language in which the instruction occurs is also the first language in the students' home, the cultural mores of the institutions are comfortable and familiar, most of the students were born in the country in which they're being educated, and perhaps most crucially, there is no easily identified cultural group dominating the bottom end numbers. The New Zealand situation is rather different.

At the 2006 census, 24 per cent of the under-18 population identified as Māori, 12 per cent as Pasifika, and 10 per cent Asian. Although this will double-count some, close to half of our students do not identify as being solely European, in an education system founded on European traditions and values.

It's a proportion that's growing. Pasifika and Māori students dominate the educational tail. National Standards data for 2012 shows Pasifika students trail badly in reading, writing and maths. Only 57 per cent of Pasifika students met the standard for writing, for example, against a national average of 70 per cent. Māori, at 60 per cent, are also significantly behind. At the other end of school experience, 87 per cent of Asian school leavers have Level 2 or better, compared with 80 per cent of Pākehā, 65 per cent of Pasifika, and 55 per cent of Māori (note the switch between Māori and Pasifika results here). Hekia Parata, the Minister of Education, has targeted our Level Two achievement rate, aiming to raise the proportion of eighteen-year-olds with this qualification by a quarter to 85 per cent. It's a laudable aim, and as the Minister has said, this will largely come about by changing the achievement profiles of Māori and Pasifika students. So, it seems that our reading of the international data needs to be slightly modified. Although socio-economic inequality is a significant driver of educational inequality in New Zealand, the effect is particularly pernicious for Māori and Pasifika students.

Part of this might be to do with the way poverty manifests itself. While children's developmental paths are remarkably robust and a great deal of middle-class angst over home environment (how much television is too much, when should music lessons begin, what is the right age for an iPad?) is nothing more than recreational anxiety, there is an obvious limit. At a certain level of neglect, violence, drug exposure and domestic chaos, long-term damage to intellectual capacity occurs.

There is a point at which material poverty translates into a poverty of spirit: families and indeed communities come apart at the seams, and children simply aren't provided with the minimum requirements of safe developmental environment. In such cases, while education can do a certain amount to address the deficits, it's an extremely expensive and labour-intensive process, and nobody should be surprised when we fail. In this regard, it might be that part of our educational tail is a function of the kind of poverty we've allowed to become embedded. Some support for this view can be found in the fact that other indications of child safety, be they levels of preventable disease, abuse or youth suicide, all show New Zealand doing poorly by international standards. It could well be that schools are failing the most vulnerable students for exactly the same reason that hospitals or justice systems are apparently failing them. Which is to say part of the solution to underachievement will lie forever beyond the reach of the school. What that solution might look like is beyond the scope of this essay, but it seems worth noting that the benefit cuts of the mid-1990s, which at the time felt brutal, have never been restored, and that the Working For Families scheme, which provided some protection for the children of the working poor, has never been extended to the children of beneficiaries. As a society, we seem oddly comfortable directing punishment at the most vulnerable, and it's hard to believe history will judge us kindly for it.

IT'S A MISTAKE however, to conclude there is nothing schools can do about underachievement. While the allure of the *Once Were Warriors* cliché is great, it's not the case that all our underachievement can be laid at the doorstep of the broken. Although the broken homes narrative simultaneously serves the needs of the talkback right (close the borders, sterilise the ferals) and the dinner party left (we can't expect them to achieve, poor things) it leaves far too much unexamined. Over the years I've taught many students who have struggled to acquire academic skills, and only a small portion of them have fit the profile of the damaged child. In my experience, most of our failing students are capable of learning. They're curious, they can think through problems, very often possess strong social and verbal skills, and their families care for them deeply. Poverty is part of the equation, to be sure, but only part. And given that education provides a means of breaking the poverty cycle, it's important not to let schools off the hook entirely.

One area that's certainly worth looking at more closely is literacy. Most children, if left to their own devices, will learn to speak and listen just by being exposed to the language. This is an incredible thing to witness, as any parent knows. Children quickly cope with grammatical structures so complex that even the experts struggle to explain them, and they do it in whatever language, or languages, happen to be on offer in their environment. They're language geniuses, each and every one of them, although by the time they reach secondary school very few of them believe it. They're more inclined to think they're not very good at communicating, because in schools the currency of language is not the spoken word, but the written one. And unlike speaking, a facility for reading and writing doesn't emerge spontaneously.

In evolutionary terms, speaking and listening are innate, while reading and writing are cultural add-ons, skills we've developed by co-opting existing capacities. And that means this ability is much more vulnerable to environmental influences. Learned skills like literacy (or golf, or violin) refine with repetition. Some children grow up in homes that are full of books. They are read to from the youngest age, and develop an ear for the peculiar rhythms and conventions of the written word. They have the shapes of letters pointed out to them; subconsciously, the adults around them sound out words, breaking them down into phonetic units. We, the middle-class parents, almost without thinking, train our children to succeed in the written world. And so they get ahead, just as the child who's surrounded by music, dance or song appears to have a natural aptitude.

By contrast, Pasifika children spring from a culture where the spoken word, rather than the written word, is king. In terms of reading and writing, they start school well behind the average, and given how much of what happens in education relies upon the written word, that gap has a tendency to reinforce itself. The fundamental mismatch between communication in the home and communication in school, places them at a severe disadvantage.

There are things we can do to break this cycle. One is to attempt to level the playing field through early intervention. From books-in-homes programs, to increasing participation in early childhood education, to throwing far more of the teaching resource into the early reading/writing experience, there are ways of assisting literacy assimilation.

Closely related is the emerging role digital communication plays in literacy development. Here we may be moving towards a more level playing field, in that smartphones, tablets et al don't come with generations of user traditions, in the way that books do. It's not impossible that these sorts of devices will become commonplace in homes where books never were. After all, it's happened with televisions, and it would be interesting to measure whether there's as big a gap in visual literacy. I suspect there isn't. As digital interaction becomes the dominant mode of written communication, then, it could be that within a generation one of the mechanisms of exclusion will break down.

The obvious problem with such optimism is affordability. At the moment, information technology is something of a privileged kids' preserve, and part of the reason is surely financial. If, in our headlong rush to modernise, we neglect to address this, then a tool that has the potential to dramatically reduce inequality could end up having the opposite effect. A policy priority has got to be ensuring equality of access. One low decile school, Point England in Glen Innes, Auckland, has provided a wonderful example of how this might be done, setting up a free Wi-Fi service for those living in the zone. Smart thinking of this type will be hugely influential.

To the extent that literacy is the problem, surely the policy priority is early intervention, which might be paid for by moving money away from the tertiary and secondary sectors, and into pre-school and early primary. Secondary teachers will scream, but you ought to ignore us. Next, you actively encourage the teaching and assessing of a much broader range of communication skills and lastly, you think long and hard about how to ensure the digital age doesn't become another mechanism for protecting privilege.

LANGUAGE MATTERS, AND so do expectations. The biggest change you notice, in moving from a low to high decile school, is the students' sense of what is possible. Kids move on to become lawyers, filmmakers, airline pilots and politicians, because nobody ever told them they couldn't. And they know people who are already doing these things: friends of their parents, older brothers and sisters. In high decile schools, far less work has to be done to motivate students, because they already sense the value of education. They see the way it has opened doors for the people they know, and they want through.

Often, in a low decile school, the opposite is the case. We can tell them they ought to work, because good grades are the passport to a life of choice and opportunity, but if they're never met a person who, having achieved at school, went on to reap the rewards, it's an awfully hard sell. This effect is exacerbated when identity is so readily defined by race. To be Pākehā, Asian, Māori or Pasifika is to already belong to a group, and the problem of 'nobody I know ever became a doctor' gets the added sting of 'and nobody I know who looks like me ever became a doctor either.' Students gravitate naturally towards those areas where success and status seem most assured, and many judge in advance that place is not the classroom. So they develop their alternative social structures, mimicking expertly the rituals of measurement, competition and exclusion we practice in the school. Further support comes from the kinds of positive discrimination programs that get the political right so easily riled, the targeted scholarships, and indeed quotas. Again, we need more of it, and we need it soon.

Even more insidious than low personal expectations, are the low expectations that we in the teaching profession also have of Māori and Pasifika students. Given that nobody goes into the profession wanting to do damage, it may well also be the area where the biggest gains can be made. It's not the case that the teaching profession is inherently racist, although that incendiary term does get thrown about when somebody's looking for attention. The problem is much more subtle than that. Probably the biggest impact we make on our students is through the feedback we give them. Education is essentially a process of observing, critiquing and giving hints for future progress. Sitting beneath every such interaction is a calculation of the student's capability and potential. If you think a student has just handed in their very best work, you're more likely to focus on the strengths than the flaws. As one teacher recently put it, ours is the task of making an A- seem a failure, and a C+ feel like a badge of honour. We manage student progress by setting goals that are both challenging and achievable.

The better we are at making such judgments, the more effective we are as teachers. Unfortunately, the human mind is an incorrigible pattern maker, and without us even realising, we use all sorts of markers to help us form our expectations. From the way a student dresses, to the eye contact they give us, to what their older brother was like, to, inevitably, skin colour. For most of us, in the past, Māori and Pasifika students failed in our classrooms in greater numbers than their peers. And that makes it tremendously difficult not to adjust our expectations downward when the next brown face walks through the door. The students know it, and so their own lowered expectations are reinforced by the style of feedback and interaction they are given. Talk to them and they will tell you, with a great degree of accuracy, who believes in them and who doesn't. The habit of underestimating is so ingrained, and so subconscious, the only way to reverse it is through deliberate and repeated practice. Te Kotahitanga is one program that, amongst other things, works to this principle, and it appears to have had significant success. So there's another place where change could occur, and it's not massively expensive. But, because it's about changing habits, in this case the teachers', it requires constant practice and reinforcement over a long period. Very often, programs like this are embraced enthusiastically at the start, but it's difficult to maintain the momentum.

There are other things we ought to do in this regard. Although, by international standards, we're very lucky in that the difference between schools isn't great, that's a profile that's shifting. The increasing obsession with getting one's children into the right school, and the way the media has played accomplice to our hysteria, hardly helps. We see house price premiums in certain school zones, and the clear effect of white flight as parents seek to protect their children from the reality that ours is a Pacific nation. The imperative must be to maintain high quality public education across the board. Similarly, the current fashion for streaming classes very often has the effect of sorting by race. It has to be worth looking at the mechanisms driving this particular fashion.

FINALLY, ONE LAST fish and chip story. I remember once being interrogated while I waited for a burger. The dentist-to-be's mother was interested in my financial status. How much did I earn each week? What did I pay in rent? How about petrol, groceries? As I gave my apologetic answers I could see her doing the calculations. Eventually she arrived at the crucial question, 'So, how much you save each week?'

I shrugged and mumbled 'not much', which translated into 'nothing at all' in both our languages. She couldn't hide her surprise, but was polite enough to keep her disdain in check. I imagine she thought 'stupid, lazy, white man.' Certainly she struggled to understand how one could care so little for the future. And that's the thing about education. Ultimately it's an investment, its rules stacked in favour of those who instinctively value current sacrifice for future reward. For my part, I have always enjoyed playing in the moment, following my interests and curiosities and assuming tomorrow will look after itself. These days it is my lot to watch some of my peers from university, where I studied economics, appearing in photographs in the business section of the newspaper (I flick through it on the way to the sport). They appear far wealthier than me, they wear suits and determined smiles, and no doubt their handshakes are firm. Not once though, have I thought I'd rather be them.

Which is a roundabout way of saying academic success should be seen as a means, not an end. A great many of our best students suffer from anxiety disorders, and are so attuned to external approval that they have lost all sense of what it is they want. We see international league tables and instinctively read the top as good and the bottom as bad. But schools do so very much more than provide academic competency. It's far more important our children can make friends, care for one another, and find reasons each day to smile. Politicians will tell us that unless our students can keep with the Finns or the Koreans, we'll lose our economic competitiveness, but, if I may make brief use of my degree, it's a misleading argument. Competitiveness is a thoroughly misunderstood concept, relying as it does on a false analogy. Productivity is far more a function of capital investment than education. The fool with a truck can shift an awful lot more dirt than the genius with a wheelbarrow.

And so, when next you consider our educational tail, and feel an urge to wonder how it is we can better teach the Māori and Pasifika communities, you might also reflect how we could better learn from them.

The 2012 PISA data released after this essay was written shows a significant drop in overall attainment levels for NZ students, while the inequality issues identified in this essay remain.

Bernard Beckett has been a secondary school teacher for more than twenty years. He has taught economics, mathematics, English and drama. He is also the author of ten novels, and has written on the philosophy of science.

Tectonic Z

Creating a zone of hope

Rod Oram

OF all developed countries, New Zealand is one of the most dependent on its natural environment for earning its living; and we have lived well, thanks to the bounty our ancestors discovered here some seven hundred years ago.

Ours was the last large land mass humans settled. We remain a small population spread thinly across two spacious islands, and many small ones. Ranked by people, we are the world's 124th-largest country. Ranked by land we're seventy-fifth.

Where we stand in the world matters hugely to us. Our location creates our cornucopia, defines us, challenges us and gives us unrivalled opportunities. But our current economic model is hitting its limits. It is generating escalating environmental, social and cultural strains. It will not provide well for us over the next seven years, let alone seventy or seven hundred.

This is our paradox of poverty amid plenty. Bar oil producers, we have per capita the highest stock of natural capital in the world; and ours is a world of ever-scarcer resources. Yet we're struggling.

To see the New Zealand problem, it is best to stand back about ten thousand kilometres – not east or west, north or south but straight up in space. Don't worry. A couple of clicks on Google Earth will get you there. Just keep an eye on the altitude in the bottom right hand corner. Don't over-shoot or you'll miss the radical, exciting future the view also affords New Zealand and its Pacific neighbours.

We live on tiny specks of land where the Indo-Australian and Pacific tectonic plates meet. The fault line gives us earthquakes and volcanoes, and one of our names – The Shaky Isles. But the tectonic pressure also creates our mountains. These intercept oceanic air currents to give us rain; the rain erodes the mountains to gives us soil. Our mid-hemisphere latitude gives us long growing seasons. The oceans give us fish and moderate our climate.

Set against these great advantages, however, we have three big disadvantages: ours is a tiny economy; we produce commodities; and we are a very long way from major markets.

Take the dairy industry. Growing fast over recent decades, it now accounts for over a quarter of New Zealand exports. It also has an impressive 40 per cent share of global trade in dairy products. Almost all dairy products are, however, consumed in the country where they are made, only 7 per cent of total world dairy output crosses borders. So, while the percentage is impressive, New Zealand has only a tiny share of the global dairy industry.

Yes, the growing middle classes in China and elsewhere are consuming more dairy products. But world output grows by more each year than the entire output of the New Zealand dairy industry. The national herd of 4.8 million cows is already degrading waterways and land suitable for dairy expansion is severely limited. There is no way industry can keep up with international demand. Producers in countries with ample land, such as the US and Brazil, meet most of the growth.

The second problem is the inherently low value of commodities. Some can be turned into valuable products such as infant formula. But it is the brand owners, not the product makers, who capture most of the value.

We were confronted by this reality early in 2012. Nestlé, the world's largest food company, paid US$12 billion for the infant formula business of Pfizer, the US pharmaceuticals company. Pfizer only owned the formulations, brands, distribution and powerful market positions such as an 8 per cent share of Chinese purchases. But New Zealand captures only a small part of the value it helped Pfizer, and now Nestlé, create.

Almost all of the product was, and still is, made by Fonterra, the co-op that processes almost all New Zealand milk. It pays its farmer-shareholders the commodity price for the milk used in the formula, while the modest toll-processing and packaging fee it gets for making the formula contributes a miniscule sum to the small share dividend it pays its farmers.

This poverty trap, evident across the economy, is captured by the World Economic Forum's annual Global Competitiveness Rankings. One of its key measures is the nature of a country's competitive advantage. This is expressed as a scale of one (low-cost natural resources) to seven (unique products and services). On this, New Zealand scored 3.8, meaning we rely on lightly processed commodities, and ranked thirty-sixth in the world.

A second measure is more important. It expresses the sophistication of a country's value chain, again on a scale of one (extraction of resources) to seven (direct relationships with final consumers). The higher a country is up the chain, the more value it captures. Again, New Zealand scored 3.8, ranking fifty-eighth.

The more farms we sell to overseas investors, for example, the worse this problem gets. Last year, Shanghai Pengxin, a Chinese conglomerate, bought a portfolio of farms from the receivers, after the New Zealand owners had gone bust, buckling under heavy debts.

Shanghai Pengxin plans to use its farms and third-party processing plants in New Zealand to supply its supermarkets in China. Being an integrated producer, it will create and capture value all the way from farm to cash register. Very little of this wealth will stick to the ribs of the New Zealand economy. It is an exact replica of the century-old British meat baron model that enriched the Vestey family and British investors but left only crumbs for the colonial locals.

The fact New Zealand ranks twenty-fourth in the OECD in terms of GDP per capita is a testament to efficiency and long work weeks, not to value creation and capture.

IT COULD BE worse, as it is for Australia. Its competitive advantage ranks it thirty-fourth, again reflecting heavy dependence on commodities. But it languishes at 105th on the value chain ranking because its iron ore, coal, gas and wheat are irredeemably undifferentiated and unprocessed commodities.

Australia is wealthier than New Zealand thanks to a larger domestic market. Yet it is a seriously suboptimal one by global standards, and the economy is suffering from Dutch Disease. This nasty affliction strikes when booming commodity sectors suck capital and labour from the rest of the economy, drive up the exchange rate and make the rest of the economy uncompetitive, as the Dutch learned when they fleetingly profited from North Sea gas in the 1960s.

Like New Zealand, Australia urgently needs to learn how to create and export sophisticated, high-value products, not commodities. Currently it generates only 18 per cent of its GDP from exports, which is remarkably little for a small country of 23 million people. New Zealand earns about a third of its GDP from exports. This matches the current global average for trade's contribution to economic activity. But New Zealand has stagnated at this level for three decades while the global average has climbed from 17 per cent. In other words, New Zealand has been losing market share, and the dominance of commodities continues to impoverish us.

New Zealand's third big disadvantage is its distance from major markets. We can easily and cheaply ship low-value commodities long distances. But it is proving incredibly difficult to turn ideas into sophisticated, high-value products and services in New Zealand and get them out to the world. It is even harder to run overseas operations from New Zealand.

Of course, ubiquitous, nearly-free internet and social media allow us to communicate instantly with others around the world. But physical proximity and high population density are critical to generating science and ideas, then commercialising them. We can connect from afar but it is not the same as being there. As Richard Florida and colleagues wrote in a 2007 paper 'The Rise of the Mega-Region', the top forty mega-regions make up about just under a fifth of the world's population, produce two-thirds of economic activity, 85.6 per cent of patented innovations, and four-fifths of the most-cited scientists. They reap ideas, not resources.

These three big disadvantages mean New Zealand is struggling to earn a big enough, resilient enough living in the global economy. Consequently, we are running a large and growing current account deficit, funded by selling off assets to overseas owners and ramping up private sector overseas borrowing. Thanks to this growing stock of debt and the flow of interest and dividend payments offshore, New Zealand's net international financial liabilities are the sixth highest of the thirty-four members of the OECD, according to International Monetary Fund data.

At some point, our creditors will start worrying about our ability to meet our obligations. Meanwhile, a third of our children live in households experiencing some level of deprivation, and on average Māori and Pasifika New Zealanders live shorter, unhealthier and poorer lives than Pākehā.

THE SOLUTION, OUR current government believes, is incremental growth of the existing economic model. Just look at all those middle class Chinese and Indians, it says. If only we could sell them more UHT milk, milk powder, infant formula, wine, lamb chops, holidays and university degrees we'll be rich. It has set some big goals, such as doubling exports by 2025, to move from a third of GDP to 40 per cent. The government's Business Growth Agenda is attempting to deliver this and the strategies of most companies in the major exporting sectors are equally limited in their thinking about producing more of the same.

Two problems arise. First, the simple arithmetic of doubling exports, even in strong sectors such as dairy, won't work. They are growing too slowly to achieve that goal, many in the primary sector would run out of land and other resources before they got there. For example, the government is pushing fourteen big irrigation projects around the country at a cost of some $12 billion, on and off farm. But government-commissioned analysis by the New Zealand Institute of Economic Research shows that the investment would only lift agricultural exports by 17 per cent towards the government's goal of doubling by 2025. Worse, many of the projects outside Canterbury would struggle to meet their cost of capital without substantial government subsidy.

Second, the government eagerly negotiates free trade agreements. But there is more to export success than access. There are few government policies or corporate strategies designed to shift New Zealand up the World Economic Forum rankings of value creation and capture.

Don't be fooled by the trade headlines. Yes, exports to China rose 26 per cent in the year ended June 2012. But total exports fell 2 per cent. New Zealand is selling fewer goods to fewer countries, and becoming very dependent on one.

New Zealanders know this trade pattern well. For almost 150 years, New Zealand was hugely dependent on British buyers of food exports and on British suppliers for imports. New Zealand was, as historian James Belich noted at the 'Catching the Knowledge Wave' conference in 2001, two small, fecund islands dangling below the equator 'like the Empire's testicles'.

That cosy, but confining, relationship ended abruptly in 1973 when Britain joined the European Economic Community. New Zealand spent the next thirty years learning how to export and import more widely. But since signing the free trade agreement with China in 2008, China quickly became our number-one customer and number-one supplier. In just five years, it has displaced Australia as our largest trading partner.

This is not a tirade against foreign trade, investment or the Chinese. Rather, it is an argument for mutual benefit. For example, Shanghai Penxin's application to buy New Zealand farms failed three of the critical tests of the Overseas Investment Act: it failed to bring new technology or skills to the country – indeed, it hired Landcorp, an NZ State Owned Enterprise, to run the farms for it; it failed to create jobs – other than two trainers of farm hands; and it failed to offer skills in the Chinese market that the local dairy industry lacked.

The government approved Shanghai Pengxin's purchase though, on the grounds that the free trade agreement with China guarantees investment reciprocity. Of course that is desirable, but the current situation is grossly imbalanced. While Shanghai Pengxin's investment was an economic negative for New Zealand, Fonterra's investment in farms in China is a massive benefit, bringing skills, capital and ultimately a billion litres of milk a year to Chinese consumers.

NEW ZEALAND NEEDS very different strategies to thrive. How can we achieve global scale in a few fields? Create sophisticated, high-value products and services through science and other intellectual and cultural pursuits? Connect and collaborate intimately with communities of like-minded people around the world? Above all, how can we be true to who we are, what we are and where we are as a nation?

We can see the answers from ten thousand kilometres up in space. The tectonic plates carve a giant Z across the Western Pacific from the Equator to near Antarctica. In the middle is 5.8 million square kilometres of ocean, an area equivalent to three-quarters of the land mass of Australia. Entrusted to New Zealand under the United Nations' Law of the Sea, it is the fifth largest national oceanic resource in the world. It is twenty-two times the land area of New Zealand. It is so big, we almost catch up with Australia, with twenty-eight times the New Zealand land mass. But Australia's oceanic resource is only 1.4 times that of New Zealand.

This is a monumental responsibility. All oceans are precious for the life they hold and their influence on the planet's ecosystem. New Zealand's oceanic resource is home to 14 per cent of the world's marine species; of those more than 60 per cent are unique, the second highest level of endemism in the world after Antarctic waters.

These life forms are essential to the healthy functioning of the oceans but also for the help they might be to humankind. As Professor Chris Battershill, who leads the coastal and marine ecosystem work at the University of Waikato's Environmental Research Institute points out, of thirty-one marine leads for anti-cancer drugs, New Zealand has contributed three. One is a breast cancer drug in pre-clinical development from a local sea sponge.

We know astonishingly little about the oceans for which we are responsible. We've studied less than 6 per cent of our seabed so far, Dr Michael McGinnis of Victoria University estimates.

So far people around the world have turned to the oceans only for fish and some offshore oil and gas. But as a rising human population puts ever more demands on dwindling terrestrial sources of food and minerals, people will seek to massively exploit the oceans.

Worse, climate change is already creating an even bigger threat to oceans. Use of fossil fuels is pushing up carbon concentrations in the atmosphere, thereby raising temperatures. Oceans are absorbing a disproportionately large share of the heat and atmospheric carbon, causing warmer and more acidic water in surface layers. These changes are already causing damage to many coral reefs, which are by far the most intensive and biodiverse ecosystems in the oceans.

Most frightening of all, no scientist knows how to reverse these profound impacts, notes Sir Jonathon Porritt, a world leader on sustainability. In his latest book, *The World We Made: Alex McKay's story from 2050* (Phaidon, 2013), Porritt extrapolates from existing new and better technologies, and economic and social trends already apparent to describe how humankind solved many, but not all, of the increasingly intense climate and other sustainability challenges impacting us now and deepening fast. But ocean acidification and heating are by far the two most sinister for which Sir Jonathon sees no solution.

On a more encouraging note, he believes humankind will make some progress on improving the health of ecosystems, though still falling short of substantial recovery and restoration. Areas of high biodiversity will be crucial to these processes. He identifies the Pacific Islands as one of the largest biodiverse regions in the world.

So let's make this vast area and its peoples a zone of hope across the Pacific's tectonic Z from the Solomon Islands east to Samoa and south to Antarctica. This embraces some of the most precious but threatened places on the planet, such as islands which will be made uninhabitable by rising sea levels; and Antarctica where nations might try to carve out sovereign territory and exploit the land and sea once the continent's international treaty becomes open to renegotiation and modification in 2041.

We and our neighbours, though, will have to learn radically new and better ways to work together, to agree on enduring values, to progress science and conservation, and to use resources wisely so we can create sustainable wealth in every sense of the phrase – environmental, social, economic and cultural.

Yet, this will be a very natural thing for us to do. We are oceanic people. We can reconnect with our past and together create a better future.

THE WORLD BUSINESS Council for Sustainable Development provides one of the clearest, most comprehensive guides in its Vision 2050 document. This lays out the main shifts we need to achieve across people's values, human development, economics, agriculture, forests, energy and power, buildings, transport and materials. Quite simply, they represent a scale, speed and complexity of change far exceeding anything humankind has achieved in its history to date.

Young New Zealand leaders in business and other fields have produced a local version of Vision 2050 with the help of the World Business Council. Released early in 2013 it offers a blueprint for a New Zealand of six million people living very well within a restored ecosystem. Member companies of the Wellington-based Sustainable Business Council are working on turning ideas into actions.

To make this work, there is a need for a new type of company, fast growing and resilient with new business models that enable them to thrive in world markets. Such vanguard companies have begun to emerge over the past decade. They are distinguished by five hallmarks: inspired products and services offering unique value; originality of business and culture, born out of their New Zealand roots; smart and varying strategies for diverse international markets; astute management skills to acquire and develop human and technology skills, and capital; and the confidence and skills to collaborate with whoever they need, wherever in the world. Companies like LanzaTech and Xero, to name but two.

LanzaTech was founded in 2005 by biologists Sean Simpson and Richard Forster to develop new forms of biofuels. They targeted industrial waste gases as their raw material, not food crops, or crops from land that could have been used for food. Their first success was capturing carbon monoxide from the stacks of the New Zealand Steel plant, south of Auckland, and bubbling it through water so bacteria could produce ethanol.

The company was backed first by Sir Stephen Tindall, who channels some of his profits from his The Warehouse retail chain into his ambitious portfolio of start-up companies. LanzaTech has gone on to secure more than US$120 million of venture capital from investors including Vinod Khosla, Silicon Valley's leading clean tech venture capitalist, and Sir Richard Branson, who sees the aviation potential of the fuel. The first commercial-scale plant was scheduled to start production at a Chinese steel plant in 2013.

LanzaTech demonstrates two fundamentally important themes about technology in a sustainable world: first, it is closing a loop. Rather than spewing carbon monoxide into the air as a greenhouse gas, it is recycling it into a synthetic fuel, thereby displacing new carbon that would have been released from oil, gas or coal; second it is using biological sciences, which are more in tune with the ecosystem and New Zealand's greatest scientific expertise.

Xero was founded in 2006 by Rod Drury and colleagues to devise online accounting services to replace conventional accounting software that was fiddly, frustrating to use and hard to update, particularly for small companies. Its ambition is bold: 'Our mission is to materially improve GDP globally by making small businesses more productive.'

At an early stage in its development, the company floated on the New Zealand stock exchange, giving it more funds for growth. In the first half of its 2013–14 financial year, it reported that its paying customers rose 89 per cent to 211,300, which increased operating revenues 87 per cent to NZ$30 million. When it announced in October 2013 it had raised a further NZ$180 million, its market capitalisation was NZ$2.3 billion.

It is very rare to see a New Zealand company grow so fast at home and abroad. The benefits to the wider economy are numerous, staff increased from 278 to 584 over the past twelve months, across its offices in New Zealand, Australia, US and Britain.

More significant than the growth is the fact that some of Xero's competitors, the big multinational companies selling traditional accounting software, are informing their shareholders that Xero is a risk to their businesses.

Xero shows it is possible to devise in New Zealand a ground-breaking service for a huge yet very conventional market, and take it rapidly out to the world.

These two companies are commendable and encouraging trailblazers, which hopefully will serve as role models for others. But we have a very, very long road ahead before we begin to reap the rewards of deep sustainability in our terrestrial and marine environments.

SUCCESS WILL FEATURE the likes of global centres of research excellence, surrounded by clusters of enterprising global companies, in the likes of dairy nutrigenomics, marine-based pharmaceuticals and marine ecosystem monitoring and management.

Such scientific and commercial success will only happen, however, if we pioneer radically new and effective international institutions. One example is the Global Research Alliance on Agricultural Greenhouse Gases, which the New Zealand government proposed at the UN's 2007 Copenhagen climate negotiations. The aim is to reduce emissions by turning them into nutrients that will help increase food production.

The Alliance now has thirty-six country members and three observers including the EU. Together, the countries account for 70 per cent of global agricultural greenhouse gases (GHGs), which in turn account for 15 per cent of total GHGs. The three workgroups of the alliance are Livestock, led by NZ and the Netherlands; Croplands, led by the US; and Paddy Rice, led by Japan, with New Zealand serving as the Secretariat for the Alliance.

New Zealand has a history of such initiatives. As one of the architects of the United Nations after World War II, the country continues to play roles there and in other international bodies such as the World Trade Organization. New Zealand was also credible and useful in climate change negotiations until the current government emasculated the Emissions Trading Scheme through a wide range of exclusions and other breaks for emitters and made a feeble commitment to emissions reduction.

The biggest challenge, however, would be to help pioneer a new international body that would bring together the nations of the western Pacific, from the Solomon Islands down to Antarctica, to ensure we are all responsible stewards and wise users of these critically important marine and terrestrial ecosystems.

Around forty thousand migrants a year arrive in New Zealand, with most settling in Auckland. The top countries of origin are the UK, China, the Philippines, Fiji and South Africa. Those classified as skilled migrants account for just under half, bringing their valuable talents to the country. India is the largest source of such migrants, followed by the UK.

This power of lives and cultures coming together suffuses Auckland. I see it daily as a business journalist. Take Rakon. Its headquarters in Mount Wellington is a mini United Nations of very highly qualified electronics engineers. Newcomers quickly acculturate into the distinctive, innovation-driven company style at Rakon; and they quickly acculturate into life in New Zealand, making their own take on Kiwi culture.

We could build the great attributes of our people, land and sea into a new New Zealand. It would look much like our nation today but bolder, stronger, more certain of its contribution to the world and more successful.

We could remain, of course, very much ourselves. Who would ever want to be a pale imitation of some other nation? We are shaped by who we are as diverse peoples, what we are physically as a country and where we are half a world away from major centres of population.

Our difference is our gift to the world. We are inventive and creative; enterprising because of remoteness; enlivened by distinctive cultures; in touch with land and sea; small but able to efficiently run a full-service nation. In a fast-homogenising global culture in which one product, one country looks ever more like another, New Zealand is an attractive alternative, offering a different way to lead our lives, to nurture the world.

A business journalist for thirty-eight years, Rod Oram worked for publications in Europe and North America such as the *Financial Times* before immigrating to New Zealand in 1997. He is currently a newspaper columnist, broadcaster, public speaker and chair of the Hikurangi Foundation, which helps develop sustainable social enterprises.

GETTING TO YES

WILLIAM BRANDT

HE sat there staring, the book he'd been reading forgotten on the table in front of him. He hadn't had sex for one hundred and thirteen days now and any girl was starting to look pretty good but even allowing for that this girl was beautiful. He watched her move up the queue.

She bought an orange juice. As she turned and scanned the room she seemed to be looking right at him for a second. She found an empty table over by the window and settled down with a textbook. Now he could only see the back of her head. She had exceptionally clean hair.

OK. This was stupid. He was going to be late for class. He would leave. Just walk out like any normal person. He put his book in his bag and started for the door. He was not looking. Not looking at all. An unseen hand took him by the elbow and steered him to the counter.

The waitress, an older woman, took his order. *She* knew. He could hear it in the slap of her slippers. His coffee arrived and he turned, slowly. There she was, just across the room, head bowed, light falling through the windows. He started towards her, his face a brittle mask.

'Do you mind if I sit here?' His voice came out harsh and flat, as if he was accusing her of something. The girl lifted her head. He looked her right in the eye. He wasn't smiling. She wasn't smiling either.

'Yes, of course,' she said. There were empty tables all over the place. He could have sat anywhere.

He eased into his chair, making slow deliberate movements. He opened his book at random, took a sip of coffee. The girl's head was down again but there was an immobility to it. She was no more reading her book than he was.

He asked her name. Asked about her studies, where she lived. She answered all his questions promptly and fully. She was serious, direct, polite. It was like a job interview. There were pauses in the conversation, during which she sat patiently, waiting for him to speak. There was a lot of eye contact. She liked him. Her pupils were enormous. She was attracted to him. He got her phone number, said he'd call her and left. He wasn't even late for class.

NATHAN CHANGED HIS mind twice about his shirt. He bought aftershave, condoms, gelled his hair. He left home wearing a hat but turned back to ditch it.

She was already waiting on the corner - and as soon as he saw her he knew he'd made a mistake. In the cafeteria she'd been in jeans and a T-shirt like everyone else, but her idea of evening wear was a calf-length skirt and a lace-collared shirt buttoned to the neck. She had a shoulder bag and flat shoes. Makeup was at the absolute minimum. She came forward to meet him and they stood a few feet apart. She was wearing a brooch, a little golden elephant. The top of her head came only a little past his chin.

They ordered ladies' fingers in a Lebanese restaurant which was popular with students because it was cheap. Throughout the meal, which was short, she kept her hands on the table, palms up, fingers loosely curled. The fine creases of her knuckles were pigmented dark brown and her palms were the same delicate pink as the beds of her nails. Her hands were incredibly clean, like the rest of her. She was so clean he could hardly look at her.

She was relaxed, confident, and talked easily, but he was tense and withdrawn. He didn't know what he was doing here. He was wasting his time. She was full of questions: did he have brothers and sisters? Did he play any sports? What was his favourite colour? Did he believe in God? The answers were no, no, blue and no.

They went Dutch.

BY THE TIME they hit the street it was dark. It surprised him when, waiting to cross, she took his hand. They walked a few blocks, her small steps moving in and out of phase with his long ones, their palms slippery in the heat. There was no conversation. They came to a busy intersection.

Nathan stopped. 'Well,' he said, 'I live down here.' He wasn't going to invite her back. He wasn't going to see her again either. But she wouldn't leave. She kept hold of his hand and shuffled her feet. They turned right and walked a few doors to a dark entranceway beside a panel-beater's shop. She stood quietly as he fumbled to get the key in the lock.

It was a tiny room with one window opening right onto the footpath. The curtains had to stay drawn and the traffic noise was unrelenting. There was nothing on the walls, the floor was covered with unwashed clothes. In one corner was a used dinner plate, in another lay a quarter-full whisky bottle. There was a tubular steel chair, an upside-down tea chest and a dirty single mattress.

They sat facing one another, almost knee to knee. Should he offer her tea? He had no tea. Coffee? He had no coffee. He found the whisky, expecting her to refuse, but she nodded. His bluff called, he unscrewed the cap. He had no clean glasses so he swigged straight from the bottle and handed it to her. She raised it carefully, holding it steady in both hands, took a small sip and coughed. He had another himself and went to replace the cap but she held out her hand for more. They finished the bottle.

She'd taken off the elephant brooch and she was playing with it, holding it cupped in her hand. To buy some time he told her a long story about how he broke his arm once. Still she sat, not talking, not really seeming to listen. He told her about his favourite foods. He told her about concrete, how it never stops drying. He told her about his father's illness, his mother's quilt-making, about a pet rat he'd had when he was ten.

He looked at his watch; it was late. She wouldn't get a bus now even if she tried. But clearly she didn't want a bus and that was not what she was here for and there was nothing for it.

When he knelt in front of her, their heads were level. When he kissed her, her eyes were already closed, her lips rubbery, hot and dry. He got his hand tangled in her hair, yanked it and had to apologise.

In rapid stages they moved to the grubby mattress, but then she put a hand on his chest to stop him. He rolled off. She burrowed her face into his neck. Her boyfriend, she said. He'd been killed in a boating accident a year ago. They'd been sweethearts, ever since high school. She ran her fingers through his hair and brought her face very close to his as she fiddled with his collar.

Nathan looked down. She had pinned the little elephant brooch to his lapel.

TRAFFIC HOWLED OUTSIDE the window, yards away. A truck hammered past. Headlights strafed the walls. They were sweating, crammed together on the narrow mattress. The damp patch was cold on his hip, the sheets were half on the floor. His arm was trapped. Her cheek was on his chest. She lay like a dead thing, her eyes liquid and huge.

William Brandt has an MA in Creative Writing from Victoria University's International Institute of Modern Letters. His collection *Alpha Male* (Victoria University Press) won the Montana Award for Best First Book in 1999. He has been published in New Zealand, the UK, Italy, Germany, France and the United States. He teaches at the International Institute of Modern Letters.

We are all Stan Walker

Why you should have watched the most hated show on TV

Damien Wilkins

ABOUT halfway through the debut series of *The X Factor* (New Zealand) I started making some notes about why I liked the show. I should add that I liked it un-ironically, though not unreservedly; I'm not insane. Of course the show is mostly reviled. Here are some of the reasons I've heard: it's exploitative of the participants and the audience, cynical, divorced from true ideas about musical talent and embarrassingly shallow; a crass, heavily scripted overseas commercial operation in the guise of an open, local, community-minded show. And the judges? No-account has-beens or lightweight nobodies, mangling the language and looking to bolster flagging careers while posing as mentors. I get all that, agree with most of it, and yet I continued to watch. Why?

An early driver, I suppose, was connected to that aspect commentators report as finished-with; namely appointment group viewing. We have teenage daughters – a key segment of the show's target market – and we watched it as a family. (My guess is that the show was consumed like this around the country, in denial of the commonplace about atomised viewers and on-demand habits.) However, near the point at which there were six or seven contestants left, I was aware things had got strange – I was sometimes watching the live show by myself. My fellow-travellers appeared less than hooked, drifting in and out of range – even *talking* through some of the judges' comments. I stayed to the end, where I was rejoined by the fair-weather cohort. Jackie won. She cried. Woop-de-shit. See how easy it is to slip into hostility. Still, it's worth noticing that the result, for the viewer at least, wasn't really the point. Winning isn't the object of our contemplation. Losing might be.

THE NOTES I made on the show, in truth, don't amount to much, certainly not a full-scale defence but they did issue from a sense that the denigrators – wise and knowing and cruel and right – were still missing something pretty great. I doubt there's been a more emotionally engaging piece of NZ television in years than those first episodes of *The X Factor*. Two recurring themes I noted: breast cancer and poverty. I don't know how many aspirants were singing for dead mothers, lost wives – maybe I'm inflating the number but grief seemed everywhere. So did poor people.

The host Dominic Bowden, not yet transformed into the suited suavery of showtime, prised open almost by accident some searing biographies as he walked among the waiting. (Something haunting, too, about that waiting, everyone slouched on chairs, lying on the carpet, drumming against walls – unspeaking family groups or couples or solitary figures, collected as if pre- or post-disaster, as in a horrible, huge transit lounge.)

Speaking of disease and mortality, later the show would make its required trips to Auckland's Starship Children's Hospital where it was painful to feel the affective distance between dialled-up illness and the random strikes in that roll-up crowd of hopefuls who had nothing but their sudden awful stories. Even deep into the finals, when a member of boy-band Moorhouse, showed us his smartphone video message from a child with cancer – the child of a friend of his mother's, he said, trying to get some intimacy into the levels of remove – it was a desperate echo of the river of pain Dom had waded through back in the day when we didn't even know who Moorhouse was.

And this was what my note meant too, I think – that you needed to have watched all the way through to catch such an echo. Had the dreaded, diminished word 'journey' begun to make a kind of sense? For those of us long-timers, the series was epic and we did remember faces, pimples, pre-show civvies before Wardrobe arrived and the judges could say things like, 'I like what you're wearing.' Maaka Fiso, a finalist, auditioned in baggy T-shirt and shorts and looked awful. Turned out he scrubbed up well (and possessed my favourite voice of the show). We knew them back when.

The slump towards groomed emotion, photo ops, product placement – the Coke segment was particularly sickening – made it harder to like anyone walking around in this world but investment is a strange thing; you're locked into returns. You want to see why you bother caring when dreck is all around.

The casual detracting glance sees slick formula in every move but this series was oddly, interestingly messy, productively mismanaged. Two finalists (including the eventual winner) were tossed out and then, in turns I can't be bothered to remember, asked back. The mess didn't end there. Again it was easy to find nauseating the judges' confident talk of 'your place in the market' but this was a piece of commerce repeatedly bothered by notions of 'art'.

When one of his acts was eliminated, Daniel Bedingfield cried at another judge: 'I thought *you'd* vote for art!' (From what I've read of Bedingfield, he considers himself an artist, with a significant history of industry abuse.) We quickly knew who the artists were – they were mainly white and played acoustic guitars. Memorably, Mel Blatt at the audition stage complained, 'What is it with all you people and your bleedin' guitars!' – Mel was definitely not an artist. The brown singers weren't immediately artists; they had voices which were 'gifts'. Stan Walker called Whenua Tapuwai's voice 'anointed'. Brownness was associated with powerful feelings, virtuosic control and unoriginality. 'I want to see you girls rapping in Kiwi accents,' Daniel told Māori duo L.O.V.E. When it wasn't wholesome (Cassie), whiteness was delicate self-expression (Eden), comic macho strut (Tom), and tameness (Anna).

But a few things made this thoroughly raced show not quite as easy to organise into the above boxes. Firstly, there was Benny Tīpene – Māori name, white act (the infernal guitar, his rumoured 'original songs', his terrible dancing, his Smiths cover). In one of the themed episodes (songs from movies), Benny was criticised by the judges for not being real enough. 'But Hollywood *is* fake,' said Benny sullenly. Of course he was talking about *The X Factor*. There was ominous unspecific talk of Benny having 'a difficult week'; he was visited by his sister for some 'grounding'. He'd been a long-time favourite but now as the judges reported back to him on a distracted performance – 'Oh Benny, is this what you've been reduced to, the only interesting thing about that was your socks' (Mel) – Benny was letting go odd yawns and glancing off to the side of the stage. For a moment it seemed he could do anything: roar, weep, run, laugh.

Whatever *The X Factor* bible says, its thou-shalt-nots finally can't fully account for the one defining gamble of the format: it's live. You see stuff before the machine can snaffle it. Of course whole swathes of its spontaneity are scripted. The licence for judges to disagree and badmouth each other, for instance, is franchised and finally not exciting. The licence for finalists to act strangely is not extended and such behaviour is usually punished and frequently exciting. Maybe, the judges warned, you don't really want this, Benny.

Dominic Bowden's mildly ribald banter (the week of 'liking bush' and 'what are you wearing under that kilt') is franchised but not two male finalists kissing each other's hands a number of times while Dom intoned the script of 'being sent home'. (Curious this almost universal infantilising formulation in reality shows: 'Leave the kitchen', 'Leave the sewing-room', 'Go straight to bed without any supper'.) I've forgotten most of the performances but I remember Benny and Tom's thespie hand-kissing. Before Tom exited, the host suggested that it was a very tense moment but the two lads were grinning goofily, and when Tom's name was announced as the loser, he looked positively delighted to leave. It was unclear who'd got the better news.

This was also the night of Benny's rather beautiful and saving reading of schmaltz classic *I Can't Help Falling in Love with You*. That struck me somehow as a Māori note. In contrast, his white bro's Jim Morrison impersonation was comedy that never approached feeling but was still delivered with weird intensity so that it almost crossed into something else. Daniel Bedingfield's put-down about Tom being a pub band singer was right and wrong; a pub band wouldn't hold this guy unless he was devoid of ambition – and maybe he is. 'Wanting it' seems to count, and it was surprisingly easy to read.

THE KEY MATERIAL, then, which casual watchers or avoiders miss or avoid, is not repellent industry grooming but nuanced, dynamic response to shifting moods. Grant the performers agency and the show becomes more than watchable.

Alongside the rote statements ('I'm just going to take those criticisms as fuel'), there was a palpable drama of striving and doubt that, unlike, say, the manufactured malice of so many other reality shows, didn't rely on competitiveness. The competition among the judges to mentor the winning contestant was weak enough but it failed to find any purchase in the acts themselves. Unlike other reality shows, *The X Factor* contestants aren't invited to comment on each other, to confess to camera some behind-the-scenes nastiness. The vibe is family, clean. The contestants' parents come to the live shows. 'Yes, we've very proud of him.' Nor does the format, unlike say in *MasterChef*, centre authority around experts. The judges aren't really in control. Who knows – industry-wise, it might be Sony, to whom the finalists are all apparently contracted, calling the shots. But affective power is another matter and, under these conditions, that sort of power is more diffuse and mysterious; it's also capable of defeating the judges, who occasionally voiced pique: 'I know you've got a fan base but I just don't get you'.

The performers did also seem genuinely supportive of each other and not at all isolated in their mentor's camps: Cassie (Girls) said she regarded Moorhouse (Groups) as her fathers on the show. Jackie (Girls) had that thing for Tom (Boys). More than this, when they gathered together on stage at the end of each show, it was a motley bunch. You couldn't say there was a shared body shape, a norm of attractiveness. Tom looked like he had false teeth; there were big stomachs, short legs. Loveliness was there too, of course, though not decisively so. A group of singers such as this made me think that showbiz is and always will be about freaks, oddballs, misfits, queers, characters prepared to dress up for us and for themselves, characters saved from other lives. 'I don't know what I'd be doing if I wasn't here,' said Whenua, who was constantly told he wasn't connecting with the audience and ended the phone poll as runner-up.

TRANSFORMATION IS WHAT *The X Factor* deals in. Critics naturally see coercion everywhere (clothes, song choices, staging) but the format is so open about its coercive tactics it's hard to feel affronted. It's also patronising at best to treat the testimony of those inside the beast as anything except genuine. Jackie, it seemed, had grown in confidence: 'I'm a completely different person. I'm happier.' Remembering her anxious, near-demented early self, the assessment had merit.

Of all the reality shows, *The X Factor* makes the most powerful and natural connection between what the contestant has to do and what the viewer experiences. I mean it requires considerable adjustment of one's reality to fully compute the significance of an adult making a cupcake. But someone singing live – that has a head-start. Another way of saying this is that song itself is about transformation – the singer's and ours – with the process astonishingly fragile, resting as it does in phrases, breaths, the chemistry of diaphragm, larynx, body. 'You sounded a lot better at rehearsal,' the judges said. 'You were closed up just then.' On a good night, visibly, audibly, the cupcake of song appears out of thin air. And of course we can't choose transcendence; it chooses us. Who knew that a weightless tune from the wretched *Twilight* films could be an emotional highlight? I certainly didn't think the weightless Anna would make anything of Stevie Nicks' *Landslide*.

THE LAST PUZZLE for me in my *X Factor* 'journey' was Stan Walker. In 2009, Stan won *Australian Idol*, or as he referred to it on this rival product, 'another show'. Readily lampooned, his self-mocking appearances on TV comedy shows around the same time as *Idol* proved he was easily ahead of the satire. Radiant, kind, silly and limited but frequently forceful and articulate, humble but also grand – he was the undoubted star of the show. When Moorhouse performed one of his anonymous songs Stan was briefly overcome ('I am not crying! These aren't tears!'). He often said, 'I'm speechless, eh.' He communicated delight and practiced decency, sometimes in a cringe-making way: 'You look beautiful,' he told fourteen-year-old Cassie, before quickly adding, 'but not sexy.' He told Anna (over twenty-fives), 'You look hot, eh, but not in a skanky way. Some people dress like that are skanky.' He always seemed surprised into emotion or statement. I found his clutzy openness winning though I have no further desire to investigate his music. 'You and me come from the same place,' he told Whenua. 'Look at you! You're in the final!' Then he said something interesting. 'People think it's because you're Māori I like you but that's not it. I like you because of your voice, bro. Because of what you do to me inside.'

That 'same place' Stan mentioned couldn't fail to resonate with any viewer up-to-speed on Walker's back-story. Born in Melbourne to Māori parents, the family moved back to New Zealand and Stan grew up in a Mount Maunganui household marked by poverty, alcoholism and violence; in interviews he's described it as 'like *Once Were Warriors*'. Both parents spent time in jail for drugs and Walker was a thief and troublemaker. He was also sexually abused by a relative. He's said that moving back to Australia, and turning to religion, saved him. Before entering *Idol*, Walker was a shop assistant at a menswear shop in Coolangatta. After winning the competition, to protect his financial interests, he set up his own company, Stan Walker Music Pty Ltd, run by his mother, April. Australia may have saved him but his return to New Zealand was, infectiously and revealingly, an identification with voice: 'Over there,' he said in one interview, meaning Australia, 'I have to talk proper. But now I'm back here in Aotearoa, I can just be me!'

If there's one thing I'll remember from *The X Factor*, it's Stan's – sorry, can't find a word for it – in my original notes it's 'Māori-ising'. Anyway, I liked the eruption of that into middle NZ; liked it in my own house too. He repeatedly identified himself and others as Māori. The first line of his Twitter bio was 'i love Jesus' (sic) but his crusading here, thankfully, found a better topic. My favourite moment was when he said to Jackie early on in the live shows that he'd always thought she was 'this little white girl' but he'd just found out her dad was Māori. Jackie grinned and looked at the floor. Was anything else ever said about her Māoriness? The Greymouth haka that ended her local town performance before the Grand Final was perhaps the only other signal. (Whenua's local return was to his Christchurch rugby league club; Benny Tipene's Palmerston North home was a farm with chickens.) The signals then were muted or not depending no doubt on the normal patterns of each person's life (and their choices about what they wanted to show of those patterns) but make no mistake, this was triumphantly a brown show.

Stan Walker grasped that at once and made sure we did too. In another interview, he spoke about 'the shame buzz': 'Sometimes you know, within the Māori community especially, people are held back by shame and a fear of succeeding.' He saved the best line for last though: 'It was the move to Australia that actually helped me,' he said, before slyly turning the solemn admiration into something more complex and funnier too, 'because Australians are shameless. They've got no shame at all.'

THERE IS, OF course, that final question, which detractors love: what lies at the end of all this? Surely, in voting and watching, we were colluding in a vast empty promise. Setting aside the way the question assumes naivety and ignorance on the participants' part – belied, for example, by Benny Tīpene's post-show media appearances ('I got what I wanted out of the show') – and looks to deny them the chance we all have to fail spectacularly, it's still worth asking. What kind of model of success, for instance, do the judges' own music careers offer?

Most of the guest stars were almost laughably transient. One whose name I've forgotten was asked his advice for the contestants. 'Enjoy it now cos it could all be gone tomorrow!' he said, and meant it. Haunted by art but ruled by contingency, fleetingness, the scrap heap, this was always going to be an inauspicious setting for credible tales of lasting transformation. With vicious transparency and utter realism, the judges each hoped to avoid the 'over twenty-fives' section as mentors. The word 'over' said it all. Predictions of a quick return to obscurity look accurate.

Yet for months of prime-time episodes, *The X Factor* – pure global product – sent a messy local version into the mainstream and in its anxiety-laden self-image showed us as complicated and involving a picture of our aspiring selves as we'll see all year. In this picture a lot of us have secret talents alongside our secret lives of pain; a lot of us are also not very well-off and brown – even if we're white.

Naysayers also forget what even young Cassie knew – that performing a song is itself so chancy and so mysterious, that all bets are off until the last note sounds. How outrageous to want 'a career' from something so flimsy, elusive and charged. Week after week we saw people lose the fight to – key word for the series – 'connect'. The rare successes were startling surprises, making Stan Walkers of us all.

Damien Wilkins is the author of seven novels, including *The Miserables* (Harcourt, 1993), which won the New Zealand Book Award. In 2013 he won a Laureate Award from the New Zealand Arts Foundation and published a new novel about Thomas Hardy called *Max Gate* (Victoria University Press). He is the Director of the International Institute of Modern Letters at Victoria University, Wellington.

Open road

No pain, no gain

Brian Turner

WHILE still a squirt, and a year or two before I started going to primary school, I often stood beside next-of-kin and others at the Caledonian Ground in Dunedin, beside adults who were shouting, 'Go, Alf!', or 'Go, Alan!' Both Alf and Alan were prominent top-class cyclists. They were my first sporting heroes, and watching them, being around them, excited my love and fascination for cycling.

So my desire to explore highways, byways and tracks and to head down roads not taken or less travelled goes back a long way now. A desire to follow tracks and roads zigging and zagging up and down hills, diving into valleys and disappearing in the far blue yonder was an irresistible part of what drove and has driven me for more than fifty years. And it's why I went mountaineering and fishing, and why I still ride a bike, am entranced, often, by the highways unreeling before me. Moving, and moved, I'm often mulling a little over what's behind and what may be in store. Cyclists know that out there there's a lot more to see than many of us ever realise, will ever notice, and there's a special pleasure in getting there using your unique, one and only engine made up of heart, lungs, sinew, muscle and bone. And when you come home, and people ask you where you've been, and you tell them, sometimes they're disbelieving. Especially if they're mainly, if not solely, accustomed to sitting in a metal carapace, the air-conditioning on, speeding along on four thrumming fat tyres.

On some days, the sights and sounds and smells amaze and delight. Today, in parts where I used to ride with pleasure, the land reeks – animal excrement and stinking water mixed in with silage and urine and nitrate contamination is vile. Such comes about, and we are required to accept, as the so-called 'price of progress'. So much of what is deemed essential if 'the economy is to grow', if we are 'to prosper', is 100 per cent purely disgustingly short-sighted, irresponsible and unsustainable. But…

Be that as it may, at times, when descending, say, or speeding along in a powerful tail wind, you feel a sense of liberation, even exultation; an earned freedom that both sets you apart and confirms you as part of a fraternity that most people never experience. Because…? Because it doesn't come easily. It requires work, skill, persistence, endurance, courage; because sometimes it hurts, quite a lot, especially on the climbs or into a headwind that's unrelenting, buffeting. The weather's changing, there's spitting cold rain – sometimes hard rain – and you're still an hour or more away from home. Keep going, keep going, don't give up. If you're hurting others are too… that's what I was told. I can still hear my father and others saying, 'if you want to be any good, you must learn to suffer.' In my experience that is true, for after pain and, at times, sorrow, the onset of relief and peace is immensely satisfying. And you're left in no doubt that it has been fully earned. How many, I wonder, of the more conspicuously wealthy know in their hearts that much of what they have acquired is not earned, has come at others' expense. The greedy, here and elsewhere, as George Monbiot put it, 'kick against the prohibitive decencies we owe to others'.

I SPENT MY childhood years in Dunedin, at the head of Otago Harbour, in southern New Zealand. Dunedin, and the south, has always been my homeplace, my heartland – no matter where else I have lived. We, my brothers and I, and my parents and uncles and cousins were active and sporty. I and my brothers weren't the sort of kids who, when asked where we'd been and what we'd been doing, answered, 'out' then 'nothing'. We were active from dawn to dark, were encouraged to 'get out and play'. What wonderful childhoods and teenage years we had: stimulating, challenging, adventurous. No prissy, overly protective 'elf 'n safety' then. How lucky we were. Years later, but before I passed thirty, I was sure Flannery O'Connor was right to have said that if you want to be a writer, you have to come from somewhere. Just like if you want to be any good at sport you have to have had the right background, the right kind of tutorship and encouragement.

My father's father, Louis, hailed from Birmingham pre-World War I. He was a soccer fanatic, but he liked other sports too. My cousins, the Larkins boys, Jim and Alan, liked rugby and cricket and athletics especially. But for many years it was cycling, both track and road, that stood out for me. In our family, for a decade or more, every winter in the years after my father, Alf, returned from World War II early in 1946, we followed cycling road races on Saturdays. When in Italy he claimed to have met the great Gino Bartali, and he often spoke of another Italian legend, Fausto Coppi. Then there were French, Belgian, and Spanish stars whose names rolled off the tongue. One threw in a few others – for example, the Australian Russell Mockridge and the great English track sprinter Reg Harris. So when I started riding myself in 1955, as an eleven year old, I often fantasised, imagined I was in break-away groups with Italian stars, high in the Dolomites, and hurtling down the switchbacks and straights below the cols. I saw myself grazed and sweaty, at times mud-streaked and almost completely spent, crossing the line victorious, hands above my head, thousands of fans cheering me. In my case I realise now that in some ways I looked to emulate others and hungered to achieve things in sport that struck me as admirable and memorable. I suppose I was looking for the validation that comes from having achieved excellence borne of hard work, persistence and, frequently, considerable courage. I think my brothers, Glenn (a cricketer) and Greg (a golfer), tended to think similarly. We believed in giving your utmost, that there was no substitute for skill, and that you ought to play fair. That there was no glory without honour. And, in my case, and especially Glenn's, we believed 'chipping' one's opponents, or 'sledging' as the euphemism has it today, was often plainly abuse, nothing more, and as such contemptible.

As a small and spindly boy I could go a bit, was frisky. Right from the beginning I loved the open road, loved the wind in my hair, the sun on my face, the clouds, the vistas, the smells of the countryside and the views of both the coastal and inland hills of my beloved Otago. In years before I'd heard of Walt Whitman, or read his 'Song of the Open Road', I was smitten by the roads before me, the smoky blues of the fabled inland Otago hills beyond the Maungatua Range west of Outram, and the Silver Peaks and Kakanuis further north.

I had yet to begin to read poetry, and it was years before I found Louis Simpson – no cyclist as far as I know – and responded with an 'Oh yes, so true', to his assertion 'At the end of the open road we come to ourselves'. He wasn't, of course, specifically writing of cycling, but he was alluding to reaching out, making discoveries, often unexpected and illuminating. What I did not know, did not believe therefore, as I do now, is that for one such as me the road is neverending, seldom smooth, but always absorbing, sometimes magical and deeply stimulating and – believe it or not – uplifting and satisfying.

ALF WAS A racing cyclist, and a good one. He was a member of the Dunedin Amateur Cycling Club, a sprinter with a good tactical instinct, who was once the Otago-Southland sprint champion. He also competed in road races but with less success as he didn't have the time to 'put in the miles' in training.

Born on 3 April 1922, Alf worked in a bike shop before he sailed off to Egypt in 1943, then on to Italy. I, born in March 1944, was nearly two before he came home to Dunedin, saw me, and began cycling again. Alf was a star on the old track at the Caledonian Ground in South Dunedin, a cold and windy and smoke-raked industrial area in days when working class people like us felt integral and genuinely part of a society that valued skilled tradespeople, and still made things for ourselves that lasted instead of importing loads of junk from overseas.

Before long my cousin Alan Larkins, a skinny teenager, was turning heads both on the track and the road. He twice won the New Zealand junior (under 19) road race championship. A remarkable feat. He also won medals on the track. I wrote about these early years in my memoir *Somebodies and Nobodies* (2002). But for reasons there's no time to explore here, I stopped racing in 1957 when I entered the third form at Otago Boys' High School.

Then, after a varied sporting career that included playing field hockey for New Zealand, I made a comeback to cycling about forty years later, in the mid '80s. I wanted to see if I could still *ride*.

One day, soon after I'd turned 50, I asked my father if he was booked up on Saturday. 'No, why do you ask?'

'I'd like a ride to Miller's Flat in Central Otago.'

'Why?'

'Because I've entered for the Kelvin Hastie Memorial road race from there to Mosgiel.'

'You're mad. There's a veteran's race out at Outram, why don't you do that?'

I said I was still competitive and if I got a reasonable handicap I reckoned I had a chance.

The race started between 10.30 and 11am. Neither warm nor cold, a bit of a sou'westerly tailwind at times. I think I was off three marks from the front which seemed about right to me.

The first ten kilometres are is flat and our bunch was going well, lapping smoothly. I felt okay but not too perky.

Then for several kilometres the road is up and down, demanding in parts. We flew down the big hill between Rae's Junction and Beaumont at between seventy and eighty kilometres per hour. A car came up alongside us and a passenger shouted at me, 'You bastards are mad'. I smiled. Yes, I thought, but it's *thrilling, is it ever*.

About twenty minutes later we climbed the Beaumont Hill. It's a killer. On and down through Bowler's Creek, then the main street of the old goldfields town Lawrence, and on through Waitahuna, all ups and downs until the top of the Mānuka Gorge.

We'd caught a few of the earlier starters by then. I got some food and another drink bottle from my father at the roadside feed station before we raced down the tricky gorge and out on to the Tokomairiro plain and shot through Milton. Ah, eighty kilometres gone and some tail wind for most of the last forty.

I wasn't feeling great. I wasn't feeling out of it either. I kept sipping drink and nibbling. Through Waihola and on across the Taieri River at Titri before bypassing Henley. Along the flood-free highway we were riding swiftly. The guns behind were having trouble hunting us down.

We caught the leaders with fifteen kilometres to go. When we crested the short hill at East Taieri, about three kilometres from the finish at the Mosgiel Railway Station, there were eight of us. Three I remember: Charlotte Cox, a leading woman nationally and a good friend of mine; another, younger, veteran Tony Chapman; and a youngish guy known as Toddy.

Someone attacked and strung us out. We turned the 90 degree corner into the finishing straight; two kilometres to go. Tony attacked. I went straight to the back of the bunch and sat there being sucked along. Tony eased and Toddy went. I thought this was good. I was on Charlotte's wheel. She moved up and then with about 300 metres left she went for it. I changed up a gear and realised this was very good indeed, for me. About 150 out I went past her as hard as I could and within 50 metres knew I had the race won.

Past the line I freewheeled and coasted along for a few hundred metres then turned around and slowly rode back towards the finish line. There, on my left, leaning against the driver's door of my car, was my father. He had both hands on his head which was down a bit. As I stopped beside him he muttered, 'I can't believe what I've just seen.'

I found it hard to believe too. Charlotte drifted by and said, with a wry smile, 'You bastard.'

WINNING 'THE HASTIE', as it's known, is a big deal in Otago cycling. Kelvin Hastie won the first Tour of Southland, way back in 1956. He'd been a hero of mine. He died young, of cancer. He and Alan Larkins were rivals on the road.

I'd won a few other races before the Hastie, and I won a few after that, but the Hastie's the most prestigious of them, for me, to this day. I still have hopes of winning another race, sometime, somewhere, but they are all in the category deemed unlikely. But who knows?

Brian Turner is a former New Zealand hockey player and has published best-selling sports biographies, many other books and numerous collections of poetry, including most recently *Just This* (Victoria University Press, 2009). He has received many awards for his writing; including the Te Mata Estate NZ Poet Laureate 2003–05, the Lauris Edmond Memorial Award for Poetry 2009 and New Zealand Prime Minister's Award for Literary Achievement in Poetry 2009.

Whale Road

Things to do in Iceland

Kate Camp

THERE are so many reasons that, when you look at the metres-long, meaty wound in the side of a whale, you don't want to think of a vagina. Teenage you says: gross. Feminist you: offensive. Literary you: obvious. But there it is, a gaping dark red metaphor surrounded by busy men in overalls. And just to take the analogy one great unacceptable leap forward, you have been scared all along about the smell, will there be a fishy smell, or a bloody smell, or some awful mix of the two? At best it might be a straight-up meat-and-bone smell, like the smell of your brother-in-law the butcher. And although, as it turns out, it never gets that strong, there's something about the fear of it, the anticipation, that is nauseating anyway. You know that somewhere under your feet, they're boiling down the sawed up bones and fat and rending them into oil, and just the thought of that sloshes around in your stomach.

'Do you want to see a dead whale?' was the first thing Brynja asked me, after showing me how to work the hot tub. 'To see how big he is,' she added, perhaps responding to a blankness on my face. We agreed that when the boat next came in, and her husband was working, she would let me know and I could drive down Hvalfjörður – whale fjord – to see it being 'cut up to pieces.'

The boats went out, and they came in. They're steam boats, brown, white and black, with a red star on the funnel. I found out later they're powered by 20 per cent whale oil, something that I remember Melville commenting on in *Moby-Dick*. Not that that's saying much, since he pretty much comments on everything. My old university tutor tells people I once said in class: '*Moby-Dick* would have been a great book, if it wasn't for the whale.' I don't remember saying that, but it sounds like me. I love *Moby-Dick*. But I know large parts of it are terrible. It's like Meatloaf: you have to love it *because* it's bombastic, not despite that fact.

Anyway, so the boats go out and the boats come in. The water is grey and choppy, but waveless, like a lake. The landscape here is all about the movement of light and shade. That makes it sound quite busy and beautiful, but it's really just that there's nothing else for it to be about. There are no trees. No snow at the moment. The *mountains* are what we in New Zealand call *hills*. So the big show is the light and dark patches, bits of summer and winter coexisting and interchanging.

I become obsessed with how you see a strip of landscape between each slat of the blinds, which together make up the whole outside world. I imagine rendering it as a tapestry, a long, thin strip of the world sliced up and joined back together. Or you could put it on a loop, like a fan belt, and have it turning on an engine at the Venice Biennale.

I should probably find something to do.

The first day I go down to the whaling station, Thorvaldur isn't working. I stand up on the bank with the other tourists, it's a well-known Thing To Do In Iceland, to stand on the mossy cone-shaped hill above the whaling station, and watch a whale being flensed. I use the word inside my head with a great deal of satisfaction. The boat is docked at the pier (wharf? jetty?) a hundred metres or so away. I expect to see it circled by a whirlpool of gulls, but there's just a few, doing lazy circuits, or waiting in the water.

It takes me ages to realise that they're towing the whale in towards the concrete ramp, underwater. Then I see the hook that's attached to it, like a harpoon, though I'm not sure if it really is one. It's moving through the water making a very small ripple. Under the surface I can see the white-with-black-stripes body of the whale. A yellow digger on the side of the wharf has a kind of hook attached to the end of it, a bit like the claw things that people have attached to a prosthetic arm, or used to. It's not hooked over like a child's letter j, but just sort of bent at the end, like a cheese knife. They use this to manoeuvre the body into place, so it can be dragged up the ramp. They get it into position, and then a couple of guys walk down and put a rope round the tail. I know from a friend that they wear gumboots with spikes on the bottom.

One of the great things about Iceland is that it is rarely slippery underfoot. Unlike in New Zealand, where, if you venture into the bush, you are forever slipping on wet grass, slick rocks, or mud, in Iceland you almost always have great grip. It's the volcanic soils, free draining, and the lava, which is rough and porous, and the moss, so deep your feet sink into it. Even now, standing on a hillside on a forty-five degree angle, where ideally one leg would be ten inches shorter than the other, the moss gives you traction and you can stay upright, and winkle your iPhone out of your pocket without falling on your arse.

I am not going to go on about how people have to photograph everything, no one can just *experience* the world. No one ever could, of course. Even Hillary pissed at the top of Everest. People are despicable and I'm one of them. So they start butchering the whale, and I take some pictures and videos and eventually I get bored and go home. Herman Melville I ain't.

A COUPLE OF days later, Thorvaldur knocks at the door. I pretend I haven't just got out of bed. He has those big, puffy men's hands, and when I shake the one he offers, even though I can feel it's hard on the surface because he's a farmer, the main sensation is that it's soft and pillowy. He says they are bringing in a whale, and I can drive down and meet him at the station, if I park my car he'll take me in. We talk for a minute about the beagles, the one that always wants to go walking off everywhere, and the one that stays close by. We squint at each other, in the manner of people who talk close to a body of water. In the ditch behind the cottage, little mini clouds of steam come up from the geothermal outlet.

When I get into his maroon Toyota Hilux, the smell is of my uncle: cigarette smoke and man stuff. The dash is covered in curled up pieces of paper, as one would expect. Yes, I can take photos. No one is surprised that you would want to, and no one is ashamed. At the Little Whale Museum up the road, the promotional photo is of a man in orange overalls, cutting up a whale on a lovely sunny day. But today it's grey, like at the start of *Moby-Dick*. It's *mizzling*.

Of course you want to feel sad when you see a dead whale, pulled up from the ocean deep. But instead you feel sort of, huh. And, yeah, that's what a dead whale would look like. I try various things to make myself feel sadder, I look at what I think is a wound on the whale's white underside, where there seem to be some pink guts poking out. How sad, its guts are poking out. Then Thorvaldur says, looking sheepish, *it is, what do you say, a woman?* It's a female, and what I thought was a wound is its vulva, and the two marks on either side are its nipples. I think about whales having sex underwater, it must be hard when there's nothing to press up against, what's to stop the female just floating away? And the male must have to be upside down. But then, they're probably looking at us thinking, you poor godforsaken wretches hooked up to all those wheels and machines.

And then I do feel a bit sad, because as they pull the whale up the ramp, its black-and-white-striped under-jaw is deflated, exactly like a soccer ball that's been left out in the garden over winter. It's just sort of dented in on itself, and you know it should be round and full in its black-and-white stripey-ness, like the sail of a Viking ship. The skin of the whale is getting all grazed from being dragged on the concrete, so you can see red patches on the black and white. There's a little boy, about three, in his mother's arms, watching the whale go up the ramp. A man is trying to take a picture of him with the whale in the background but he's not co-operating.

We walk round to get a new vantage point. There are stairs up the side of the fuel tank, rusted metal stairs, and I know I was raised in the romantic tradition because I want to photograph the rusted stairs, and the sea-faded plastic crates, and the piles of broken down machinery. Thorvaldur tells me a bit about the history of the whaling station, how it was originally part of an Allied operations base in World War II, which is why there are so many fuel tanks, and how the owner is the son of the original owner, who set up the station in the 1950s.

All the meat is exported to Japan, and I have a vague recollection that whale meat became a source of protein there after the war, in the devastation after the war. But like many of the facts I know, it's possible I made that up.

I think for a minute of a man I heard about, either the luckiest or unluckiest man in Japan, who witnessed the bombs fall on both Hiroshima and Nagasaki. A river full of bodies is what I remember, and he was in a car factory, and how you can see through your eyelids when the bomb goes off.

THE FIRST THING they do is measure the whale with one of those yellow builders' measuring tape things. It's not that big, about the size of a bus. I mean, that's big for an animal, and at times it seems to be a geological feature rather than a corpse, but it's somehow smaller than I was expecting. I guess when you hear amazing whale statistics – a heart the size of a VW Beetle – they are usually about blue whales, and this is a fin whale.

The northern fin whale population and the southern fin whale population don't mix, Thorvaldur tells me, which is why there are so many fin whales in the north, while in the southern ocean they may indeed be quite depleted. I tell him about how many whales there used to be in Wellington Harbour, that people wrote in to the paper complaining that they were keeping them awake, spouting in the night. Those were right whales, called that because they were the right ones to kill.

After they've measured the body, they cut out a bit of flesh and put it in an orange box, that's the scientific part. Then they start to cut up the whale. Later at the whale museum I read that the flensing tools and whaling techniques were brought to Iceland by the Norwegians. The tool looks like a hockey stick with a curved blade about the width of a machete. Wearing spiked, dark-green gumboots a man walks along the top of the whale, cutting into the body with a kind of sweeping motion. Other men cut off the fin and it falls on to the tarmac with a wet *thwack*.

The layers of whale are very distinct, the black skin, the white fat, and the dark, dark red flesh. 'It's a lot of meat yes?' Thorvaldur asks, once they've cut the cave-sized, mouth-shaped opening in the side, and that's exactly what I'm thinking. You get a feel for the wealth that a whale represents, a mountain of food that you don't so much butcher as *mine*.

All in all there's probably a dozen men working on the body. When a slab of meat is cut free, a couple of guys hook it then drag it off. I don't know why but I'm surprised how heavy the slabs seem to be. One man is running the winch, which is steam operated, so he's standing in a cloud. He's wearing a blue surgical-scrubs-type cap and blue gloves, and he has a face like a French actor, by which I mean, he has a mobile face, with deep, creamy lines. The winch is used to bring the heavier pieces of whale towards the rending area, where they will be cut up and pushed down into a pool of water to be boiled.

I'm watching the French actor man talk to Thorvaldur, and enjoying the vaguely health-spa feeling of the warm steam on my face, when I realise that they've started flaying the whale. Having cut into the blubber and attached hooks, they're now peeling the outer layer off the body with the winch, like taking off a wetsuit, or pulling the chicken skin off a drumstick. My dad keeps pliers in the cutlery drawer for that exact purpose. Within half a minute the whale's been stripped of its black skin and white blubber.

They cut the outer layer into sections, and when the pieces of the skin and blubber hit the tarmac, the flesh part spreads out like a kind of liquid jelly, still attached to the blubber and skin but sort of spilling and pouring across the ground, and then pulling back. I check myself for signs of sadness or disgust: nothing. Next time I look over at the whale, its jawbone is being winched up into the air, making it look for a minute like some kind of odd cathedral.

I ask Thorvaldur about the whale jawbones on the beach by the cottage, which I imagined had washed ashore. 'I brought them there from the station, to get white,' he says. 'Maybe I can make something with them.' He says he drove them home on his tractor. I want to tell him about the whale skeletons I've seen, at the museum in Wellington, and in Oxford, and how they are hung with invisible threads and how they resemble buildings, meeting houses, or architectural plans. But I know no one wants to hear about something better, somewhere else. So I say: 'you could make a gate with them.'

It's starting to drizzle now. Most of the tourists have left the hillside: after the first half hour of watching a dead whale you feel like you've seen as much as you need to. Now that we're really into the body of it, they start up the saw. The blades are like those ones you see in old photos, of men cutting down the kauri forest. They don't have handles though, just a long stretch of triangle teeth, and they fit into a steam engine that moves them back and forth. The noise is a kind of grunting clanking, and with the billowing steam it's very dark satanic mills, very *Tess of the D'Urbervilles* threshing machine. They cut the pieces of bone and fat and what I suppose is cartilage into suitcase-sized chunks, then use long metal-ended sticks to poke them down holes in the concrete.

As we leave, they're cutting up the outer parts of the whale into neat squares. The top layer is ribbed in black and white, like some kind of rubber, and then there's a creamy white layer, which I assume is the blubber, and then a thin, liquid-jelly of bright red flesh. The squares, each about the size of an oven door, look like huge pieces of Louise cake, with their neat layers.

I realise the asphalt is slick underneath my feet, and I can see I'm walking, not necessarily on blood, but on some kind of membranous slime. I know it's my last chance to feel horrified and I take a deep, searching breath in through my nose, probing the air for something awful. I can smell blood, and fish. But it's fine.

I had a dream about whales once. My feeling is that, by definition, any dream about whales is magnificent. This one certainly was. My dead friend and I were standing on the deck of a hillside building, looking out across the ocean towards the setting sun. As it went down, the waves became transparent, and in the apricot light we could see whales, surfing in towards the shore. At least, they had the huge, black bodies of whales, but in the light we could see they had the affectionate faces of dogs.

Kate Camp is the author of five collections of poetry, all from Victoria University Press: *Unfamiliar Legends of the Stars* (1998), *Realia* (2002), *Beauty Sleep* (2006), *The Mirror of Simple Annihilated Souls* (2010), which won the 2011 *New Zealand Post* Book Award for poetry, and *Snow White's Coffin* (2003). *Snow White's Coffin* was written in 2012 when Camp held the Creative New Zealand Berlin writer's residency.

booknotes
UNBOUND

www.booknotes-unbound.org.nz

NEW ZEALAND BOOK COUNCIL
Te Kaunihera Pukapuka o Aotearoa

*The online hub for New Zealand books and writing,
featuring articles, commentary, author interviews
and new writing from the best Kiwi writers.*

James Brown

Green light

In the deep south, the winter light is clear as beauty.
There are no half measures – it stares you in the face
until you look away. But there is also imperfection.
I must insist on imperfection. I stand before the mirror
freshly bathed, my fearful lack of symmetry
half defying gravity. Full moon and waning crescent:
a smile is a scar, a scar a crescent smile.
Evening mist and wood smoke sharpen
their wispy fingers. The air is crystallising.
In Bluff, you can buy a house for $35,000.
Rotten teeth wax into a waning southerly.
There is news of an earthquake in Wellington.
More northern lies. They take our power
and now they want our 'resilient spirit'.
Do we really need more finely turned description
to help us admire the beauty of their imagination?
Nothing much else seems to be happening.
Should I describe my sex life, the pearl in my oyster?
The witching hour approacheth. As a child,
I mutilated my Barbie to customise her beauty.
I stare at the sky. Perhaps the southern lights,
which I have never seen, will turn green with envy
as we roil like ferrets in the frost.
Karen, who's lived here all her life,
has never heard of them, but Edna claims
she saw them last Monday from Oreti Beach.
What was she doing out there in the dead of night?
She smiles her gap-toothed smile.
It is hard to know what to believe.
The moon, where I doubt anyone has ever set foot,
comes up and bathes my eyes
with its single milky breast.

James Brown's latest poetry collection is *Warm Auditorium* (Victoria University Press, 2012). He has been a finalist in the Montana New Zealand Book Awards three times. He teaches the Poetry Writing workshop at the International Institute of Modern Letters at Victoria University and works as a writer at Te Papa, New Zealand's national museum.

Christchurch Christmas, 2012

ANNE NOBLE

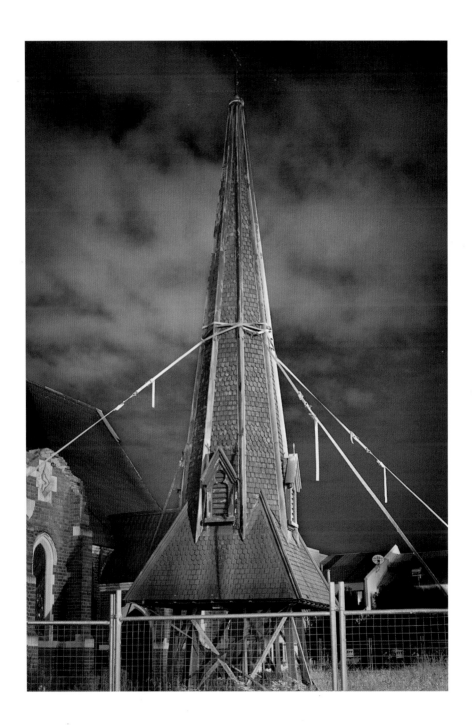

Anne Noble is Distinguished Professor of Fine Art at Massey University, Wellington, and one of New Zealand's most highly regarded photographers, producing comprehensive series of work, spanning landscape, documentary and installations incorporating still and moving image. In 2009 she received The Arts Foundation Laureate award in recognition of her contribution to the visual arts in New Zealand.

Amending the map

A city of becoming

Sally Blundell

WE almost forgot. The manicured gardens, the orderly course of the Avon River, the neat grid of streets – the very structure of this Church of England settlement built on the founding principles of faith and learning encouraged a form of environmental amnesia. Despite earlier experiences of flooding and tectonic movement, the city, we thought, was solid. Solid as a rock.

But Christchurch, the Garden City, the city on the Plains, an Antipodean outpost, some still say, of nineteenth century England, is a place of wetlands, of flax and fern, grassland and swamp forest, bulrush and bird life; a watery terrain of springs and waterways draining into the Ōtākaro (Avon) and Ōpawaho (Heathcote) rivers.

The reminder of this landscape, long buried under the city's paved footprint, was sudden and brutal. On an early September morning in 2010 a 7.1 magnitude earthquake ripped open pastureland, kinked country roads, and toppled buildings. Remarkably no one was killed. Five months later, on 22 February, 185 people lost their lives in a smaller but more violent quake close to the inner city. Buildings crumbled, vehicles were crushed, hilltop homes teetered on eroded cliffs. Throughout the city, but particularly along the river corridor, liquefied silt bubbled up into backyards, springs appeared under carparks, riverbanks slumped, underground waterways collapsed, roads buckled into ribbons of broken seal, burst pipes and twisted bridges. Swathes of land, especially in the eastern suburbs, were assigned to the newly desig- nated 'red zone': areas deemed too damaged, too vulnerable, for 'practical and timely repair'.

Over that single sunny lunch hour old place names acquired renewed relevance: Avonside, Avonhead, Springfield Rd, Wetlands Grove. In the city centre the landmark Christchurch Art Gallery, opened in 2003, has as its Māori name Te Puna o Waiwhetu, referring to the spring, *te puna*, nearby.

We have the language, but it is a language that speaks to an older landscape.

'There are about eight thousand springs under the city,' says landscape architect and inner city resident Di Lucas. 'We have all these wonderful meandering streams and wetlands. But people had forgotten that this is where the springs emerge in the [Canterbury] Plains and feed the Avon.'

These features, teeming with food and rich in natural resources, attracted the first peoples to this southern region. Long before the first Europeans nosed their whaleboat into the shallows of the Avon River in 1840 three waves of Māori *iwi* (tribes) from the North Island – Waitaha, Ngāti Māmoe, then, in the mid-1700s, Ngāi Tahu – were drawn to this area to catch eels, whitebait, trout and ducks, to gather fernroot and bulrush and to harvest the *harakeke* (flax) used to make clothing, ropes, mats and *mōkihi* (rafts). By 1800 an estimated five thousand Māori lived in central Canterbury, mostly in the higher, drier regions of Kaiapoi and smaller settlements on Banks Peninsula, using the land that is now Christchurch as travel routes and seasonal campsites.

In 1836, Captain William Rhodes, fresh from buying land in New South Wales, looked over the Port Hills that separate the port of Lyttelton from the Canterbury Plains and observed that the land was largely 'swamp and mostly covered with water'. Over a decade later English surveyor Captain Joseph Thomas thought otherwise. He found the site at the head of Lyttelton Harbour originally chosen for the new settlement planned by Canterbury Association founders John Robert Godley and Edward Gibbon Wakefield to be too cramped, the cost of required reclamation too high. He too looked down on the Plains, noting not only swampland but also vast expanses of potential farmland, a navigable river and good stands of forest.

The first street plan, drawn by assistant surveyor Edward Jollie in 1850, carefully avoids, or crosses at the shortest point, the myriad of streams that run through the selected site. But as the city grew the land was cleared and drained. Springs and tributaries were diverted, piped or built over, old stream beds filled in. Stands of tī kōuka (cabbage trees), once used to guide travellers through the often-treacherous swamplands, were cut down.

'WE WILL LEARN from this,' says Lucas of the earthquake. 'Now for the first time people are thinking about the land beneath. These old stream corridors are a natural feature. You don't mess with things like that.'

But mess we did. A map of the worst hit areas of the inner city correlates almost exactly with the fine web of creeks and streams underlying Jollie's 1850 gridded street map.

Today the city is full of strange sights. A building facade leans into a mesh of scaffolding, banks of shipping containers protect insecure walls and vulnerable roads, a rooftop rests fully intact on an inner city lot, a backless theatre reveals rows of tiered seats. The city centre lost 80 per cent of its buildings. Its skyline is low and spare, its streets scattered with traffic cones, detour signs and improvised car parks.

Christchurch is a city of becoming – a transitional space caught between memory of the past and hope for the future, an urban centre awash with empty sites, temporary gardens, impermanent artworks and community projects. Alongside a rash of sanctioned and unsanctioned street art, billboards advertise new developments, sandwich boards promote relocated businesses, wire fencing serves as an unofficial noticeboard for messages of mourning, strength ('Kia kaha', we read, 'Stay strong') and protest against processes of insurance, repair and rebuilding that seem too intransigent, too disconnected, too 'top-down'.

Out of this dramatically altered landscape a new city is being planned. In May 2011 some ten thousand people used Post-it notes, video clips, Lego creations, and questionnaires to pitch their suggestions for the revamped inner city as part of the council-run Share an Idea expo. The resulting draft city plan was presented to the government, which passed it on to its new arm, the Canterbury Earthquake Recovery Authority (CERA), established in the wake of the February earthquake to lead the recovery of the city. The same act that brought CERA into being also appointed the South Island's principal iwi Ngāi Tahu as a strategic partner in the rebuild alongside the Crown and local council. Under the legislation the required recovery strategy must be developed in consultation with, and with input from, its governing body Te Rūnanga o Ngāi Tahu (TRONT). Already this tripartite arrangement is taking form. The new plan for the inner city includes a commitment to recognise Ngāi Tahu heritage and places of significance, to 'incorporate and showcase Ngāi Tahu cultural identity and values' and to 'integrate the Ngāi Tahu narrative into the new city through planning and design of the anchor projects and precincts'.

Co-governance arrangements between iwi and the Crown are not uncommon. Such plans are in place for specific natural features such as the Waikato River in the North Island and Te Waihora/Lake Ellesmere in the South. In 2013 the Crown and central North Island iwi Ngāi Tūhoe signed a co-management plan for Te Urewera National Park, by which full control of the 212-hectare estate will eventually be ceded to Tūhoe. Various acts of Parliament, beginning with the State-owned Enterprises Act of 1986, include the obligation to take into account the principles of the Treaty of Waitangi, signed by the British Crown and about 540 Māori *rangatira* (chiefs) in 1840 and long considered New Zealand's founding document. Since the 1970s 'honouring the Treaty' and, more recently, 'Treaty partnership' have become the catch cry for political aspirations and new regulatory frameworks.

But this is Christchurch, often described as a transplanted corner of empire, a postcard-perfect tour bus destination complete with weeping willows, nattily dressed punters poling visitors up the Avon and an architectural legacy dominated by a now-diminished suite of neo-Gothic buildings including the former university, now the Arts Centre, and the ChristChurch Cathedral, currently the subject of a vociferous save-or-raze debate.

As Mark Twain wrote during his visit in 1895, 'Christchurch is an English town, with an English-park annex, and a winding English brook just like the Avon – and named the Avon… Its grassy banks are bordered by the stateliest and most impressive weeping willows to be found in the world.'

This reputation is exaggerated. Native plantings have been a feature of the city since the 1860s; the subsequent pattern of suburban growth with its fraying edge of single-storey, single-family homes is more American than English; the surrounding expanses of flat paddocks and braided rivers stretching across the Plains to the pile of mountains that form the Southern Alps are uniquely New Zealand.

While the city's population of 377,000 does comprise a higher proportion of New Zealand Europeans than other New Zealand cities, its diversity is growing. Projections for 2021 put the Māori population at 38,800 (up 37.6 per cent from 2006), the Asian ethnic population at 52,100 (up 73.7 per cent) and the Pacific population at 16,000 (up 52.4 per cent). The 'European/Other' ethnic group is projected to reach 326,600 – an increase of only 4.3 per cent.

THE EARTHQUAKE OF 22 February 2011 left Te Rūnanga o Ngāi Tahu homeless. Its large inner city building, Te Wai Pounamu, was shaken, closed, marked for demolition. TRONT migrated westward, to the control tower of the historic Wigram Aerodrome, once the site of a nineteenth-century *pa* (village) occupied by Ngāi Tahu, then home to the Royal New Zealand Air Force. Now, in a tight but full circle, it sits again on Ngāi Tahu-owned land. Here the office of Mark Solomon, the youthful-looking *kaiwhakahaere* (chair) of Te Rūnanga o Ngāi Tahu, looks down on a sea of new houses, tiled rooves, pocket-handkerchief lawns, street names, many in *te reo Māori* (Māori language), alluding to the area's aviational history. This is Wigram Skies, SOLD signs everywhere, one of three new residential developments being built by the iwi in and around the city.

The eleven thousand earthquakes that have battered the city over the past three years have changed attitudes. No one, explains Solomon, complains about students after the Volunteer Student Army took to the streets with shovels, rakes and spades to clear silt-ridden yards and gutters. Similarly the unpaid efforts of the 'Farmy Army' have breached the long-standing urban-rural divide. In the immediate aftermath of the February earthquake Māori wardens knocked on close to ten thousand doors, delivered around 1,500 food packages and huge amounts of water, addressing the needs not only of Māori but also of migrants and Pākehā.

'There is no such thing as colour or racism in a disaster,' he says. 'Every-one is equal and because everyone pitched in it has broken down a lot of silly barriers that were there before.'

He describes the potential of the new cultural and visitor centre, Te Puna Ahurea, planned as a symbolic entrance to the city in Victoria Square, once the main site of trade between settlers and Māori. Such a centre, he says, will give form to the traditional Māori value of *manaaki*, meaning offering support or the hand of friendship.

'Everyone thought it was just for Māori but we're saying no – we want a cultural centre for all cultures, something everyone is comfortable with. We are not a monocultural society, we are not bicultural society, we are multi-cultural. Before the earthquake I would have said every Māori kid in the city comes with a stigma – and that stigma is that they are Māori. That attitude is rapidly changing.'

But inserting a 'Māori chapter' into the city-wide rebuild, the biggest economic development project ever undertaken in New Zealand, is not so straight-forward. Key anchor projects identified in the new plan for the city centre, including a green frame bordering the east and south of a condensed central business district, a new convention centre and cultural centre and the Papa o Ōtākaro/Avon River Precinct, provide ample opportunities to acknowledge Ngāi Tahu history and to connect 'past traditions to future aspirations', but these 'past traditions' are complex.

Throughout the 1840s and 1850s, European settlers in Christchurch relied on Ngāi Tahu, particularly the Ngāi Tū-āhu-riri hapū which holds *manawhenua*, or tribal authority, over the city from its historic home in Tuahiwi in North Canterbury, to supply provisions brought in from outlying regions and traded in Market (now Victoria) Square. Following the signing of the Treaty of Waitangi the Crown purchased the South Island through a series of deeds, the largest being the Canterbury Purchase of 1848 by which the Crown bought twenty million acres (about eight million hectares) for £2,000. One of the conditions of the sale was that Ngāi Tahu communi-ties would have continued access to *mahinga kai* (food and resource gathering places), including the large village settlements of Puāri and Tautahi (from which the Māori name for the city, Ōtautahi, is derived), now lying within the city boundaries. But, in relying on a narrow translation of these *mahinga kai* as 'cultivations', access to many of these vitally important sites was denied. Land was privatised, titles sold. Repeated claims for continued access to these areas were dismissed.

In 1986 Hēnare Rakiihia Tau, *ūpoko* (head) of Ngāi Tū-āhu-riri, filed a claim with the Waitangi Tribunal on behalf of the Ngāi Tahu Māori Trust Board. The claim was presented in nine parts, known as the 'Nine Tall Trees of Ngāi Tahu'. Eight of these represented different areas of land purchased from Ngāi Tahu, while the ninth represented Ngāi Tahu's mahinga kai. The resulting report formed the basis of the landmark settlement between Ngāi Tahu and the Crown, including compensation valued at $170 million (about 1.5 per cent, suggests Solomon, of what the tribe had lost), first right of refusal on all Crown land being sold, an apology from the Crown, opportunities for cultural redress (the protection of customary rights guaranteed under the Treaty and Deed of Purchase) and a 'top-up' mechanism to ensure Ngāi Tahu's position is maintained relative to settlements negotiated by other tribes.

By the time of the earthquake almost fifty thousand people identified themselves as Ngāi Tahu, making it the fourth largest tribe in New Zealand and the largest in the South Island. Its asset base is in excess of $809 million with significant interests in tourism, seafood, farming and property.

HOW IS THIS story of settlement and encounter to be 'intertwined', as the recovery plan states, into the redevelopment of the central city? Under the heading 'Complementary elements', the plan suggests markers to identify historically important Māori sites, art works by Ngāi Tahu artists and new plantings of indigenous flora as possible ways of integrating 'the Ngāi Tahu narrative' into a city previously dominated by an imported English aesthetic.

Ngāi Tahu Chief Executive Officer Arihia Bennett says such visual acknowledgements give the iwi more relevance within the city. 'It gives us a sense of identity, it enables us to be valued with integrity, that we are part of this landscape.'

I ask her to imagine a hypothetical five-year-old child, starting school today and graduating in twelve or so years. 'That child will grow up seeing, touching, *feeling* that he is part of this city. I want children to see this Ngāi

Tahu identity as the norm, not as an afterthought or add-on but something that it is integrated through all stages of thinking from conceptual to turnkey.'

But some fear Māoridom will be presented through a generic, largely decorative iconography based on the arts and crafts expression of North Island Māori and not applicable further south (Ngāi Tahu communities, for example, traditionally had little carving in their buildings). In *Memory and Place: geographies of a critical relationship* (2004), Steven Hoelscher and Derek Alderman argue that 'geographies of memory', traditionally circulated in material form or through performative arts and cultural displays, 'are frequently called upon to support the specific kind of conquest and domination associated with colonialism.' Such 'imaginative geographies', to borrow the phrase of Edward Said, pay 'negligible attention to the actuality of the region's geography or its inhabitants, but more accurately reflected the fantasies and preoccupations of colonising agents'.

To avoid an incorrect and potentially alienating misreading Te Maire Tau, director of the Ngāi Tahu Research Centre at the University of Canterbury, is arguing for an aesthetic that refers specifically to Ngāi Tahu and Ngāi Tū-āhu-riri, the descendants of those originally allocated land in the Kaiapoi Māori Reserve under the Canterbury Purchase.

Such an aesthetic, he argues, need not be rooted in the 'mythic world view' and rituals of pre-European Māori. Rather he is looking to a contemporary expression of Māori design and architecture within a city founded on imported English principles.

'We want a twenty-first century aesthetic that is Māori-settler, not swimming with the dolphins, spiritual stuff. Ngāi Tahu need to see their community valued and respected in the city but equally important is that they understand the value of Pākehā settler communities in Christchurch. There's no point in putting in customary values that don't resonate with Pākehā. The tribe's rhetoric right through is we have committed to the Queen and the British Empire [through the Treaty] – we are not going to go backwards from that. But what were the values when English settlers came here? Once we know that we can engage, we can see where to bounce, test and synthesise.'

So the sturdy, bronze monarch, currently staring down visitors to Victoria Square, the site of the planned new cultural centre, will stay? 'Everyone thought we were going to chuck her in the river but, no, she is a fundamental part of the Treaty.'

Tau has been preparing the historic background for the development of the proposed Papa o Ōtākaro/Avon River Precinct, a broad tract of land weaving through the city centre on both sides of the river. The draft plan presents it as a place of cycleways, pathways and cafes, with artworks by Ngāi Tahu artists and 'cultural markers' identifying the importance of this waterway to Māori.

But to have any real relevance such visual references need to be grounded in the specific values associated with a much older landscape, the landscape of Lucas's eight thousand springs and the life they supported and attracted. Already the plan suggests enhancing springs and waterways and improving water quality to encourage the return of native birds, create additional habitat for fish and eels and allow for the planting of orchards along the river, so upholding the mana of Ngāi Tū-āhu-riri as *kaitiaki* or guardians of Ōtākaro/ Avon River and the importance of *kai*, food.

'Māori culture is based on food,' says Solomon. 'Food and access to it. It is what governed us. So the river is one of the focal points for us. You cannot have access to mahinga kai without water and for us the wetlands are the filter systems for rivers, the breeding ground for many species. I'm not in favour of taking out all the exotic [plants] around Christchurch – we are not called the Garden City for nothing – but I'd like to see the Avon planted in natives. A corridor showing our visitors this is what Canterbury used to look like.'

Architect Huia Reriti works on behalf Te Rūnanga o Ngāi Tahu as advisor on some of the planned anchor projects for the city. To translate the traditional values implicit in mahinga kai, he says, is to incorporate more meaningful elements than, say, traditional Māori arts and crafts appliquéd on to European built structural forms. Rather than adopting 'complementary elements', he says, the rebuild requires an aesthetic rooted in a relationship that is as equal as it is specific.

The expression of a uniquely Ngāi Tahu aesthetic, he argues, has yet to be defined. Across the country 'traditional Māori art' tends to be expressed as basket weaving, wood carving, *kōwhaiwhai* (the usually abstract patterns painted on the rafters of Māori meeting houses) and the 'Air New Zealand koru thing'.

'But we are more parochial down here, we don't use global views of Māori in this city. We don't want a Sky Tower here [as Auckland has]. We don't want *tikanga* [customs] from Wellington or Rotorua which don't fit our conditions and history. If it is global it will be a wishy-washy watered-down aesthetic. I'd like to think this new city will engage both European and Māori culture equally. It is as simple as that – we are equal partners in Treaty of Waitangi. The future of that combination is what interests me. Hopefully it will forge something new or something we haven't been aware of before.'

He gives as an example Australian architect Glen Murcutt in his ability to use modern materials – glass, concrete, corrugated metal – while also paying attention to Aboriginal references to the seasons, the movement of the sun and the moon, light and wind.

'We have to get rid of the narrative of legend telling. It is wrong, on so many levels. I don't do the whale legends, I don't do the story-telling. I don't want it to be bullshit. Some of this stuff gets too esoteric, but to leave out fundamentals like food and drink is a bit strange – put in indigenous stuff and leave out the kai? What's that about? There must be something about the natural bush we walked through as a nomadic tribe that had beautiful space and texture that had nothing to do with who was killed in battle there. So why can't we design an aesthetic that encapsulates the factual story rather than this oral history, a mutually agreed vision of shared values, history and culture celebrating a shared colonial past?'

WE ARE NOT talking 'complementary elements' here. Increasingly the conversation is veering towards a shared story of encounter, historic factuality and social values. The role of Ngāi Tahu in the city rebuild is being recognised as an opportunity to address more long-standing problems, exacerbated by the earthquakes but indicative of a long-standing disengagement that impacts on the wellbeing of Māori communities and *whānau* (extended family).

From behind his desk, at the former Wigram Aerodrome control tower, Mark Solomon rolls out the numbers. In 2010, for example, only a quarter of Māori school leavers were qualified to attend university compared to half of the non-Māori school leavers. 'Can we survive as a first world nation based on a workforce of labourers? Absolutely not. We have to turn our nation around.'

To meet the requirements of the city-wide rebuild Te Rūnanga o Ngāi Tahu, in partnership with the Christchurch Polytechnic Institute of Technology and Hawkins Construction, have developed He Toki ki te Rika (an adze in the hand), a Māori trades training initiative to provide entry into jobs and trade apprenticeships.'I say to all the kids on the training program, getting your ticket as a tradesman is the start but stay on the waka [canoe] with us – we'll put the training resources in front of you so you can become the supervisor. And when you are the supervisor don't get off that waka, we'll put training packages in front of you that turn you into the manager. And when you are in the manager's role, stay on that waka because we want you to become the planner.'

Similarly steering the conversation away from design, motifs, decorative elements, Arihia Bennett points to the pressing need for more housing, a result of the earthquake and the establishment of the red zone but also the loss of historic reserve land. Already Ngāi Tahu is working with the government and outside agencies to develop a model of affordable housing for families currently reliant on emergency, shared or temporary accommodation. Operating within a wraparound program of social services and pastoral care, the venture, says Bennett, is aimed not at corporate return but at social return. 'This is not about property development, it is about whānau development. It will allow communities to stay together through rentals and low cost housing, all mixed in so people feel part of that community.'

WE RETURN TO our child of the future, living in a city far different from the deflated cityscape we see today. 'I'd like them to be looking at a city that they feel in their *puku* [belly], in their heart and in their head, is part of them,' says Arihia Bennett. 'I would like that five-year-old child to have grown up knowing they are strong in their identity not only as Ngāi Tahu but as Christchurch citizens, that they are part of this city.'

To establish that sense of belonging the city cannot, will not, simply stand up, dust itself down and restore its familiar paved footprint. That footprint, broken apart by eleven thousand earthquakes, has exposed an older landscape, a landscape instrumental to the telling of the story of migration and settlement of early Māori, the resourceful gaze of Joseph Thomas, the subsequent history of cultural encounter and the physical and social development of the city. Landscapes of memory, Derek Alderman and Joshua Inwood write, 'anchor and bring historical legitimacy to the identities of social groups, but they also serve as a conduit for debating what (and whose) view of the past should be remembered' (2013). In Christchurch's council chambers and government offices, in universities and a former airport control tower, the challenge of identifying and giving tangible form to these multifarious and still unfolding stories are being debated. Through the strategic partnership of the Crown, the local council and Ngāi Tahu the result, it is hoped, will not stop at aesthetically appealing add-ons or 'complementary elements'. Nor will it settle on a static landscape mired in memory and memorialisation. Rather this debate, if given adequate time, research and opportunities for discussion, will allow for a new and distinctive reconstruction of architect Huia Reriti's 'mutually agreed vision of shared values, history and culture', a vision that anchors memory in a specific, authentic and ever-changing environment.

Sally Blundell is a freelance journalist and writer in Christchurch. In 2009 she completed her PhD, 'The Language of Silence: Speechlessness as a Response to Terror and Trauma in Contemporary Fiction', at the University of Canterbury. In 2008 her book, *Look This Way: New Zealand writers on New Zealand artists* (Auckland University Press), was short-listed for the New Zealand Book Awards.

Portrait of an artist

Photographer, documentary-maker, storyteller

Glenn Busch

Before you began writing people's stories you were a photographer, how did that happen?

For part of every year now I live on a boat. Those who know about boats, particularly old boats such as ours, understand the merit of someone who can do things. On the river where we live someone who can fix an electrical problem or resurrect a dying diesel engine is king. My father, in the time I lived with him, was the same. A man who could make things, and make things happen. A man who could put his mind and hand to any problem, nut it out, make it work, find an answer.

As much as I admire such people I cannot claim the same for myself. I'll have a go at things, as most Kiwis of my generation will, but I'm no expert. I left school at fourteen, working anywhere I could find whenever I was in need of money, spending it when I had it, on whatever took my fancy.

In the winter of 1971 I was twenty-two years old and living back in Auckland when something happened that changed the way I thought about the world, an epiphany that took my life in quite a different direction. One day, quite by chance, I found myself in room full of the most extraordinary people. Portraits, made by the wonderful photographer,

Gyula Halász, known to the world today by the name he derived from his Transylvanian birthplace, Brassaï. It would be true to say that the work I stood looking at for many hours that day astounded me and even before leaving that room, I realised a transformation had taken place.

When did you know for certain you would become a photographer?

I heard a voice behind me saying, 'Hey! Hey! Over here.' It was early morning in the Auckland fish markets. I'm surrounded by the smell of king fish, mullet, snapper. Strong fluorescent lights illuminated the whole area, bouncing off water that coated the floor, the walls, the tables and the men who work there. I turned towards the voice and standing there was a man with Stalin's moustache but not his face. He was wearing a European cap over a shy, gentle expression. He had kind, shining eyes and held a large fish. 'Take a picture of this,' he said, happy and a little bashful at the same time, and so, I did as I was told.

Later that night in the dull red light of my dark room I watched hopefully as the image slowly emerged in the developer. I remember saying, 'Yes,' very loudly, then taking a deep breath and turning around in a full circle before looking at it again. I was both very happy and surprised. This was the first picture I had made that seemed to have a life of its own. Shimmering there in the developer was the story of that moment. A picture made of silver, light and shadow. It seemed to both hint at the future, and suggest the past. His – and perhaps mine also.

When did you first start to use text?

I was always interested in listening to people's stories. My photographs have always been of people; I was never that interested in anything else. I tended to work slowly and with the cooperation of the people I photographed. Usually that entailed listening to their stories, often for many hours. A couple of years after making that first picture I was offered an exhibition. At some point during the time I was putting it together I remember having this sort of Dick Tracy fantasy: wouldn't it be great if you could look at a portrait and then press a button on the wall and out of a little speaker would come the story of their life. I even tried it in a half-hearted sort of way. I got as far as recording someone's story on a large old reel-to-reel recorder I borrowed from a friend. A couple of days later she came and retrieved it while I was out, and promptly taped over everything I'd recorded. I gave up on it then and didn't think about again until years later when I started working on my first book, *Working Men* (1984).

Why did you decide to use text and image together at that point?

As I said before, my youth had been spent labouring in various industries, mines, factories and so on, in both New Zealand and Australia. For a lot of reasons I have a great deal of respect for many of the people I worked with over that time which is why I wanted to make the book. I began at the Christchurch gas works just before it was to be pulled down. The photographs I was making there were of working men, but the reality was that they were soon to be made redundant. One of the men in the book, John Dale, I photographed while he was temporarily employed demolishing his place of work. Talking to these men, listening to what they were telling me, it became apparent that the pictures were not going to be enough, there had to be something more. Their own thoughts and feelings were the obvious answer.

Part of the power of your text is that it doesn't appear to be mediated by a third person, even though the controlling hand of the author stands behind the work.

My technique, if you can call it that, has evolved over a long time. I was always rather bored reading those strictly academic oral recordings that included questions. I'm sure they are made for good reason and with the best of intentions, it's just that I prefer stories, and in particular stories about how people feel. In the beginning I simply removed my own voice and moved things around a bit. These days I do a lot more. As anyone who has seen a transcript of an interview knows, a lot of what is said doesn't make that much sense written down. Innuendo, gesture, subtleties that abound in the spoken word are missing. The form of a discussion is a very different thing than the form of a written narrative. These days I try to construct an interesting and informative text from the words I have collected; always, of course, being careful not to change meaning or intent. My job here is much the same as when making a photograph; to try and shape what has been told to me into a readable story. One that holds both the reader's interest and conveys, in a meaningful way, what the person wanted to say.

How did the Avonside project come about?

It happened because we were asked to do it. In response to the Christchurch earthquakes, Lawrence Roberts – whose own home in the suburb of Avonside had been seriously damaged – began writing *avonsideblog*. It was an impressive undertaking that kept his friends and neighbours as well informed and as up to date as possible amid all of those devastating changes taking place in their community. I got involved, along with my two collaborators, Bridgit Anderson and Tim Veling, because Lawrence knew of the work of *Place In Time*, the Christchurch documentary project I started in 2000. He simply asked if we would record the experiences of those in his community – a community that was about to virtually disappear – and we said yes. There were no guiding principles, Christchurch is where we live and it felt like something we could and should do – so we did it. Over about a year I talked at length to around sixty people in a fairly small area. One person would introduce me to another, the person next door, a friend or relative in the next street, some I met at a street barbeque organised by Lorraine Marshall and Paul Watson. Tim photographed the changing landscape of the suburb, Bridgit made portraits of the people I spoke to.

The Christchurch Arts Festival became interested at a fairly early stage. The fact that there are no large indoor exhibition spaces presently in Christchurch helped shape the idea of large outdoor panels. It is a way of exhibiting that *Place In Time* has used before. I'm not opposed to art galleries but I like the idea of putting our work into places that give the best opportunity for large numbers of people to see it. We had one show a few years ago about a Christchurch community that we put up in their local supermarket. Forty thousand people walked past it in two weeks and a large percentage stopped to take a look. There is also a perception that people dislike large amounts of text with images in exhibitions. From my own experience over the years this is simply not true. If the text is interesting and has relevance to the viewer, they will stand for long periods of time and read it. *The Press*, Christchurch's daily newspaper, published a four-page liftout about the Avonside exhibition the day it opened.

The work on Avonside has not finished with the exhibition. Tim continues to photograph the changes as they occur in the landscape. I have been working on shaping much longer versions of the stories. What will happen to them? I'm not sure. I would like to see it become a book, I love books, but maybe it will just end up on our website, placeintime.org. Who knows? Whatever happens to the work I like to think of it as a tribute to those people who, having lost so much, were so generous in the way they have shared their own private and emotional experiences of this disaster. It is a significant gift and I am grateful to them for allowing me to be a part of it.

As told to Lloyd Jones

Glenn Busch began his working life re-treading truck and car tyres in an Auckland factory. Since that time he has lived and worked in many different places, and since the 1960s has been using a camera – and later a tape recorder – to gather the stories of people he meets along the way. He is a senior lecturer at the School of Fine Arts, University of Canterbury.

MEMOIR

Place in time

Abridged interview from the Avonside Project

Pamela 'Judy' Ross

COWLISHAW Street: I took it out on him. He wasn't even here to take it out on, but I'd go out to the cemetery and I'd curse and swear at him and say why aren't you here to help me get through this. To cuddle me. I'm by myself and trying to do it all alone. I used to get so angry.

I lived my first nineteen years in Invercargill, and then I moved up here to Christchurch. That's when I met him and I knew I'd be here for good. We had three children. Our first was a son who passed away when he was only three months old. That was…that was so terribly hard.

Then we had our two daughters and we bought our home and everything was good for a time until the arthritis came. Rheumatoid arthritis, I got it real cruel, and it's been with me now for more than thirty years. Not being able to get down on the floor and play with them, change their nappies…you wanted to be involved like any mother but that was the beginning and it only got worse.

First it was my knees, they didn't want to replace them because they said I was too young but in end they had to be replaced and then it was the hips and then it was the shoulders. In the past ten years I've had nine replacements. At the moment I'm waiting to have my toe amputated. When I go through a detector at the airport they're groping me straight away, I've got so much metal in me. You don't need to be a rocket scientist, you've only got to look at me. I've got a letter about it all but nothing stops them.

The noise when it came was quite a shock. I was in bed and only had a moment to wonder what it was. Then it started, the whole house shaking and shaking. There wasn't much I could do about it by then except stay where I was. I just pulled the blankets over my head and told myself it's got to stop sooner or later. Trouble was it seemed to go on forever. Finally it did stop but inside myself I kept going like mad. I could feel my heart racing. Of course there was no power, no torch, nothing. Finally I managed to get myself out of bed and into the front room, sat on my chair there. Every time there was an aftershock I got myself over to the doorframe and stood under it.

My neighbours from next door arrived shortly after and God it was good to see them. I felt so relieved when they came through the door. At first I'd felt like I was just on my own, you know, and that's really hard. Like I was saying before, hard not to be angry, even when it's nobody's fault. That's just being human I guess, the things we feel. Anyway, we got into the wardrobe then and found my old phone, which worked, not like those useless new ones. So that gave me something. Then some previous neighbours of mine came round and took me back to their place for a few hours.

The rest of that day was a bit unreal. You wouldn't believe it but I had a wedding to go to that day. I actually thought the wedding would have been cancelled but no, they carried on. Everyone tried really hard to focus on the bride and groom and not to talk about the earthquake. Actually it was a lovely wedding. They couldn't use the hall they'd booked but everyone went back to the bride's parents place and we had a feast. Finally we all came home. I mean everybody was just so tired. I came back to reality then. No power still and the cracks in the road… I found that all a bit difficult and eventually I took off. Went down to Invercargill and spent some time with my family there.

I WAS A bit scared coming back to Christchurch. After having that time with my family and friends, I felt the loneliness of it and, yes, to be honest, I was also a little afraid. There wasn't much choice anyway, I had to be here for my rheumatologist and this is where my partner is. I mean he's in the cemetery so it's not going to worry him, but for me it's another story. I'd never want to leave him.

The second [earthquake] when it happened was really awful. I couldn't get up. I was in a bank and had been thrown from one side of the room to the other. The whole side of my body was bruised and I'm lying there a bit dazed and it's all so random until suddenly it hits me, where's Marley? Where is she?

It was lovely, she had come from Australia to be here on her birthday and she was due to fly out on 23 February. And on the twenty-second I had just dropped her off in town to do a few things. 'Don't worry,' she said, 'I'll either walk home or get the bus.' So off I went, headed back home until I remembered I had some things to do at the bank. I'd been putting this job off and I thought, stop procrastinating, just go and do it. So I there was, at the Eastgate Mall, when it happened.

I knew my other daughter, Jade, would be all right. She works in early childhood and I knew where she'd be. That she'd have to focus on the kids, put all her energy into that, and so I felt she would be all right. But I didn't have a clue where Marley was. People were screaming, people were being carried across the road to the Medical Centre there. I tried to get her on my phone but they had all crashed. Then, as I got to my feet, I watched the whole side of The Warehouse building fall down. Everything was so much dust and rubble.

I wasn't allowed to go back to my car. I had to leave it there. In the end I managed to get a ride with a lady from the bank. She used to live round the corner from me. She got me as far as the Dallington bridge, then it was walk. Well, I couldn't do it. I had jandals and tights on and I got halfway up Retreat Road and there was another big aftershock. I grabbed this fence and I was screaming and screaming and this lovely lady came out and yells to me, 'Just hang on, just hang on.' And when it stopped she said, 'Where are you going?'

I said, 'I've got to get home. I've got to get to Cowlishaw Street. I don't know where my daughter is.'

'Okay, okay,' she said, 'I'll go and put my gumboots on and I'll take you.'

If it weren't for her I wouldn't have…well, I wouldn't have made it. She was marvellous. And when I got home my daughter was there. She'd already got home and couldn't find me. I was so pleased to see her. She'd been in Cashel Mall where all those people died. That shook me, that really shook me. Someone must have been watching over her.

AGAIN THERE WAS no power and the place was trashed. Absolutely trashed. Some kind people from the neighbourhood had come around on pushbikes looking for me. That was nice. The truth was I was feeling pretty confused. I just sat on the chair out there and I didn't know what I was going to do. I wasn't thinking straight at all. So when an old friend that lives out by Oxford rang up and said 'I'm on my way, I'm coming to get you,' I was more than happy to go. We went out there and stayed for three days until finally I flew back to Invercargill once more.

When I got back we were still on generated power. Hell, they've only just taken the portaloo away and they weren't much fun. It wasn't just the toilet situation; it was the weather as well. We had snow and every other thing you can think of. Well because of my arthritis I can't fit into shoes, and snow and jandals are not the greatest combination. I ended up having to use a bucket.

I had some counselling after that. That wasn't an easy time, total devastation really. Total grief. Like I was saying before, when my partner passed away it took forever to get my head around it, the loss of him. Then it took ages to get around losing my family home. It took forever to get used to this place and I know there's people a lot worse off than me. People lost their lives. Others have lost their homes and their businesses. I know all that, but I did need that counselling and it helped me. Helped me a lot.

Then June happened. Two [quakes] in one day and that threw me back again. The first one wasn't so bad. I managed to stay calm. The doctor had said to me, if you're sitting down and there's a shake, stay there, don't try and get out because you could fall over. 'You don't want that,' she'd said to me.

Well, after, I did go outside and I thought, I coped, you know, I coped with that one. Later I was talking to a lady walking past with her dog. 'That's the big one for the day,' she said. I was standing by the front garden there and just as she left my sister sent me a text asking how I was. I was trying to text her back when the next one came and knocked me over. I got caught up in the rose bush there and because my skin's really thin it was just ripping off like tissue paper. A young guy down the road came running over and rescued me. Got me untangled but I was a bit of a mess.

I came back inside to another shambles. Outside too, bricks had fallen off the wall. If I'd been around that side of the house, I don't know what would have happened. It made me feel sick to think about it.

I'VE BEEN HERE two years now, I've managed to settle into it and I thought, this is where I'm going to be. This is my place. But will it be now? The hardest thing is not knowing anything at all. What will happen to me? Will I be zoned green and have my home be fixed up. That is what I'm praying for. Not that I believe in praying too much but that's what I would really love to happen.

Anyway, nothing is going to happen overnight. It's going to take years and years and years. I don't know that I'll still be alive when it's finally all sorted but I'm alive now and so I'll go along and make the best I can of it.

Mental well being, that's what we need and yeah, these earthquakes have given it a bit of a kicking. I'm getting a lot better now but in the beginning no, it wasn't good. At night, when it was time to pull the drapes, I didn't like that. I wouldn't get into my pyjamas. I wouldn't even go to bed. I'd sit in that chair all night fully dressed. I'd have my emergency bag and my medications and I'd never lock the door. I was too scared to lock the door. I'd be awake looking at the clock, 4am, that's okay. Then it would be 5am. Oh well, if we have a shake now there will be people up and around. Six o'clock was even better. Then it would be 7am and I'd got through another night.

When I finally got the counselling it helped to knock that sort of thing on the head. I get to bed now and have a night's sleep. I still miss having someone to wake up to. To know that whatever comes I'd have someone to help deal with it, that would be good. But I'm trying not to let those things pull me down. I've already been down a road to hell and back. Now I want to get over this thing and get back to where I was. If I wake up with a shitty feeling I open the window and say out loud, 'You can just bugger off, get out of here.' Sometimes life can seem cruel, or at least a bit unfair. But look, while I may be going to have my toe off, I've still got two legs. I'm not in a wheelchair. I can still drive my car. I've still got a voice. Just to be able to have my wee house. To keep my independence and have my own wee home here… that's all I'd ask for. I hope I can have that.

A short time later Judy's home was relegated to the red zone. It will be demolished.

As told to Glenn Busch as part of the Christchurch documentary project, *Place in Time*.

Vincent O'Sullivan

There, being Monday morning

'So why's he dead?', the reasonable
and polite enough query as children witness
from the distance, the body moved to a van
with white sides and frosted panes.

I was born, there's no question of that.
I am in a dozen framed photos on this
table or that mantle. The clothes alter in each
picture, the face grows more attentive, you

can tell what school from the crest on my cap,
you can tell the girl beside me with the wind
in her veil like an angry invisible bee
is very happy that morning. Where? is another

of the many reasonable questions. 'You've got
me there,' I say. There is a copper beech
bigger than the house it broods over, I have
sometimes thought of it as caring, which

of course is my fantasising, a tree being simply
that. There, at another time, was a jetty,
a village with five syllables in its long
Welsh name. There were good and bad places.

There was sitting in a car watching children scamper
to another car, that was the saddest *there*;
and walking by a river, its broad dark current
bearing chunks of pumice from volcanoes,

a woman once said were like skulls in a hurry.
From a hundred examples I might give you
I select a handful at random, a sample
of what may occur on particular days.

I appreciate that addresses, next of kin,
official forms – they are yours to attend, I'm
sorry. The last witness, only this morning,
walking a spark of pure temperament

on an orange lead, her glancing back,
walking on, 'getting on with life'. Is that
an answer, now I'm discovered? A considered
decision. Don't let the children see.

Not that they spoke of it back then

She would tell him, 'Put your shirt back on,'
this inarticulate man, slow as a child,
slower as a man, who picked flowers coming
home from school, who kept milk bottles
with bursts of orange shrapnelling membritia
on his window sill, that's when he was a man.
She'd tell him that about covering himself
when he scythed the paddock smooth enough for bowls,
not giving a damn to be honest about it,
his kindness to animals, his gift with children,
the gentle stories he told that bored her –
she wanted roughness and hardness and if he wanted more
well fine, whatever it was. What she'd tell him
though, 'The visitors are here in the driveway,'
and he'd know all right why she told him, his moving
gradually towards the shed, sweat gleaming
so much more than Christ's on the parlour wall.

Vincent O'Sullivan is a novelist, poet, short story writer, biographer and editor. His poetry collection *Us, Then* was published by Victoria University Press in 2013, and his new stories, *The Families*, is due early 2014. He lives in Dunedin.

First, build your hut

New Zealand's missing great nineteenth century novel

Lydia Wevers

WHERE is our Marcus Clarke? Henry Handel Richardson? Rolf Boldre-wood, Ada Cambridge, Tasma, Henry Kingsley, Joseph Furphy? Why don't we have the rich history of three-deckers and popular fiction that adorns the literary history of Victorian Australia? In the late 1890s a clerk on a large sheep station in the North Island wrote in one of his many letters to the local paper that it was high time someone wrote a 'really good novel of life and manners in New Zealand'. But literary history as it was taught to students of my generation maintained that New Zealand literature did not begin until the 1930s – 1932 to be precise – when a group of young men in Auckland published a magazine called *Phoenix* and ushered in literary nationalism. In any case the novel was not the preferred genre of the fiction writers of the 1930s who, following Henry Lawson and the Golden Nineties, liked the short story. It has taken us till 2013 to get a big, fat, juicy nineteenth century novel – I refer of course to Eleanor Catton's Booker Prize-winning *The Luminaries*.

What was actually written in the nineteenth century in New Zealand was long regarded as embarrassing, as Jane Stafford and Mark Williams have observed in their re-evaluation of nineteenth century New Zealand literature, *Maoriland: New Zealand Literature, 1872–1914* (Victoria University Press, 2007). Even with a fresh eye, it is still hard to find more than the occasional halfway decent nineteenth-century novel in the slim shelf of bad novels, before the end of the Victorian era. The scarcity of novels in nineteenth-century New Zealand is one of those puzzles that makes you speculate about cultural temperament and the history of colonisation. There is no doubt that New Zealanders were reading voraciously in the nineteenth century. As JE Traue commented in his 2007 essay, 'The Public Library Explosion in Colonial New Zealand', the rate of book ownership was high: 'the number of volumes per head of population between 1873 and 1896 varied between one book to 1.72 people and one book to 3.05 people, more than for the colony of Victoria, the richest in Australia with a much larger population, in the late nineteenth century.'

But what New Zealanders were reading was not novels written by other New Zealanders, or about New Zealand, possibly because there were hardly any to choose from and what there was still does not attract much admiration. The novel generally agreed to be the first written and published in and about New Zealand, Henry Stoney's *Taranaki: A Tale of the War* (1861), was a crudely fashioned tale that according to Joan Stevens exploited local dispatches and mixed them with a 'violently sensational' plot. After all, as Stevens caustically asked, with J Fenimore Cooper, H Rider Haggard and GA Henty to copy, what could go wrong?

> You needed only the hero, preferably of officer caste, a Māori princess
> or a settler's daughter or both, tribal jealousies, a tohunga or two,
> some military skirmishes, a few bloodcurdling yells, and the trick was
> done. Mix well with muskets and inaccurate Māori, and serve up to a
> London publisher. *The New Zealand Novel 1860–1965* (1966)

Most novels written about New Zealand in the 1880s and '90s are depressingly full of these 'local colour' formulas. Of course there's Samuel Butler's *Erewhon* (1872), but can a utopian novel of ideas really be claimed for New Zealand literature in the way that *For the Term of his Natural Life* (1874) or *Such is Life* (1903) are Australian? *Erewhon*, an almost-anagram of *nowhere*, is clearly not aiming for an actual country. George Chamier's *Philosopher Dick* (1891) is, according to Joan Stevens, the 'most mature' of New Zealand novels before the end of the century, but this 'shapeless holdall' has never been a household name, confined rather to conference papers and graduate students. It is not until after the turn of the century that some of the better-known 'nineteenth-century' novels appear, such as William Satchell's *The Greenstone Door* (1914) and Edith Searle Grossman's *The Heart of the Bush* (1910), a writer and a novel rediscovered by feminism.

Does a nation get the literature it deserves? The rest of this essay will fly some kites about why New Zealand has a famine and Australia a feast.

One of the crucial differences between our countries is the eighteenth century. The invasion of Australia by the British navy in 1788, nineteen years after Cook, a year before the French Revolution and during the terms of office of Thomas Jefferson and Benjamin Franklin, means that when Marcus Clarke began to publish *His Natural Life* (later published as *For the Term of His Natural Life*) in the *Australian Journal* in 1870 there was already almost a century of local colonial history to draw on, and a century of the novel. As novels grew in importance and length during the first half of the nineteenth century, so did the appetite of readers for fiction, and both these developments were synchronous with the growth of the Australian colonies. Those who arrived on the rocky shores of Sydney Cove on 26 January 1788 had varying degrees of literacy, but they brought with them their powerful and developing print culture. Perhaps more importantly, they also brought eighteenth-century attitudes towards people. Slavery was not abolished for another forty-five years, and its bedfellow, the forced exile of unwanted people, continued even longer. Violent conflict, both internal to the punitive authoritarianism and class warfare of the penal system and external, in the treatment of Aboriginal and Torres Strait Islander people, fills the early colonial history of Australia. Conflict is always richly full of narrative possibility. Add to this the serial publication of the three-decker novel, which was perfectly suited for long-range transport, and the boom of bestselling 'sensation' novels in the 1860s, which vastly grew both the readership and the income of authors, and the market was ready for the fruits of Australia's imaginative soil – convicts, goldfields and bushrangers. The long eighteenth century might have ended by the time Marcus Clarke's novel hit the booksellers, but the penal colony of New South Wales had participated in it, and many of its ideas and systems had influenced Australian development, such as the adoption of Jeremy Bentham's panopticon at Parramatta Prison and at Port Arthur. Clarke, a journalist, based *His Natural Life* on convict letters, diaries and official reports he researched for a series of articles on convict days, and visited Port Arthur where parts of the novel are set. It was published in three volumes in London in 1875 and sold almost 45,000 copies over the next twenty years.

SO WHY DIDN'T the New Zealand mix of goldfields, migration and war have a similar result? There seems to be enough fodder in the events of the New Zealand Wars and rags-to-riches accounts of goldmining to fuel the stamina required for a long novel, but the New Zealand novel of the nineteenth century is a far punier thing than its trans-Tasman cousin. The best known novel about the New Zealand Wars was in fact written by an Australian – *War to the Knife* (1899) by Rolf Boldrewood – and while there are a variety of novels set on the goldfields, from Benjamin Farjeon's *Shadows in the Snow* (1866), to another Australian, Vincent Pyke's *Wild Will Enderby* (1873), none of them achieved the length, circulation or fame of *His Natural Life*. A scattering of romances, like *A Rolling Stone* (1886) by Clara Cheeseman, a three-volume pioneering love story, are among the slim pickings on the New Zealand scene. Very few of the novels which Joan Stevens lists in her 1961 history are still read, and it is notable that Stafford and Williams's revisionist *Māoriland* does not reclaim any of them. Instead they extend the nineteenth century to 1914 and feature Edith Searle Grossmann, Katherine Mansfield and Henry Lawson. The novel makes a start on life for earnest only in the twentieth century.

Was the New Zealand colonial temper more attuned to practical rather than imaginative engagement? Certainly some versions of our twentieth-century national character, such as Barry Crump's a 'good keen man', the taciturn repressed men in Frank Sargeson's stories or the ways in which we celebrate tight-lipped heroes would suggest so. Another factor might be scale. By the time of Federation in 1901 the six self-governing Australian colonies had rich histories of their own and some regional variation. New Zealand was the seventh possible member, and one of the smallest potential states, and though it promoted itself as a whole world in miniature – a wonderland of fjords, mountains, hot and cold lakes, volcanoes and thermal pools in one easily traversed country – perhaps scenery didn't do as much for fiction as floggings and chains. New Zealand also had a smaller, more distinctively English and Scots (as opposed to Irish) population and prided itself on its many resemblances to the Mother Country, in Charles Hursthouse's phrase, the 'Britain of the South'. But was this our undoing? Did we need more miscreants, adventurers, and ne'er-do-wells? More of Captain Starlight and less of Edward Gibbon? More Irish ballads and more blarney? It is hard to escape the conclusion that New Zealand was an altogether tamer, more parochial and strait-laced place, and yet...

If I ask what a shelf of New Zealand Victorian novels might have looked like, there is the world of bestselling nineteenth-century fiction to play with. What if New Zealanders had produced their own versions of some of the runaway hits of the 1860s? How about *Lady Barker's Secret,* by PE Gammon, a lady novelist required to earn her living by her pen after the untimely death of her gold-prospecting husband. It is a novel about an English gentlewoman living on a high country sheep station with her second husband. One night a shepherd arrives at the door in the middle of snowstorm with a child in his arms. They are taken in and the Barkers, who have no children, take over the care of the child, a little girl called Nell. Eventually it emerges that the child is Lady Barker's illegitimate granddaughter, born to the daughter she abandoned as a child. Plot resemblances to a famous novel of the 1860s are entirely coincidental. And perhaps the next on the shelf is *Wiremu Twist* a three-decker by a freelance journalist, Roderick Stickens. The novel relates the story of a small Māori boy abducted by sealers who escapes the ship in Sydney only to land in a gang of thieves. Taught to be an accomplished thief himself, he is eventually apprehended and shipped to Norfolk Island where he meets, in the penitentiary, one of his iwi. They break out together, commandeer a whaleboat and sail it to New Zealand where they reunite with their whānau. Or how about Willie Hollins's *The Greenstone,* a novel in which a sacred piece of greenstone is stolen from its Māori owners by an avaricious ethnographer. Bringing bad luck to everyone who comes into possession of it, it also inspires tremendous greed, revealing the shallowness of colonial society, and its ruthless dismissal of what it perceives as inferior cultures. And a different literary history could have been ours as well. As the 'well-known scholar and historian' Dr Digby Cromwell might have written in his 'masterly' history of nineteenth century New Zealand fiction, *To the Genre Born* (1973):

> These three novels, *Lady Barker's Secret, Wiremu Twist* and *The Greenstone* illustrate how the great patterns of nineteenth century fiction can transfer across vast oceans and be reinvented with all their generic characteristics intact, drama, adventure, sensation and the deepening plot, but subtly transformed, like Prospero's island, by strange airs. The family separations, colonial encounters and ethnological cupidity of early colonists are magisterially described in these major works, rightfully claimed as the beginning of an important new literature, and now canonical works read by every schoolchild and university student in New Zealand.

Instead, our actual colonists were carefully selected by 'systematic colonisation' and perhaps too focused on making money from their small holdings (or their large sheep stations) to have the energy or emotion for writing big novels. All they wanted after a hard day's dagging or clearing bush was to make dirty thumbmarks on the pages of the newest H Rider Haggard and fall asleep by the fire with a cup of moonshine. Perhaps if Eleanor Catton's astrological murder mystery, *The Luminaries,* set in the frontier West Coast town of Hokitika in 1866, replete with prostitutes, Chinese goldminers and scheming men had been published in 1893 instead of 2013, it might have joined the bestseller lists with *Lady Audley's Secret, Oliver Twist* and *The Greenstone.* But it seems that slow-to-burn New Zealanders have taken more than a century to start filling up the bookshelf with the riches of our Victorian past.

Many of the things New Zealanders don't like about Australians – brashness, in-your-face competitiveness, a gloating arrogance – are also attitudes which in the nineteenth century allowed for big ambitions and big clashes and also big novels. And some of the things Australians don't like about New Zealanders – our genteel pretensions, sense of superiority about our origins, smugness – are also inhibiting to big acts of self-expression. But we also did a lot of plain hard work in this deeply forested landscape, such as chopping down the Ninety Mile Bush Lawson describes near Pahiatua, though it is work many of us wish we hadn't done now. And we also spent a lot of time and emotion, and not always in good ways, on living, marrying and warring with Māori. Perhaps the story of the missing New Zealand novel in the nineteenth century is not to do with the cramping effects of bourgeois ambitions rather than the dramatic potential of floggings and chains but the energy expended on the heart of the bush. Did that take all the imagination and energy there was? Wasn't there time to look up and out to the vast distances beyond the present, or to imagine stories that reached out from the point of contact? Didn't anyone have time to put pen to paper over the many months it takes, even at Trollope's rate of two and half thousand words a day before breakfast, to push out that missing three-decker? You can only write the novel after you have built the hut to write it in.

For more on the changing face of New Zealand expression, read 'The New Zealand voice' by Laurie Bauer in the e-book *Pacific Highways: Volume 2*, available free at www.griffithreview.com

Lydia Wevers is the director of the Stout Research Centre for New Zealand Studies at Victoria University of Wellington. She has published widely on Australian and New Zealand literature. Her most recent book is *Reading on the Farm: Victorian Fiction and the Colonial World* (Victoria University Press, 2010).

Cliff Fell

Encounter above the Hurunui

A cloud river above the Hurunui
and on the plane there are two Māori bros –
one sitting with me until he could shift
to the seat just behind with his brother,
long lost, of course, they've not met up in ten
years and now happen to clamber into
this cabin almost together. They're both
in love with Hope, the flight attendant: Well,
why not, who wouldn't be?…she's got to be
the prettiest flightie I've seen in years,
the first of them says, a wisecracker with
his well-timed one-liners, he was down in
Lyttleton last night doing stand-up, an
open mic, I should be on TV, says
he, and he should, but is a fisherman
who works for Sealord, goes out on the Dawn
Something, whose skipper is Chubby Someone
or other, a good man, he says, the cloud
breaking up as we head north across the is
of the island – the is of it. I've got
my sunglasses on for the first time in
weeks and Hope is now serving us bottles
of water, I saw you make eyes at her
behind those sunnies, Haddock says – his name,
the first one who was sitting next to me –
as she passes to the back, But, she's mine,
Cliff – I've lived in hope of her for years, and
now she's found me, you're not stealing her, mate,
Aue, the younger one says, you're dreaming,
bro, you haven't a hope in hell, Nor heaven,
for that matter, I add, as she passes
back to the front, In fact, you're hopeless, pal.
Aue, he grins and laughter falls away
through the fuselage to the bony folds
of mountains below, where we gaze down at
the line of a long white road, the dust an

etching of someone's intention to move
across the big land, it must be the man
who helped himself to what had been before,
who took block and tackle, a new straw hat
and two teams of oxen to break the place
open, fetched water from the crooked tarn
and wondered at times where it was going,
this road – or where you are going, poem,
or where we're all going, the big question
that no one can answer, not the shadow
of the plane, a black cross that moves over
the land like a gun-sight, nor the white clouds
of river broken up, nor my mother
who walks with painful awkward grace, Did she
recognise you, Haddock asks, who's learned that
I'm back from seeing her, Yes, Well that's good,
so I guess she just farts when she walks, right? –
Of course not, I say, though sometimes it's true,
as he well knows and I cannot deny,
so laugh with him and his dark laughing eye,
the great city of his audacity,
as he gestures down at the land's ascent,
says: It gives the meaning to being here,
mate, or something like that, he who's going
soon to sea, his brother to court for gun
trouble, It's you and Tama Iti, āe,
I say, and I like Jesus with these two
jokers at my shoulders, going with them
in this cruciform plane, we're all counting
cars on the highway now, the shelterbelts
of Wakefield, we are going to the end of
the runway, we're gazing at Hope's face.

Cliff Fell's two collections of poems are *The Adulterer's Bible* (2003) and *Beauty of the Badlands* (2008), both from Victoria University Press. The first was awarded the Adam Prize and the Jessie Mackay Prize for Poetry. He lives near Motueka in the upper part of Te Wai Pounamu and teaches at Nelson Marlborough Institute of Technology.

ESSAY

Simply by sailing in a new direction

The search for Storyland

Kate De Goldi

IN October 2012 several dozen writers from New Zealand appeared at the Frankfurt Book Fair where New Zealand had been nominated as the 'country of honour'. We had been gathered for a series of literary events, part of a full-throated piece of cultural diplomacy which would, it was argued, assist increased sales of New Zealand books and promote trade and tourism.

It was interesting being amongst it all – the cultural presentations, the operatic pavilion display, the anxious literary egos swelling and dying a dozen times a day – interesting and often unsettling. The gap between the writing act and the representation of one's self and work at a festival is usually disorienting. But this was self plus work plus, somehow, *the national literature* at the biggest and most glamorous book sale in the world. The stakes felt both high and absurd.

The panels convened addressed key ingredients in NZ literature – the short story as a quintessential NZ form, the preoccupation with the landscape, isolation, the gothic social substrata – and a contemporary snapshot was gamely attempted, too. It was hard to know what the Europeans in the audiences made of it all. For a New Zealand writer participating and observing, it seemed both spirited and a little splintered. Sometimes, listening in the audience or expatiating on stage, I experienced an odd disassociation. What, if anything, *did* we and our work add up to collectively? A fluent narrative of the national literature was impossible because the writers gathered could never represent such a thing – if such a thing existed. And if such a thing existed it was liable to have the whiff of dogma…

Nevertheless, reaching for some organising principal, some cohesive description or distillation of our literature was a constant tic. More than once in print and broadcast prior to the Festival I had offered the metaphor of the braided river. The Waimakariri's varied passage from mountain to sea corresponded very tidily, I suggested, to the history of our literature. The current polyphony of voices, themes and forms matched perfectly the river's voluptuous spread and division across the Canterbury Plains.

At Frankfurt I developed a ruthlessly glib version of Braided River Theory even as I regretted its broad sweep submerging nuance and singularity, and as I blushed at the very Kiwi inevitability of a geographic analogy. Like all metaphors it recedes a little on close scrutiny but it did the job well enough, I suppose.

Back at home in front of the blank page a *national* literature is usually the last thing on one's mind. And, despite my generally enthusiastic contributions to the collective presentation of the NZ story, the Frankfurt expedition offered a powerful reminder that one's writing life and imaginative urges are at times only loosely connected to the grand cultural narrative. The sites from which imaginative exploration might lift off are not often where a country's best-loved literary orthodoxies might have them. Ironically, this was pointed up beautifully at Frankfurt in a panel devoted to a celebration of the life and work of Margaret Mahy.

WHICHEVER NARRATIVE OF New Zealand literature one subscribes to, one thing about the country's writing seems inarguable: it is a heavily realist tradition. There have been little outbreaks of surrealism, thin seams of spiritual writing, and a strain of tall story – or fable – lingers in some children's writing; the overwhelming mode though – particularly in fiction – is realism. The novels of Janet Frame – by common consent the country's greatest writer – have an intensity and preoccupation with language's freighting that brings them close to a kind of altered reality but that is more a function of her own and her characters' fevered interiority than a true departure from the world as we know it. In a Frame novel we are still in the material world, however fragile our grip.

Mid-century children's fiction also ploughed a determinedly social-realist-jolly-pastoral furrow, and even with the maturing of children's fiction in the 1980s and a body of work that moved beyond adventure and romance clichés or the name checking of native fauna and flora, still the imagined world was a resolutely concrete one. The brightest stars in this new wave were four writers born in the 1930s – Jack Lasenby, Joy Cowley, Maurice Gee and – the supernova – Margaret Mahy, all of whom have spoken often over the years about the powerful influence of childhood experience on their later work and the relationship between childhood *reading* and their own writing. There are many correspondences, too, between Lasenby, Cowley and Gee's writing for children – small town settings, lurking threat in the natural world, unreliable adults, to name just some – and their fictions have a depth and stylistic sophistication that sets them apart from other work of the period. In particular – and this perhaps sealed their appeal with librarians, teachers and parents – their work is planted in a recognisable, often provincial, New Zealand: bush, beach, mangrove swamp, rural town, kitchen table…

At Frankfurt, though, it was the work of Margaret Mahy (who had died some months earlier) that provoked the most interest. The panel convened to discuss her legacy shared the stage with Mahy herself, who was there on film. As ever she was the best representative of her work, and flush with insights on the anarchic lives of story and language. The panel (three authors for children, including myself) on the other hand, struggled, I thought, to get out from under the usual pieties about the writer. A reluctance to wrestle with the body of work – to go beyond the facts of Mahy's biography, or enthusiastic anecdotes about her generosity and whimsicality – has been marked amongst Mahy's immediate colleagues: the children's writing and reviewing community. It has always struck me as odd that the most frequently used epithet for Mahy is 'NZ's most-*loved* children's writer.' However true, it seems a default position and is more to do with the person than the work. So it was on the Frankfurt panel. This is in part due to a general hesitancy – or inability – to engage critically, to move beyond description, plot rehearsal and age recommenda-tion, that bedevils the NZ children's book world. But I think a more likely reason for the evasion is the paradox Mahy and her body of work represent: New Zealand's most famous writer is also a writer whose work is in so many respects ardently un-New Zealand – or at least ardently not the New Zealand we have, over time, assumed is the proper subject and setting for our fiction.

Mahy's initial efforts to be published in New Zealand tell the story most graphically. Her early subject matter (imaginative adventure, magical transformations) and settings (meadows, forests, the ocean blue; childhood); a tone that was by turns lyrical, buoyant, astonished; stories and poems with a parade of pirates, witches, giddy librarians, wild animals, monsters, kings and crumpled parents; the sheer vaudevillian energy of the whole – all these ensured that she was, in a very real sense, unrecognisable to mid-'60s trade publishers as a *New Zealand* writer. The cultural nationalist conversation of the previous decades had solidified to a consensus around the proper job of New Zealand literature: reflecting the country's remoteness, its landscape, and the people moving about in it right back at the reading public. Mahy, characteristically, had a wry acceptance of the difficult prospect she presented to publishers: she was a writer with a 'fault line' running through her, a writer who lived in New Zealand but whose imagination had been ignited by 'another mongrel country where the Wild West and forest of wolves and lions melted into each other,' – in other words, Storyland.

'I am made and formed by what I read,' Mahy said, very firmly, to me once in an interview. That formative reading childhood was exactly what you might expect of a New Zealander through the '30s and '40s: an occasional New Zealand novel or poem, but, overwhelmingly, the European tradition – nursery rhyme, fairy tale, adventure story, epic poetry, nonsense verse and the classics of English literature. Later fantasy from Tolkein, Mervyn Peake, Angela Carter and others were important for Mahy, but a long view of her work suggests it was the co-ordinates of fairy tale, the philosophic under-pinnings of myth and legend, and the explosive power of magic that really formed her imaginative DNA. Storyland – supercharged or enchanted – was, paradoxically, the place where the important moments of *human* thinking and growth could be most thrillingly explored: magic was a literary agent enabling what would become Mahy's fictional stock-in-trade: characters experiencing astonishment, transcendence and, above all, transformation.

As a reader she was 'committed to otherness;' as a writer, her own versions of otherness – teenage enchanters in suburbia, ordinary families with spellbound children, malevolent sorcerers come to town – represented *imaginatively* true ways of being. They were the most convincing vehicles for her exploration of the deeper parts of her psyche and the profound myster-ies presented by 'real' life: love and disappointment, guilt, exaltation, small human weaknesses, the puzzle of family and the conundrums posed by talent and power.

NEW ZEALAND WRITING not being given much to this kind of form or subject matter, and largely deaf to stories without obvious local colour or geography, it is small wonder that Mahy's initial offerings to publishers met with bafflement. A novel, story or poem, 'dealing direct with life,' was a more recognisable – and marketable – proposition. Direct dealing with life is one of a number of slightly imperious edicts throughout poet Allen Curnow's introduction to *A Book of New Zealand Verse* (1945). This piece and the introduction to Curnow's 1960 anthology have the heat and purposefulness of manifesto and were received as such by a writing and publishing community keen to identify and demarcate the emerging culture. We have 'lived so long at a low intensity,' wrote Curnow. And, 'in New Zealand we lack capacity for the tragic emotions, pity, wonder, or terror.' The work Margaret Mahy submitted regularly throughout the '60s offered a startling counter to that writ. *Wonder* – or astonishment (a word she used constantly) – was the very fuel that powered her writing engine. But until 1969 the only publication able to accommodate her singular voice was the *NZ School Journal* and even its editors had to go into battle on occasions with others in the School Publications office.

The fairy tale structures and characters Mahy used so often as prompts and grids for her later novels were also the configurations she used to explain her own life. An insightful teacher was 'the magician who gave me something to live up to. I will never forget the fairy-tale feeling of being recognised at last for what I felt I was – a writer and a reader...' Similarly, reading in 1969 the letter from Franklin Watts in New York offering to publish simultaneously five of her stories as picture books, made her feel 'like Cinderella entering the ballroom and being seen at last in her true beauty.' International recognition having the peculiar hold that it does in New Zealand that particular transformation enabled Mahy's proper entry into the reading public's consciousness; thirty years later, with an extraordinary list of global publications, two Carnegie Medals, and scores of highly successful early reader titles, she was a household name.

In fact, by the 1980s when Mahy was able to devote time to full-length novels, a door had opened between Storyland and New Zealand. Her protagonists were planted in a recognisable geology or cityscape (Banks Peninsula; the outer suburbs of Christchurch), though on the page places are subtly transfigured – a humming animism is always just beneath the surface of a Mahy narrative. The metaphoric possibilities offered by the Peninsula's volcanic crater and the Port Hills are superbly exploited, for example, in *Catalogue of the Universe* (1985) and *The Tricksters* (1986). In *24 hours* (2000) Christchurch's grid-patterned inner city is discernable, though the story and its subtext are riffing joyously on *Alice in Wonderland*. Suburbia had been a lively hunting ground for Mahy in her story collections and novellas – crowded of course with dragons, witches, magicians, and pirates – but now, writing at length, she found more gristle there: families wrangling the past, disturbed teenagers, venal public figures, feckless or disturbed parents, predatory strangers.

All the same, in customary New Zealand literary terms, and notwithstanding the absorption of the local, there is still something formidably *other* about Mahy's longer fictions. They are tightly plotted and full of texture, the pyrotechnic and musical word play of the shorter fiction gives way to a more business-like sentence making. But the moments of crisis and understanding have the intensity of operatic arias and duets – with all the pity and terror and wonder allegedly disavowed by the culture Mahy lived in. And form is perfectly congruent with content – and perhaps this is the heart of the work's difference – because Mahy's subjects are the big existential questions. Her stories are page turning and immersive because of what is happening to the well-drawn characters, but also because they are always conducting arguments with philosophical and moral weight. And not only are these novels unabashedly intellectual – a rarity in NZ fiction for young people – they also insist on the supernatural as both a legitimate device and subject for a novelist.

I READ MY first Mahy young adult novel, *The Changeover* (1985), when I was twenty-five and was thoroughly disconcerted by it, even faintly outraged. I still have the copy with my peevish underlinings and marginalia; I would toss it out but it's such an entertaining example of youthful hubris and the fall-out from a heady romance with literary doctrine. Thirty years later it is so clear to me that when confronted with Laura Chant and the boy witch, Sorry Carlisle, my own internal cultural fault-line staged a major spasm.

Like Margaret Mahy I, too, was decisively formed by my childhood reading – a torrent of books from the trans-Atlantic children's literature renaissance of the postwar period. From an early age I longed, in my secret self, somehow to permanently inhabit those fictional worlds and in time I understood that this would have to be done by writing, by emulating – in a way that was categorically my own – the subjects and sentences of those writers. My identification with that literature was so total that I shifted my 400-odd children's titles from flat to flat throughout my late adolescence and twenties. Since my early teens I had also been hoovering up literature for adults from around the world, but it was the children's fiction that operated as an orienting scripture, a Talmud I repaired to regularly for instruction and which, I am quite sure, shaped my true writing self. Aside from the occasional school text however, until I was twenty-one, New Zealand literature was unknown country. In the early '80s I began studying it at university and, almost overnight, with all the conviction of a late convert, I became a card-carrying literary nationalist. This was all very fine – one should know the literature of one's country – but, being a great one then for a binary view of things, an embrace of 'New Zealand' seemed somehow to require a rejection of whatever the country was I'd emigrated from. I sold all my children's books and contemplated Frank Sargeson. And when, with my newly sovietised lens, I first read *The Changeover* I could only see it as fiction that failed properly to represent the apparent verities of NZ writing I now so zealously championed.

These days, when I re-read the book I see what I couldn't allow myself to acknowledge at the time: it is a very fine addition to a strong tradition of children's speculative fiction. Mahy, like other great exponents of the form – Jane Langton and Madeleine L'Engle in the US, William Mayne, Penelope Farmer and Diana Wynne Jones in the UK (whose work I had been bred on) – had fused the philosophic and the supernatural with the quotidian; she had let loose the unearthly in suburbia in order to explore matters that puzzled and propelled her: the nature of courage and sacrifice; the invention of self; the question of evil. Twenty years of writing has allowed me to properly understand that one's writing genetics aren't to be denied. One is born into – and *reads* one's way into – a country of the imagination, and sometimes the topography of that place has only a little in common with the place one physically inhabits. As I have moved circuitously back to my own imaginative land – childhood – so, too, have I seen clearly and greatly appreciated the contours and morphology of Margaret Mahy's.

OF COURSE, SOME writers have the coordinates of their imaginative world well fixed early on; they know themselves and their intent and they do without the messy business of exile and repatriation. They recognise the other inhabitants, too. When Elizabeth Knox read *The Changeover,* at the same age and in the same year I did, she knew at once that Margaret Mahy was a writer with immense significance for her and her own writing life.

Even if Knox had never spoken or written about Mahy as an important imaginative lodestone it is abundantly clear once you read her fiction, particularly her young adult novels, that Mahy's voice and subject matter and the speculative form she worked within have been a powerful influence. Knox has a quite singular voice and is propelled to the page by her own unique cluster of psychological and intellectual preoccupations. On the page, though, and in her broader fictional intent, there are intriguing echoes of the older writer, not the least being Knox's sustained exploration of the immaterial and a notion of a kind of magic that has substance, that is, in one sense, profoundly real.

Knox's description of the effect on her of *The Changeover* and *The Haunting* (1982) is revealing: 'with Margaret I understood I'd met a writer who was *for* me. She was a New Zealander and, reading those two books, I felt that she was building a room in New Zealand literature where I wanted to go, be, hang out, get comfortable.' She had no difficulty seeing Mahy as a New Zealand writer – quite the reverse – and it was important to her that there existed *in* New Zealand an exemplar of the kind of literary fantasy she herself wanted to write. No fault-line for Elizabeth Knox.

Why do you think Margaret was important? I asked Knox once, when we were discussing Mahy's effect on the writing culture. 'Because she was *there*,' she said, with immediate and characteristic conviction. For Knox it was entirely personal. Mahy was a necessary compass, an instrument of orientation within her own country that enabled her to set about her particular fictional project with confidence.

Knox grew up thoroughly aware of New Zealand literature and its exponents. Her father, Ray Kox, was the editor of *New Zealand's Heritage,* a significant social history of the 1970s. Writers and Wellington intellectuals were on the periphery of her family life. Moreover, writing things down and making story was a fundamental family habit. Building fantastical worlds in a Wellington backyard or flat was a perfectly straightforward and integrated act. When Knox read *The Changeover* she was already at work on her first novel, a ghost story making assured use of the Nelson landscape. Recognising Margaret Mahy as a home-grown literary ancestor sealed the deal for future work.

That first novel, *After Z-hour* (1987), is a fascinating read in the light of the body of work that follows. The story has a persuasive realist setting: the bush and weather and buildings of rural Nelson are powerfully evoked. Six characters needing shelter for various reasons assemble in an old house with a history, their back-stories, motivations and interactions duly revealed. So far, so familiarly New Zealand. But where the novel – and I think the author's real interest – roars into life is with the troubled ghost (a World War I soldier) and more powerfully still with the man-boy, Kelfie, a kind of medium for the ghost and the first of many dangerous and alluring young men, real and unearthly, that walk moodily through the pages of Knox's novels. Interestingly, the house where most of the action occurs has a 'repelling' quality – it seems at times nearly to disappear from view, to be, in some way, unavailable to the folk who need shelter. In *Mortal Fire* (2013), Knox's most recent young adult novel, a fully realised – and fully fantastical – version of both house and erotically charged boy-enchanter are at the heart of the story's important moments of self-knowledge, courage and transformation.

Knox's realist outings are shapely and resonant – her autobiographical trilogy of novellas is one of the most intense and haunting evocations of childhood yet published in New Zealand – but it is as if her deepest fictional propulsions meet their proper form once she launches into full-blooded literary fantasy and the roll call of unearthly characters are set free: angels, vampires, golems, magicians and young people with nascent artistic or magical potential. From *The Vintner's Luck* (1998), onwards and particularly with the three young adult novels set in her invented republic, Southland – a re-imagined version of New Zealand – the Mahy inheritance is very evident.

In a sense, Knox's Southland novels mirror and clarify and extend the Mahy project. As Mahy's slightly angled version of Christchurch suburbia and its sometimes magically endowed inhabitants offered her the best way to move around her real subject matter, so Southland – the large Pacific island with a history and environment that echoes New Zealand's, but where magic is part of the fabric – enables Knox to continue her abiding fascination with both what it is to be human *and* everything the immaterial might mean in the human world. It is as if – to me at least – having a second writer so determinedly argue ideas through fantastical fiction I have – and in a New Zealand context – come to understand better the first writer's true endeavour. Knox has achieved that which she wished for when she first read Mahy: 'it was Margaret's *thinking* that I wanted to be able to beat into myself, or isolate myself with. Her thinking – always unusual, and always right.'

It is always hard – maybe perilous – to try and capture in words the particular music – the timbre and rhythm – a writer makes on the page. But I have been struck often over the years by a tonal similarity in Mahy and Knox. Or to put it another way, a similar musculature in their sentence making and paragraphs. I think it is something to do with *urgency* – the urgency of the ideas at play and the characters' (and their writers') most urgent need to communicate them. There are few poetical effects in the sentences; the words are less for the ear than the alert mind. It is Wagner rather than Schubert, a powerful build-up of energy rather than beautiful melody over paragraph and page; precise and elemental language that gathers a weight and force as the critical idea is pressed home. There is nothing like it anywhere else in New Zealand fiction. In Knox's work this effect is amplified by the number of individual italicised words scattered throughout the text. It is like someone tugging harder and harder at your sleeve while they explain something very important, and from time to time pushing a finger hard into your flesh to emphasise the point. 'Margaret's *thinking*,' indeed.

ELIZABETH KNOX WAS at the Frankfurt Book Fair, too – in person, but also in the film shown of Margaret Mahy during the panel. Knox and Mahy were in conversation – an exchange, however abbreviated, that did what the panel could not: here were two writers who understood each other in a vital way. Knox's questions of Mahy were mindful of the general audience but still they proceeded from the inside out, from a deep understanding of Mahy cultivated by lengthy prospecting in the same territory and with the same intent.

In all the crush and fever and ambiguity of the Frankfurt/New Zealand enterprise, and the wondering then and later just what a country's literature added up to or if there should be any calculation going on at all, it was good to think about those two New Zealanders who were writers, though not precisely New Zealand writers – in the way none of us is precisely – rather writers who have charted determinedly solo voyages, coasting in New Zealand waters but spending much time in Storyland and Southland too; and importantly, from time to time, *sighting* each other.

Knox's first Southland novel, *Dreamhunter* (2006), is dedicated to Margaret Mahy, an acknowledgement of their shared territory and purpose, and with gratitude perhaps for Mahy *being there*. And Knox's delight in Mahy and her work was thoroughly reciprocated. Mahy reviewed *After Z-Hour* with unqualified enthusiasm: 'An astonishing book, full of care, concentration, insight and power.' Concentration, insight and power are words of consequence in the Mahy lexicon, but 'astonishing' is the real oil. Here was a matter for wonder. A fellow traveller arrived in her writing country. When I think of that moment – Mahy reading Knox's first novel, meeting Knox herself for the first time on the page – I am always reminded of the scene in Mahy's novel, *Memory* (1987), where Jonny, hungover and bruised, first meets Sophie, the old woman who has been released to an altered reality, a new kind of wisdom, by her dementia. Wearing a long coat and a hat 'like a crimson chamber-pot without a handle' and pushing an empty supermarket trolley across an empty car park, she makes for Jonny as if 'he were the very one she had been waiting for.' Jonny watches, intrigued and a little apprehensive. He stands very still so the old woman can walk past him. 'But instead, she came right up to him, staring at him, as if she were waiting for him to begin a conversation. Jonny remained silent. In the end she was the one who spoke first.

"Are *you* the one?" she asked.'

References available at www.griffithreview.com

Kate De Goldi writes fiction for all ages. She teaches creative writing in schools around New Zealand and reviews literature in print and on radio. Her novel *The 10pm Question* (Longacre, 2008) has had wide international publication. Kate is currently working on a study of children's literature bibliophile and archivist, Susan Price. Her most recent publication is *The ACB with Honora Lee* (2012), illustrated by Gregory O'Brien.

The lie of the land

Jim's wife by another name

Hamish Clayton

THIS is the biography of a painting I've known my whole life. At least, there hasn't been a time when I can't remember the painting that used to hang in the long, darkened hallway of my grandparents' house on the farm in northern Hawke's Bay. This was the farm we used to visit as children for what felt like the endless weeks of school holidays. I knew the farm in all its seasons – from its calm, elegiac autumns through cold dark winters, and into the halcyon heat of summer. Because the farm is now only remembered as a fragment in a happy childhood, the richness I've remembered has surely deepened with the years. So the winters of recall are probably colder and more dramatic than they really were, the summers probably longer and hotter, and the magpies waking us in the still mornings more melodic and otherworldly.

How then, I wonder, has the painting which used to hang in the hallway deepened with the years since I last saw it? How have the years I've lived away from her watchful gaze influenced my recall? The shape of her thickset body emerges from the gloom of the spare landscape she stands against; her slab-like feet and hands and her solid, impassive stare; her dress and hat and bag, clearly the accessories of another, previous time. Even then, to the small boy I was, she was a woman who obviously belonged to a bygone age: a woman of some mythic, and in our case, settler past.

What I cannot remember – not quite, not with any clarity – is the first time I was told about that woman and the fragments of her curious history. I do remember, and so do my brother and sister, the legend of her backstory: how she came to be associated with the family through an uncle of my mother's. This was my maternal grandfather's brother, his elder by some years. Jim, despite being the older of the two, was the prodigal son, the family absconder prone to disappearing and reappearing at intervals, usually unannounced, but always with a story to explain his last period of sustained absence. Or, once, a wife.

There are variations on the story. For some reason it is my older brother's account that has formed definitively in my mind; he tells how Jim appeared in the front door one night just after teatime, during a storm in the depths of winter and nonchalantly asked my astounded and delighted grandmother if he was in time for pudding. She invited him in from the cold, set him down at the kitchen table and called to our grandfather that they had a visitor. When my grandfather entered the room he barely raised an eyebrow.

'Gidday Jim,' he said and sat down. At that point they hadn't seen one another for two or three years. They sat at the table while my grandmother brought them tea and pikelets with jam and cream and spoke as if they'd seen each other that morning.

After an hour or so of sharing news, the story goes, my great-uncle mentioned he had a wife. This was too much for my grandmother. '*Jim!* Why didn't you say? Where on earth is she?'

'In the truck.'

In later years, this became one of my grandmother's favourite stories, one to which she would return again and again whenever asked, especially in the years after my grandfather died. It was not just the story but her husband also she would remember. It was her way of being happy again. I never told her when I noticed if the details had changed a few degrees.

Jim and his new wife stayed a week and then he was off again, not to return for another ten or fifteen years. He spent most of that time in Australia working as a drover until the work ran out. That must have been sometime in the '60s. By then my mother had been born, the last of my grandparents' three children. She remembers Jim returning for a couple of weeks when she was six or seven, but by that stage the 'wife' had mysteriously disappeared. When I was a teenager I learned that most in the wider family had doubted they'd ever been married. Jim's infrequent missives home mentioned his bride less and less, until eventually all trace of her dropped off altogether. My grandparents surmised that she and Jim had pretended to be married to avoid embarrassing their hosts.

It was Jim who sent my grandparents the painting. My mother and aunt remember its arrival and my grandmother unwrapping it on the large kitchen table, witnessing her silent astonishment when she saw who it was. For it was her – Jim's 'wife' – whom my grandmother hadn't seen for what must have been the best part of twenty years. Still, there was no doubt about it. There was no letter of explanation enclosed, just a note, 'Love Jim'. They hung her in the hallway, at that northern end, in the darkness, away from the sunlight. And there she stayed, on the farm, until my grandfather died and my grand-mother moved into a smaller house closer to town. I don't remember ever seeing the painting of Jim's wife hung in my grandmother's new place, but it must have been somewhere. She wouldn't have discarded it. But nor do I remember it emerging after she'd died and as her children set about dividing her things between them. Somehow it faded out of all reckoning.

But now, and in a curious way that I cannot quite understand, the paint-ing has returned to us again.

First, a confession: I have never stolen anything before in my life. I remember being dared to once in a toy shop and failing utterly to silence the inner conscience and forge the steel will required. But this time the conscience intervened with the opposite effect; I felt I couldn't *not* take the book with me. Because you've heard what the painting meant to me, how it sat like a cornerstone in my private, family mythology, you will, I think, understand.

I'd been tramping through the Egmont National Park in Taranaki, on the west coast of the North Island – the obverse side of the island from the farm where I'd spent those idyllic childhoods. I was all alone. The walking wasn't too strenuous, and the day was beautiful. The only thing that weighed on my mind came a couple of hours into the walk when I realised I'd forgotten to pack any reading matter. I crossed my fingers there would be something in the hut. Most huts have books left in them by previous trampers for the next to enjoy. My fate was in the hands, or at least the readings habits, of my fellow trampers.

When I got to Kāhui hut it was empty except for me. And a dozen or so books. Thank God, I said aloud to the empty room. I made a cup of tea and changed into warm, dry clothes – there had been a few river crossings through the afternoon and though I wasn't cold having walked for six hours, I was soaking below the waist. When I was comfortable, padding about in thick socks, thermal long johns and a couple of jerseys I perused the small shelf by the window.

I was relieved and impressed when I discovered a roll call of surprisingly literary names. Alongside the anticipated Stephen Kings and Wilbur Smiths, there was a Maurice Gee – the *Plumb* trilogy, which I'd read – and next to him a book of Murray Bail's short stories which I hadn't. I selected the Bail and sat at the table with a cup of tea and a packet of biscuits. When I opened the volume, there, staring at me through the screen of a grainy reproduction, like a ghost looking across the years, was our painting of Jim's wife. I've since learned of course that the painting is called *The Drover's Wife*, and that it was painted in 1945 by the Australian painter Russell Drysdale. But I knew her by another name; to me she was and always will be Jim's wife, that curiously fleeting and yet stable presence in our house and the background of our lives all through the years. In a state of virtual shock I read the short story, which Bail had named after Drysdale's painting and where her reproduction appears. I devoured the words as fast as I could. And then I read it again more slowly; and again, I think, a third time.

You see now why I had to take the book with me.

THE STORY AND the painting have become twin obsessions. I had to find out what I could about them, their inceptions and their histories. And of course, I had to find out how Jim was involved, and who that woman really was. I began by saying that this is the biography of a painting; perhaps it is more acute – more trenchant and better directed – to say that this is the biography of a painting and its reception.

I have not visited the National Gallery of Australia, in Canberra, to see where she now hangs. Curiously though, by now I have seen so many copies and reproductions that I am not sure what I would find were I to stand before her in the flesh. I've memorised the details, the composition. I know how many spare lines of trees stand in the middle distance; I know how the vastness of space behind her hangs on the line of land and sky, just as I know the slight tilt of her hat and the stoicism in her softly shaded eyes. And I know too the tiny dark figure beyond, tending to the horse and wagon, which, I suppose, the drover's wife is about to embark within. I can't help wonder if that tiny figure was meant, in some way, to be Jim.

I hazard a guess that the painting is as familiar to many Australians as the works of well-known New Zealand painters like Rita Angus or Colin McCahon are familiar to New Zealanders. Perhaps, as is the case with Angus and McCahon, there will be those with barely a passing interest in art's role in cultural nationalism but who might be able to tell you that Drysdale and *The Drover's Wife* are 'important', even if they're not able to explain why. I'm interested in that audience and the role they play, vital and inexpert, in the production of a national myth.

For like Angus and McCahon, Drysdale is a painter whose work, it seems to me, has presented certain strains of the national mythos with – we are told – such force and clarity that eventually his work has been allowed to stand in for whichever local reality it was produced in response to. The boundary between the painted landscape and the real one is thus smoothed over, erased, and from here it is hardly surprising when the mythologiser of the land is, in turn, swiftly and inexorably mythologised himself.

A few days after returning from the national park where I came across the Bail story for the first time, I disappeared into a library seeking out other traces of Drysdale. I discovered Geoffrey Dutton, a writer with whom I was not acquainted before, but whose angle on Drysdale was familiar: 'a slow, stubborn and solitary painter of unshakeable integrity [whose] loving vision of Australia [...] is entirely his own.' Except that it *isn't* quite his own, as Dutton's terms also permit: 'There are now many occasions on which an Australian can find himself in front of a man, a town street or a deserted landscape and say, "That's a Russell Drysdale."'

From the start Bail chooses to wrong-foot us, the implied reader familiar with the painting and, presumably, the place it holds in the Australian cultural psyche. And although I wasn't one of those readers until I'd discovered later for myself something of Drysdale's place in the canon, I felt I understood intuitively the ambit of Bail's story, with its concern to playfully undercut culturally constructed assumptions of identity.

Bail's narrator, the bitter Gordon, starts by addressing the painting itself, or at least its reproduction, sitting above the story's opening lines: 'There has been a mistake – but of no great importance – made in the denomination of this picture. The woman depicted is not "The Drover's Wife". She is my wife.'

Gordon notes the hidden left hand of the woman in the painting and reads sinister import in what we *can't* see: 'This portrait was painted shortly after she left – and had joined him. Notice she has very conveniently hidden her wedding hand.' Our cuckolded narrator goes on, cannily trading further on suggestion and absence: 'I say "shortly after" because she has our small suitcase – Drysdale has made it look like a shopping bag – and she is wearing the sandshoes she normally wore to the beach.'

In the space of two paragraphs Bail constructs a version of the painting's history raucously divergent from any we could expect to receive at the hands of Drysdale's critics. Gone is the determined Aussie she-battler of the bucolic legend underpinning the drover's wife and taking her place an absconding wife and mother. Gone too, for that matter, is Drysdale the honest chronicler of life in the outback; Bail effectively side-lines him, translating him into a mere bit-player, a hapless portraitist limited in range and vision. Although 'Drysdale' the fictional painter is excused by Gordon for the liberties he has taken with his subject – 'the artist has fallen down (though how was he to know?)' – he stands accused of taking them all the same: 'He has Hazel with a resigned helpless expression – as if it were all my fault. Or, as if she had been a country woman all her ruddy life.'

From here, Bail's subversions come thick and fast. Hazel, we are told, struggled with her weight and 'had a silly streak.' She lacked both class – 'A drover! Why a drover?' – and sympathy: her final words to her husband, 'Don't give Trev any carrots.' Through her, Gordon is himself a figure lampooned. He is a dentist – perhaps a career choice as respectably dissonant with the dominant tropes of Australian myth-making as Bail could imagine. And on the subject of landscape itself Bail is committed to the satirist's edge, disrupting all romantic notions associated with contemporary Australians' relationship with the land; perhaps most memorably towards the end of the story, when a train barrels along the Adelaide-Port Augusta railway line, tearing Gordon and his family from their sleep where they are camped in the great outdoors.

But underlying Bail's fun at Gordon's expense are deeper, more far-reaching ramifications. Gordon is in many respects an unwitting narrator, but it is through him that Bail reminds us of the extent of the drover's wife myth with a couple of sly nods to Lawson. For one thing, there is the snake which appears under the house in both Bail's and Lawson's short stories; although Bail's tone here is too playful, too mocking of the emasculated Gordon to count as homage; his description of the 'black brute, its head bashed in' reminds us of Lawson's take on the myth. Far more telling is the very final note which Bail strikes. Gordon's closing thoughts consider how dominant Hazel stands in relation to the 'rotten landscape' all around her. Anyone who has read Lawson will recall those native apple trees, 'stunted, rotten'. It is as though Bail has not only hand-picked the word that most represented the extent of the feeling he found in Lawson's story and thereby chosen to finish with it, but also that he has deployed it as an insult, flung on behalf of the worsted Gordon, back towards Drysdale himself, that painter of 'rotten' landscapes.

Delicately imbricated into the layers of Bail's treatment, then, are laid these subtle reminders of the power and the place of stories and mythologies as they interact with the real world. All are contingent on recognising the nature of art as artifice. For when Gordon observes of the painting that the landscape 'is the outback — but where exactly? South Australia? It could easily be Queensland, West Australia, the Northern Territory. We don't know. You could never find that spot,' he doesn't only remind us of the reality of the vastness of Australia's great hinterland, but also that Drysdale *was* a painter of mythic proportion; that if his vaunted 'new vision of Australia' has been firmly lodged in the national cultural consciousness, then it has traded on some broader, more abstract value than the particularities of this scene or that subject.

Although the fictional Gordon seems designed to subvert the critically imagined Drysdale, Bail's manoeuvring also reminds us of the reality beyond the frames of both the painting and the story.

When I read Bail's short story I was taken with how the writer had chosen to sit with us, on our side of the painting, inhabiting the same space we inhabit when we stand before it, whether we are in the gallery or looking at it reproduced on the page. Though he makes it an imagined space – situating the fictional, abandoned husband of the painting's subject before the painting itself – it pays to remember that this is a real space in the world as well. As it was, I discovered, a real space for Dutton; as it was once a real space for my great-uncle when he must have stood before it somehow, decades ago.

It was only then, considering how I'd once looked at the painting as a small boy and then again as an adult – and how Dutton had, and Uncle Jim had – that I realised what I thought Bail was really up to with his story. I contended earlier in this essay that with landscape painters of national importance like Drysdale, 'the boundary between the painted landscape and the real one is smoothed over, erased, and from here it is hardly surprising when the mythologiser of the land is, in turn, swiftly and inexorably mythologised himself.' I've realised now that it is the space of that boundary itself, that field which often seems invisible to us, that Bail writes from within. He stands between us and our perception, intervening in our reception. In becoming a new lens he thus allows that there is no one version of this painting, but potentially as many different versions as there are pairs of eyes that have looked upon it.

WHAT WOULD JIM have made of Bail's story, and its author daring to stand in his shoes? I choose to think he would've liked it, though of course I cannot really say. Whether contemporary literature was an enthusiasm Jim would've held is perhaps doubtful but this seems beside the point to me – from what I think I know of him, he would've approved, staunchly, of the playful humour underpinning Bail's take. He was, as we know, a joker.

But what was really at stake in my interest was her. I had wanted, simply, to discover what had become of Uncle Jim's wife. His 'wife'. It was only after I became frustrated with trying to find out exactly who she was that the extent of the joke dawned on me. That sending this painting back to my grandparents, this painting called *The Drover's Wife*, had been Jim's wry humour again. An acknowledgement of what everyone else had long decided they knew: that that woman hadn't been his wife. Sending that painting was no more than one of his knowing winks. I imagined him coming across a framed reproduction of it somewhere, perhaps on a visit to Sydney during those final years when he himself had been working as a drover. Perhaps he'd walked down the main street on a hot day and seen it hanging in a window. I see him pause before it in the street, struck by the uncanny likeness to a woman he'd known years ago.

I ran this theory past my family. My brother and sister were convinced, my mother and aunt less so. For one thing, they said, the painting was *never* called the *drover's* wife. Always, they insisted, it was *Jim's* wife.

'And besides, she was *convinced*…' my aunt went on as she described again that moment when my grandmother had unwrapped the painting and seen Jim's wife for the first time in years, staring at her through the picture frame.

'It was *her*,' my mother and aunt implored us, we three children who had never met Jim, far less his mythical wife.

It was only when my mother exclaimed, aiming for the emphatically rhetorical, 'Surely Jim would have explained the joke!' that a pause fell between the two sisters and they looked at each other silently.

I can still see them as they were in that moment, sitting opposite one another at the dinner table, quietly realising that a gap in the family mythology had finally been filled. But I can't help but wonder too if it was only at that moment that they realised the gap had even been there.

Notes are available at www.griffithreview.com

Hamish Clayton was born in Hawke's Bay in 1977. He holds degrees in Art History and English Literature from Victoria University of Wellington, where he is currently working on a PhD about the New Zealand novelist David Ballantyne. His first novel, *Wulf* (Penguin, 2011), won the Best First Book Award for Fiction at the *New Zealand Post Book Awards* 2012.

An A-frame in Antarctica

Getting away from it all

Matt Vance

AHEAD was a peculiar vision. Black Island appeared to levitate above the Ross Ice Shelf. A shimmering dark lake had formed below it where there had not been rain for over two million years. I rest on my ski poles and in the thin Antarctic air catch my breath. I watch the lake grow legs, fold, collapse and gently lower Black Island back in place.

On a calm day mirages are common here. Roald Amundsen and his party, who were the first people to the South Pole in 1911, saw their fair share of them. Perhaps the most famous of these mirages was seen within days of their reaching the pole. 'Our finest day up here,' wrote Amundsen. 'Calm most of the day with burning sunshine... As we were breaking camp Hassel called out, "Do you see that black thing over there?" Everyone saw it. "Can it be Scott?" someone called. Bjaaland skied forward to investigate. He did not have to ski far. "Mirage," he reported laconically, "dog turds."'

To the east of where I stand lies a black dot; not a dog turd but an A-frame hut. The hut has become an institution at New Zealand's Scott Base since it was rescued from the American McMurdo Station trash pile in 1971. The New Zealanders quickly made the A-frame hut their own. It is a small pointed gesture in the vastness of the Ross Ice Shelf, which captures the New Zealand desire to get away from it all, to simplify and make do.

Every year the A-frame is dug out of the snowdrift and roughly levelled on its skids. Inside, it has a timber panel finish, a selection of saggy couches and beds, and most of the time it contains good company. It's nearly 11 pm by the time I reach the hut but the sun shows no inclination to set. I am greeted by an artist from Auckland and a scientist from Dunedin. Like me, they have come out here for a night away from the hustle of Scott Base. They seem happy to see me. They are even happier when I produce a bottle of whiskey from my pack.

Inside the hut it is warm. We drink the whiskey. It is rough but somehow it tastes smooth. We talk with big pauses, as if the vastness of the Ross Ice Shelf itself is nudging in between our words. We talk of Ed Hillary's last night here and of Amundsen and his dogs.

On the rough timber shelf above the saggy bunk I have reclined on, there are novels and non-fiction epics of varying quality. In one of the better ones Robert Macfarlane writes, 'Ideas are like waves and have fetches. They arrive having travelled vast distances, and their pasts are often invisible, or barely imaginable.' Antarctica is one of those ideas and, like the Southern Ocean that surrounds it, has the greatest fetch of any on the planet. Antarctica is an idea that has been brewing for a long time.

It was 319 BC that Aristotle first guessed at the presence of a great Southern land. In the intervening two thousand or so years, before Antarctica was actually discovered, the resulting void proved an attractive vacuum into which rushed every conceivable theory and myth, populating a geography of hope that still persists to this day. There were Arcadian forests, lost civilisations and UFO bases projected onto the white page of this undiscovered continent. Being inaccessible, these ideas were hard to refute and proliferated like sastrugi in a blizzard.

Amongst the visions of Arcadia and UFO bases, it was perhaps John Symmes' theory of a hollow earth that was most remarkable. Symmes was a captain in the United States Army who, in 1818, expounded a hollow earth theory that gained considerable notoriety. The poles were supposed to be surrounded by a barrier of ice that protected a warm climate and super-race of people who had access through a hole at the poles to the habitable centre of the earth.

Symmes' half-baked theory appealed to the sense of the sublime so fashionable at the time. The sublime was attributed to experiences or landscapes that contained equal parts of terror and fascination for the observer. Like any good half-baked theory, Symmes' hole tended to morph and change like a mirage, growing legs and setting itself down away from the critics' eye.

The A-frame hut is as close to the utopia of Symmes' hole as it is possible to get. The hut is a human scale, triangular refuge from the white hell outside. Like Symmes' version of Antarctica, the A-frame goes against expectation. It is the direct contrast of its black to the landscape's white, its vertical to the horizontal and its warm to the cold that surrounds. The A-frame takes you by pleasant surprise.

New Zealand has grown up with Antarctica and this intimate association has imbued our concept of landscape, weather and history. Around my homeport in Lyttelton Harbour there are constant physical reminders of the departure of the expeditions of Scott. Each morning in summer my commuter ferry skirts another icebreaker bunkering before heading south, and I step onto the wharf Scott left from and pass the pub where he had his last drink. At night Antarctica occasionally visits with an icy blast from the south, which rattles the roof of my bach. Antarctica is never far from New Zealand's thoughts.

In a country that should know better, we colonise just like the rest of them. We make sense of a new landscape by furnishing it to remind us of home. The clues about how to be in this place are obscure, so instead we retreat towards Massey Ferguson tractors, corrugated iron and rugby goal posts.

Like other colonisers we attempt to name the landscape around us. Despite our best intentions, Antarctic naming has a strong sense of the absurd about it, in no part due to the violence, movement and constant attempts at illusion of the physical environment. This is not a landscape that tolerates being pinned down.

Names in Antarctica are now dished out, not to remind us of events or of people who have dwelt there, but for studious sacrifice to the world of science and bureaucracy and for seriously good politicking. Most of the named will never see their col, glacier or mountain and within a few generations, the connection will be lost in the thick volumes of the *Composite Gazetteer of*

Antarctica. It's as if the words refuse to stick to the slippery substrate they are confronted with. Perhaps because of this the colonisers of Antarctica revert to things rather than words. Things are like a comfort blanket, familiar, tangible and soft to the touch. Over the hill at the American McMurdo Station they have Frosty Boys, bowling alleys, cable TV and ATMs. The New Zealanders have a ski-field and a bach on the Ross Ice Shelf. Escape seems to be our national anthem.

I brew a midnight cup of tea for the inmates of the A-frame. From the frosted window near the kitchen the only feature of the landscape that appears to be living is the looming presence of Mt Erebus to the north. It is an active volcano, puffing wispy, white smoke from its top. Like a portrait with eyes that follow you around the room, the mountain remains the same size no matter how far you move away from it. The A-frame is manoeuvred to face it, scared to turn its back on such an eerie phenomena.

From where I sip my tea Mt Erebus looks like a child's sketch of a mountain, harmless and easy to ascend. Robert Macfarlane reminds us, 'Without doubt it is these harmless looking conical mountains that have killed the most in human history.' He was right, and this mountain is no different. On the north side the mountain hides a scar a few kilometres long that contains the wreckage of flight TE 901, which ploughed into the mountain in 1979 on a sight-seeing trip from New Zealand to McMurdo Sound. In one violent moment more New Zealanders have died in Antarctica than any other nationality.

Death on a smaller scale is a constant in this place. Below the A-frame hut is eighty metres or so of glacial ice, floating on the dark waters of McMurdo Sound. Further towards the mainland and buried some sixteen metres down are Scott, Bowers and Wilson, more than one hundred years on from their death and still on their journey home. They lie together, frozen into their sleeping bags and wrapped in their tent, where the effects of scurvy, malnutrition and frostbite ushered them into sleep. Out beyond them Oates lies curled up. Further back near the base of the ice shelf, Evans lies slumped forward as if in prayer. They are all on a journey to the sea and around five hundred years from now Scott and his companions will be committed to the deep east of the A-frame hut, somewhere near Cape Crozier.

Being alone is a rare thing on Base and a week of this intense scrutiny is enough for any sane person. The A-frame offers an escape from all of this and is the only thing that unites the current inhabitants.

Compounding this need for sanctuary in the A-frame is an equally power-ful desire to escape from the colour green – *Chelsea Cucumber* to be precise – and the entire exterior of Scott Base is painted in this gruesome fashion.

In the 1970s Bob Thompson, the then manager of the New Zealand Antarctic Programme, came up with the idea of a green Scott Base after returning from a visit to Ireland. He adored the white houses set in the green fields and thought the inverse would be just as suitable in Antarctica. The idea persists inside the buildings, which blessedly are not green, but contain pictur-esque, Andris Apse photos of New Zealand rural landscapes. The A-frame hut is free from this green obsession and merely makes its statement with the more vernacular idea of black plywood and red trim.

I doze on the saggy bed with the spectacular view. With no night at this time of year the sun merely does loops around the horizon and its perpetual presence means that sleep is neither deep, nor rewarding. The shadows it casts are the only clue to time passing.

When the shadows stretch out in a westerly direction I rise and make thick porridge to steel us for our ski back to Scott Base. I leave the remains of the whiskey bottle on the shelf next to the eclectic selection of books. It is a small koha for our sanctuary and will most likely be finished by another New Zealander from Scott Base looking for an escape of one form or another. The ever-watchful eyes of Mt Erebus follow us as we clip into our skis and glide into a slow rhythm. The A-frame hut slips behind into the white haze.

SOME TIME AFTER these notes were written the A-frame hut burnt down. A clumsy relighting of the diesel heater, a malfunctioning fire extin-guisher and the A-frame became a place of absence. The bitumen and plywood construction, dried to a crisp by years of living in a desert, went up with an audible *whoompf.* In the perpetual darkness of May the flames shot up in a funeral pyre, fuelled by saggy beds, diesel fuel and memories.

Matt Vance is a New Zealand-based writer and sailor who has worked in and around Antarctica for more than a decade. His latest book is *How to Sail a Boat* (AWA Press, 2013).

Bill Manhire

Erebus voices

The Mountain

I am here beside my brother, Terror.
I am the place of human error.

I am beauty and cloud, and I am sorrow;
I am tears which you will weep tomorrow.

I am the sky and the exhausting gale.
I am the place of ice. I am the debris trail.

And I am still a hand, a fingertip, a ring.
I am what there is no forgetting.

I am the one with truly broken heart.
I watched them fall, and freeze, and break apart.

The Dead

We fell.

Yet we were loved and we are lifted.

We froze.

Yet we were loved and we are warm.

We broke apart.

Yet we are here and we are whole.

Bill Manhire was New Zealand's inaugural poet laureate. His recent *Selected Poems* is published in New Zealand by Victoria University Press, and in the UK by Carcanet. 'Erebus Voices' was written for Sir Edmund Hillary to read at Scott Base, Antarctica, during a service commemorating the 257 passengers and crew who lost their lives on Flight TE901.

Reading Geoff Cochrane

A constant companion

Carrie Tiffany

WHEN I was a child I had two dolls in a box. Each night I placed the dolls on the floor of the box and covered them with a sheet of black paper. Sometimes the dolls required reassurance. I told them that the day was finished in their country, that it was no longer time for speaking and that all of the world was asleep.

I meet these two New Zealanders. They are brainy and handsome; they live in an old workers' cottage on the edge of Melbourne. There is a pāua shell ashtray. There are postcards of Colin McCahon. *Kia ora*, they murmur, when they pick up the telephone. I'm there one day when a relative arrives off the plane from Wellington. An old cardboard suitcase is snapped open; cake from a teashop on Lambton Quay, jars of bubbled honey, custard powder in an orange packet. The soft comforts of home… I score a slim volume of Geoff Cochrane. It's 2001 and this is how it begins.

It doesn't happen instantly. The Irish hold the ground. You duke it out, those first few years, with the American poet Donald Hall. But *Hypnic Jerks* (2005) seals it for me. I think of you each time I'm hooked back from sleep. I think of you in your crummy pad – the few forks and knives shivering in their drawer when the bus stops outside. I think of the view from your flat; pines, drainage ditches, rugby posts like gallows, wooded hills, a soft drink plant, red leaves that bounce like crisps, rain that inks the road.

I read your lines and I make you up. I foist you on to the few Australian poets and readers of poetry that I know. I take you out to dinner. I take you to London. I do a number on you in an interview for the women's hour on the BBC. The doughy host looks over her glasses at me. She pronounces *New Zealand* so archly the face powder on her soft English cheeks lifts and talcs the air. I take you to Calgary, Mildura, Ubud, Leeds, Port Hedland. I take you to Auckland where I mention you to a bookish crowd in a hotel bar. One of the drinkers is your publisher. I leave.

I read your lines and I follow them like tracks. There you are walking down the long hill towards Antarctica, watching the shunted clouds, taking in the smell of gorse fires, the sky is the colour of wet salt. I learn not to clarify. The waxy eye of the Kōwhai? She is not a bird; she is a tree with a yellow flower hanging limply penile. The poem is dead to me; the bird of my imagination forever tangled in its rhythms.

Your life is hectic, lonely, full of innocence and sin. Your books sit a-slant on the table next to my bed. The white covers are not weathering well. The dentist's chair tilts and sinks, I think of you. The extractions, the full clearance, the needle's spiteful sting. There is your knowledge of household paint, cigarette lighters, pencils, addiction.

You write and you walk. You walk to resist the abyss. You walk to the supermarket at the foot of Tinakori Hill. You walk Wellington's ribboned pavements; you walk its harboured curve. You were walking before Sebald reached the Pacific and we sat in cafés discussing the *flâneur*. I sense you in my ankles at St Kilda as I hesitate on the kerb.

News comes. You have been seen in a shop. You are thin. I hear there are stacks of your manuscripts waiting for attention on your publisher's floor. The thought of all those poems spooling out in front of you – hovering voluptuously on the brink of being read. In *Vanilla Wine* (2003) you say you have a readership of perhaps twenty-three people. I make them up too.

The world is full of people we will never know, sitting at home, coughing quietly in their countries. It can be hard to bear the thought of these people who will always be remote, never in relation. When the day is finished in my country and I pull the black sheet over my face you are already in deep night. If I can't sleep I'll reach for you. Your poems have travelled across the sea from your island to mine in a kind of double movement – a silent athletics of writing and reading. I don't believe the poems you make are a symptom of estrangement, but of over-feeling. Although, who am I to say? I made you up. But you started it, Geoff Cochrane; you started it all those years ago when you sat down in your country and began to write.

Carrie Tiffany is an agricultural journalist and novelist. She lives in Melbourne. Geoff Cochrane is a Wellington poet. His latest work is *The Worm in the Tequila* (2011). They have never met.

Geoff Cochrane

Equinoctial

        A hand's turn or two
        A hand's turn or two
And my work is done for the day.

        ~

        Behold my suit of meats
and fat tarantulas. Check out my cloak of knives
        and pinkest heliums.

        ~

        Our lilies are broken by the wind.
Broken by the wind, and then they rust.
Broken by the wind, and then they rot.

        ~~

A habit I seem to have formed (and can't afford):
Each morning at eleven, a latte at the same place,
At the same table, my own inviolable spot
        Downwind of the non-smokers.

        ~~

    Coffee. What a racket. I must be nuts.
    But I'm making an attempt to *live*, you see;
I'm conducting an experiment in living.

Geoff Cochrane lives in Wellington. In 2009 he received the Janet Frame Award for Poetry. His latest book is *The Bengal Engine's Mango Afterglow* (Victoria University Press, 2012). A collection of his short stories is in preparation.

Save over 20% with a 1 or 2 Year Subscription plus receive a FREE copy of a past edition of your choice*

☐ I would like to subscribe   ☐ I wish to give a subscription to: *(please tick ✓ one)*

Name: _____

Address: _____

_____ Postcode: _____

Email:_____Telephone: _____

Please choose your subscription package *(please tick ✓ one below)*

☐ 1 year within Australia: $88.00 (inc gst)   ☐ 2 years within Australia: $165.00 (inc gst)

☐ 1 year outside Australia: $143.00 AUD   ☐ 2 years outside Australia: $275.00 AUD

I wish the subscription to begin with *(please tick ✓ one below)*

☐ CURRENT EDITION†   ☐ NEXT EDITION

For my FREE past edition, please send it to ☐ me   ☐ my gift recipient *(please tick ✓ one)*

EDITION TITLE* _____

Select from past editions at www.griffithreview.com *While past edition copies remain in stock.

PAYMENT DETAILS

Purchaser's Address *(if not the subscription recipient)*:

_____ Postcode: _____

Email:_____Telephone:_____

☐ I have enclosed a cheque/money order for $_____ made payable to **Griffith REVIEW** (Payable in Australian Dollars only)

☐ **Card Type (*please circle one*):** Bankcard / Mastercard / Visa / Amex

Card Number: ☐☐☐☐ ☐☐☐☐ ☐☐☐☐ ☐☐☐☐

Expiry Date: __ __ / __ __

Cardholder name: _____

Cardholder Signature:_____

MAIL TO:
Business Manager - Griffith REVIEW
REPLY PAID 61015
NATHAN QLD 4111 Australia

FAX TO:
Business Manager - Griffith REVIEW
07 3735 3272 (*within Australia*)
+61 7 3735 3272 (*International*)

● The details given above will only be used for the subscription collection and distribution of Griffith REVIEW and will not be passed to a third party for other uses. For further information consult Griffith University's Privacy Plan at www.griffith.edu.au/ua/aa/vc/pp ● † Current Edition only available for subscriptions received up until 2 weeks before Next Edition release date. See www.griffithreview.com for release dates.